This book is dedicated
to the staff of the
**HAIGHT-ASHBURY
FREE CLINICS**
for the more than 23 years of
exceptional service
to their community.

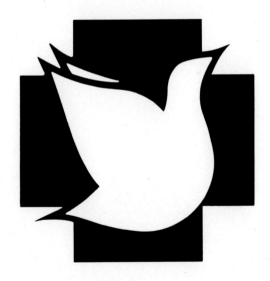

We have written and designed **Uppers, Downers, All Arounders** to serve as a factual, non-judgmental reference source about psychoactive drugs such as crack cocaine, alcohol, marijuana, crank, Valium, LSD, ice, and tobacco for those who need more knowledge about the mental and physical effects of these substances and about related issues such as drug testing, treatment, pregnancy, AIDS, and drug abuse prevention.

Uppers, Downers, All Arounders is written clearly, concisely, and simply, using more than 200 illustrations, photos, and graphs. It may be used by parents (and teenagers), employers (and employees), teachers (and students), counselors (and clients), medical personnel, law enforcement groups, and those who just want to know more about psychoactive drugs. Reviews, questions, and suggested exercises are included for those who wish to create a course on psychoactive drugs designed to meet the specific needs of their community.

Quotations used in **Uppers, Downers, All Arounders** have been culled from more than 60 hours of interviews with current drug users, users in early treatment, and recovering users.

UPPERS, DOWNERS, ALL AROUNDERS

Authors:
DARRYL S. INABA, Pharm.D.
(Haight-Ashbury Clinics)

WILLIAM E. COHEN
(Biomed Arts Associates Inc.)

Publishers:
CINEMED INC.
WEC FILMS

Production Services:
BIOMED ARTS ASSOCIATES INC.

Designer:
MIKE YEUNG

Medical Illustrator:
WALTER DENN

Available Through
CINEMED INC.
P.O. Box 96
Ashland, Oregon 97520
(503) 488-2805
or
THE HAIGHT-ASHBURY DETOX CLINIC
529 Clayton Street
San Francisco, CA 94117
(415) 621-2016

First Edition, printed 1989
Updated and reprinted 1990

THIRD PRINTING JULY 1990"
ISBN 0-926544-00-4

Pot-laced brownies give class of senior citizens high old time

By Richard Nordwind
Herald staff writer

Some senior citizens may have felt like they were dancing on air while they whirled around their ballroom dance class in Monterey Park this week, but it wasn't the fox trot that made them feel high.

Unbeknownst to the seniors, their instructor allegedly had brought out a plate of pot brownies during a pause in the class Thursday night, according to Monterey Park police.

"I was hungry, so I ate four of them. They tasted like regular pastry," said Robert Martinez, 66, of Los Angeles, who had just started attending the class at the Langley Senior Citizen Center two weeks ago.

As Martinez soon found out, those were no ordinary said yesterday. "He was just trying to relax the gro Donato was not available for comment yesterd

Beth Ryan, the senior citizens' coordinator Langley Center, said Donato had taught seni ballroom dancing for more than a year. His Thursc night class had about 30 to 35 members, she said "He was an excellent instructor," Ryan said Donato, adding, "We're canceling his Thursday ni classes immediately."

Monterey Park runs ballroom classes three nigh week. On Tuesday the center sponsors a dance. "I how this doesn't ruin things," Ryan remarked regretfu

The brownies were served around 8 p.m. along w some punch, during a break between fox trot a waltz instruction, Martinez recalled. Feeling refresh Martinez resumed his dancing, but by the end of

Reagan Will Launch Drive on Illegal Drugs in 12 Cities

By RONALD J. OSTROW, Times Staff Writer

WASHINGTON—Temporarily dropping the Administration's budget-cutting campaign, Pres-

States through South Florida, the new task forces will differ in ways respect from those used in the Fort

What Booze Do to the Bo

By DR. JOSEPH A. PURSCH

Question: Although I spent three organization recently I could not a sobriety. My wife and alcoholic because I could say I never missed a had many hangovers

While I was in tre man's talks, but all talks instead of telli d: to the human bo with what alcohol c these mental attemp think they won't wo

Answer: Most strongly emphasize get through to pa change in attitude a know that alcohol d not enabled

California Raids On Pot Growers Called Success

By Steve Wiegand
Chronicle Correspondent

Sacramento
Federal, state and local law enf terday ry — ir out No crative dustry

mated street value of more th $130 million, were destroyed Th

Lung Cancer Now Deadliest Form for California Women

By HARRY NELSON, Times Medical Writer

SAN FRANCISCO—Lung cancer has passed breast cancer as the leading cause of cancer deaths in California women, a state health

primary health problem in Califo nia," he said at a news conferen here. "It sells a product which kil but has no product liability."

Codeine is No. 1 in prescription abuse

Benzodiazepine hypnotic

Common sleeping pills can cause short-term amnesia

By H
Hears

L turn becor passe tion say

A Coast rest c

T rapid "serig claim ment prescribing of codeine compounds by

Psychology Today

A college professor and world-renowned scientist flies to London, delivers a lecture, leads a discussion and then spends the night fighting jet lag in a hotel. The next day, when he is congratulated on the brilliance of his discussion, he doesn't remember

s nearly three years

m was another neu nes Tetrud of Wat s one of the first to co

UPPER M Cocaine was f an the earl

More Victims of Fake Heroin

217 Bay Area heroin users who may have been exposed to the paralyzing toxin in the synthetic drug, and have identified 40 who have definitely injected themselves with the contaminated narcotic.

Most of symptoms o when they v and tested t Langston sai ginning to sh ingly severe ty, shuffling and cramp mark true Pa

The pati

followed at and treated have improve least tempor manent cure

L.A. Boy Br Cocaine 'R To School

Los Angeles

A fourth-grade brought a bag of rock allegedly provided mother's boyfriend, to room yesterday, and one child ate some of stance and suffered sions, authorities said.

Several others pupils Luther King Jr. Element were examined by doc none of them appeared to en the drug, officials said

School district spo For Hain said a 9-year-ol g into conv

commander cocaine wa year-old boy iven the di I the boyfrien gster to hi t about 20 for it.

riend. Roi old on $500 Los An

"We have no answers for

sion." Nc to see i medicin A: Nc the num 90% of l tion of t

Smoking Ban Ordered for All L.A. County Medical Facilities

ICK, Times Staff Writer

you're head ealth clinic in

patients and employees, Gates said Gates already prohibited smok

Drug Use by College Athletes May Be Exaggerated—Study

EAST LANSING, Mich. (UPI)—Drug use by college gely social and nd may be ex ationwide study 2,000 college es. financed by a from the NCAA large and small chools nation ducted by Wil

Those who did report usage appeared to favor alcohol, the study showed. Asked if they had used alcohol in the last 12 months, 88% percent of the athletes said either they had or they had stopped. The next highest response was for marijuana and hashish, reported having been used by 36% of the athletes; anti-inflammato-

Arizona schools went to drug testing early

By Karen Allen
USA TODAY

Arizona's major universities — the University of Arizona in Tucson and Arizona State University in Tempe — accepted the idea of drug testing and implemented their own policies

ty of adopting a conference testing policy.

Six Pac-10 schools (others are Southern California, Oregon State, Oregon and California) are testing some or all of their athletes. Washington and Washington State are the push for the go-ahead from legal ad

2 tons of cocaine seized in Miami

MIAMI — Two tons of cocaine — worth more than $1 billion — were confiscated within two hours Wednesday in one of the USA's biggest seizures ever. On Biscayne Bay, the Coast Guard chased three smugglers until they jumped overboard and abandoned their speedboat. It was packed with 1,909 pounds of cocaine. One man was arrested; two escaped. Later, police stopped a Winnebago camper and

Chemical in Decaffeinated Coffee

What chemical is used to remove caffeine from coffee? Is it harmful?

Methylene chloride, or dichloromethane, is the solvent used to

high doses (the equivalent of 10 cloves a day for 6 months).

Such hig produce bod ing and diai atastrophic nd social su

Commer ules of garl ittle of the iveness of th the manufa o destroy or gredients in nd anti-clot e totally ab icts.

Needle 'Plunged Into Arm'

Worker Sues Over Forced Blo

By Jill Singleton

A United Parcel Service employee in Oakland is suing his employer for allegedly jab bing a hypodermic needle into his arm and taking a blood test

body fluids, specifically blood and privacy of ot man's own p

Crack Addiction Sp Among Middle-Clas

Crackdown Has Little Impact

Heroin Manufacture Thrives in Pakistan

By WILLIAM J. EATON, Times Staff Writer

ISLAMABAD, Pakistan—Despite a highly publicized crackdown on heroin laboratories in northern Pakistan, manufacture of the drug in this area remains as high as ever, U.S. of

Son Afgha shifte Pakist before

The ingrec sharpl aging poppy availal kistan alway officia Kotal, opium

"Yo ton or with forcer condit

surrendered only laboratory equipment—"pots and pans" in narcotics jargon—and did not turn over any chemicals, heroin or the morphine base used to produce the addictive

police are suspected of taking payoffs to drop criminal charges against operators of heroin laboratories.

Even so, Pakistani authorities acts.

Effects of PCP, Cocaine on Unborn:

By ANNE C. ROARK, Times Staff Writer

Scientists have long known that babies whose mothers use heroin and methadone are born with drug addictions of their own as well as mental problems. But only recently have medical researchers begun to study the effects of cocaine and PCP (phencyclidine) on unborn children—and the picture they are seeing is not pretty.

The offspring of these drug users typically suffer numero irritabilit nearly c physical suspect What

pregnant women is rising rapidly. Testifying at a special hearing called Wednesday by Los Angeles County Supervisor Ed Edelman, Jean McIntosh of the Department of Children's Services said that, since 1981 her department had a 453% increase in infant and child drug problems. Only a portion of the increase can be attributed to more accurate medical tests and better reporting, she said.

Glamorous Images Nurture Harmful Views, Study Finds

Children Swayed by TV Drinking

By CANDY JUSTICE, Scripps-Howard

en Hawkeye gulped a home-

the drinking scenes chose to serve

Liver Cancer From Steroids?

Cases Involving Two Athletes Prompt Warning by Research

conflicting evidence on w steroids build strength, bu warn the hormones have found to lead to liver dama other ailments, including hea ... sterility, hormone i an imbalance immune system in

Teen-agers' No. 1 Drug: Al

120,000 Problem Drinkers Estimated in L.

By BEVERLY BEYETTE

L.A. Police to Take Anti-Drug Message to 50 Grade Schools

By RICHARD WEST, Times Staff Writer

specially selected Los Angeles police ... to classrooms of 50 city schools beginning Oct. 3 to sixth-grade students on

one crippling disease, ... and a March of Dollars" is needed to eradicate another one. drug abuse, Gates said.

When one businessman heard about Project DARE, "he wrote a check for 20,000 bucks" to

Alcohol Programs Save Jobs—a

By WILLIAM OVEREND, Times Staff Writer

He had been arrested twice for drunk driving and was suffering periodic blackouts. His personal life was in a shambles from alcohol and

the Hughes employee-counseling program, says that almost 2,000 Hughes employees have been treated for alcohol problems in the

pattern, h alcoholic d possible, th any kind of

3

TABLE OF CONTENTS

Joseph stumbles across his brain's pleasure center.

THE NEIGHBORHOOD by JERRY VAN AMERONGEN

©1986-Jerry Van Amerongen. Reprinted with special permission of Cowles Syndicate Inc.

ACKNOWLEDGMENTS

PAUL J. STEINBRONER, Film Producer/Distributor, Partner in CINEMED, for five years spent supporting, editing, and ramrodding this book which threatened to rival the Pyramids in gestation.

MICHAEL ALDRICH, Ph.D., Curator of the **FITZ HUGH LUDLOW MEMORIAL LIBRARY**, for his aid in editing the book, for the resources of the library, for his incredible store of knowledge, for his foresight in teaming up with **MICHELLE ALDRICH**, and for access to his marvelous book, **THE DOPE CHRONICLES, 1850-1950**, which provided us with so many ideas.

HELEN K. BRODERICK, Operations Manager, CINEMED Inc., for suggestions, transcripts, computer work, and the kung pao chicken that made this book possible.

ANTHONY J. PUENTES, M.D., Medical Director, Santa Clara County Health Department, Bureau of Drug Abuse Services, for his invaluable writing and editing of the Drugs and Pregnancy section of this book.

MICHAEL YEUNG, Designer, for his wonderful sense of form, the best thumbnail sketches around, and for his willingness to be disturbed after 10pm.

WALTER DENN, Medical Illustrator, Biomed Arts Inc., for the many sleepless nights it took to do the marvelous illustrations.

PAUL WARING, Photographer and Partner in Biomed Arts Associates Inc., for his help in preparing the many photos and illustrations used.

DEBORAH LOTT, Editor, for her invaluable assistance editing the book, particularly with all the deadlines, and for her command of the English Language.

ROBERT R. SAGER, Director of the Drug Enforcement Administration's San Francisco Laboratory, for his marvelous staff, a unique collection of drugs and paraphernalia, and his willingness to take the time to get it right.

MASSANI BROWN, Prevention Coordinator, Ashland, Oregon Public Schools, for her insight into the problems of drug prevention education.

MICHAEL E. HOLSTEIN, Ph.D., for his marvelous command of the English language while helping to edit the book and his long-distance English lessons.

PAUL L. STEINBRONER, President of Cinemed, Inc., for his business suggestions and financial support that made this book possible.

We would also like to acknowledge those people from the Haight-Ashbury Clinics whose energies have provided the foundation for the clinic's role as a leader in chemical dependency treatment.

DAVID SMITH, M.D., Medical Director, Haight-Ashbury Clinics, for his superb writings about psychoactive drugs and for his foresight as one of the founders of the Haight-Ashbury Free Clinics.

GEORGE R. (SKIP) GAY, M.D. & JOHN JONES, M.D., for their medical genius as the inspirational founders of the Haight-Ashbury Clinic's Detox Programs.

MIM LANDRY, Director, Training and Education Project, for the ever ready article, new phrasing, and remarkable telephone answering machine.

GREG HAYNER, Pharm.D., Director of Pharmacy Services, for his endless store of knowledge of the chemical intricacies of drugs.

MELANIE SAMPSON, Administrative Aide, for being the spirit of the Haight-Ashbury Detox Clinic since the late 60's.

JOHN NEWMEYER, PH.D. , Director of Research for the Haight-Ashbury Clinics, for being a sagacious chronicler of drug trends in the United States.

RICK SEYMOUR, M.A., Executive Administrator and Fundraiser, for his many years of service and the immeasurable devotion he has given to finding resources and funding for the clinic's varied programs.

DOUGLAS CARTER, Research Supervisor for the Drug Detox Project, for his seventeen years of dedication and hard work on behalf of the community it serves.

ANDY RICE R.N., Nursing Supervisor, for her long term commitment to the better health and well being of the clinic's clients.

TALT MALONE, Prevention Coordinator, for his guidance in this crucial area of our work.

MANUEL SANCHEZ, Counselor, for his professional expertise in demonstrating the clinic's work. *(see page 109)*

ALEX STALCUP, M.D., Medical Director, for his invaluable contributions to the clinical growth of the Detox Project Services.

CRAIG McDERMIT, PH.D., Supervising Clinical Psychologist, for continued dedication and hard work.

JOHN DEDOMENICO, Director of Volunteer Services, for the formulation of an effective and productive volunteer training program.

MAGDALEN CHANG & DAVID YONEMOTO of the Bill Pone Memorial Unit, for their very innovative work with Asian Pacific American Substance Abusers.

MARJORIE COLVIN, ELIZABETH SAMPSON, & RICHARD HALEY, for their unending dedication to the clients of the Detox Project.

RAFIQ BILAL, for his contributions to the formation of the Institute of Black Chemical Abuse with Glide Memorial Church.

HERBERT HOUSTON, Chief Executive Officer, Haight-Ashbury Free Medical Clinics, Inc., for his progressive leadership during very difficult times.

IRVING KLOMPUS, M.D., for always being there to help out in the treatment of the clinic's clientele.

PABLO STEWART, M.D., for his continued giving of clinical assistance above and beyond the call of duty.

REVEREND CECIL WILLIAMS, Pastor of the Glide Memorial Church, and **JAN MIRIKITANI,** for providing a home and support for The Glide/Haight-Ashbury Institute on Black Chemical Abuse and for their spiritual guidance in leading so many into recovery.

Special thanks to **HARPER AND ROW PUBLISHERS** for permission to use parts of their book, **THE DOPE CHRONICLES 1850-1950,** Harper and Row, S.F. 1979.

A very special note of appreciation to **ANNA EVERETT, MILLICENT BUXTON,** and the **SAN FRANCISCO MEDICAL SOCIETY WOMEN'S MEDICAL AUXILLARY** for their invaluable contribution and support in the development of this book.

INTRODUCTION

DARRYL INABA, Pharm D., Director, Drug Detoxification, Rehabilitation, and Aftercare Project of the Haight-Ashbury Free Medical Clinics and Associate Clinical Professor at the University of California Medical Center, San Francisco, California.

Since 1967, more than 30,000 drug users have availed themselves of the services of the Haight-Ashbury Clinics. In that period of time, we have seen several startling changes in the types of drugs that are used and the kinds of people that use or abuse them.

Substances like cocaine, heroin, marijuana, and PCP can no longer be considered the only drugs open to potential abuse when "legal drugs" such as prescription medications, alcohol, and nicotine have been shown to be equally liable. In addition, pharmaceutical researchers and "street chemists" continue to discover new, abusable drugs such as MPPP, MDMA, isobutyl nitrate, 3-methyl-fentanyl, ice, and freebase cocaine or its hybrid form, crack.

In addition, drug abuse can no longer be considered a hippie, ghetto dweller, barrio gang member, or Chinatown immigrant phenomenon. (Most of us use drugs in one form or another). The people who come to our clinic are from every cultural, ethnic, economic, and age group: college student, truck driver, housewife, doctor, junior high school student, hobo. For these reasons, it is the firm belief of the Haight-Ashbury Clinics that honest and factual education about drugs and their effects is the only way that drug information will be accepted by the user and non-user alike.

Since its inception, our drug detox program has focused on prevention and has developed a **"teaching not preaching"** approach to drug education. We have learned that scare tactics are not only ineffective but worse, they create a credibility gap.

We realize that psychoactive drugs and their potential for abuse represent a complex field. Thus, education about drugs and their effects cannot be completed with a one-, four-, or even eight-hour presentation. To be effective, drug abuse education requires an extended educational process. Remember, we are exposed to drugs throughout our lifetime.

We have designed this book to serve as a starting point for that educational process. It may be used as a textbook for a course on drugs or as a reference source for those committed to factual, objective drug education.

1928

HOOVER BACKS U.S. IN DOPE WAR

By Universal Service.

WASHINGTON, Jan. 21.—President Hoover today sent a message to Congress recommending $25,000 be appropriated for American participation in the International Conference on Limitation of the manufacture of narcotic drugs, to be held at Geneva, Switzerland, May 27.

The President transmitted a statement by Secretary of State Stimson, declaring the United States always has taken the lead in seeking international co-operation to stamp out the illicit narcotic drug traffic and urging the appropriation. Stimson said:

"It has been the aim of this government to bring about international co-operation in dealing with this problem, and to persuade other governments to limit the amount of narcotic drugs manufactured to the amounts essential for medical and scientific purposes."

The United States has been successful in establishing arrangements with nineteen countries for exchange of information on the movement of illicit drugs, with a view to co-operation in their suppression, Stimson said.

As an example of the magnitude of the problem, he cited the seizure of 17,500 ounces of morphine from the steamship Alesia in New York on December 15.

1921

HARDING'S PEN SPEEDS DRIVE AGAINST DRUGS

President Signs Congress Resolution to Join with Other Nations in Limiting Supply

HUGHES PLEDGES ACTION

Negotiations to Open at Once with Lands That Grow the Bases of Opium and Cocaine

By Universal Service.

WASHINGTON, March 3.—President Harding to-day signed the joint Congressional resolution urging that the United States take up with certain foreign governments the necessity for curtailing at the source the production of habit-forming drugs.

Secretary Hughes immediately pledged the "closest attention" of the State Department to the con...

1988

Bush gets word: Find czar to fight drug war

Reagan signs bill Congress imposed

By Dan Freedman
EXAMINER WASHINGTON BUREAU

WASHINGTON — Whether he likes it or not, President-elect Bush is charged with installing a drug czar in the White House to coordinate the government's $4 billion war on illegal narcotics.

The so-called czar, officially the director of the Office of National Drug Policy Control, is Congress' own answer to what it considers the Reagan administration's failed effort to curtail rising drug use and importation.

Under the drug bill passed by Congress last month and signed into law by President Reagan Friday, the cabinet-level czar will have wide-ranging ... but not absolute

— author...
ment's v...
planes, sh...
educatio...
sumption, a...
trafficking.

"Our bat...
any single p...
won by any s...
during the emotional signing ceremony in the White House. But the
...ill's tough ap-
...alled "recre-
...s well as its
... for anyone
ted killings.

1929

COOLIDGE SIGNS BILL DOPE-CURE FARMS

NEW U.S. LAW WILL HELP END NARCOTIC EVIL, SAVE ADDICTS

JANUARY 20, 1929

Rep. Porter, Measure's Author, Calls It Boon to Nation; Gives W. R. Hearst Credit

All "Drug Slave" Convicts Will Be Sent to Farms First for Rehabilitation

ARTHUR HACHTEN,
By Universal Service

WASHINGTON, Jan. 19.—President Coolidge today signed the Porter bill, creating two Federal farms where narcotic drug addicts may be cured of their affliction.

The President invited Representative Stephen G. Porter (Rep., of Penna), chairman of the House Foreign Affairs Committee and author of the bill, to breakfast with him at the White House to witness his signing of this measure, which has been described by health authorities, Federal judges and civic leaders as "a boon to the nation."

NARCOTIC DIVISION CREATED

Responsibility for drafting plans and constructing buildings is placed upon the supervising architect in the Treasury Department.

Management and control of the institutions is vested in the Secretary of the Treasury, who is to create a narcotic division in the Public Health service. This division shall have immediate control of the institutions. The law says:

"The care and treatment of the addicts there, restore them to health and train them to be self supporting and self-reliant."

The surgeon general is to co-operate with the several States in providing information and assistance in creating similar State institutions.

United States attorneys are required to report to superior...

for
...tific
...cted
the
...taken
up with Great Britain, Persia and Turkey, India, a British possession, produces considerable quantities of opium.

Reports from London already indicate a growing British appreciation of the drug menace; and the negotiations with the English Government, it is known, will receive considerable popular support on both sides of the Atlantic.

BLOW AT COCAINE

The second group of negotiations will be conducted with the Netherlands, Peru and Bolivia, relative to the coca leaf and its derivatives, chiefly cocaine. The island of Java, a Dutch possession, produces coca leaves.

Secretary Hughes' deep interest in the drug problem assures prompt action in carrying on both sets of negotiations.

Following the signing, President Harding sent the pen to Representative Porter, of Pennsylvania, author of the resolution.

1986

Political Jockeying

Reagan, Congress Call for Drug War

Washington

House and Senate leaders and President Reagan called for bipartisan cooperation against drugs yesterday while all sides continued to maneuver for the political spotlight on what is becoming a major issue of the 1986 campaign.

Despite the talk of bipartisanship, the House, Senate and White House are not close on the size and scope of an anti-drug program, with the administration wanting to spend a few hundred million dollars and some members of Congress talking of a billion and a half or more. The potential cost of some congressional proposals could turn the administration against them.

"It appears to me that that's not going to begin to be nearly enough," he said.

Dole said that he also favors spending beyond the administration's target.

Administration aides said later that the president's program might grow. The $250 million figure Miller used did not include the cost of a proposal to permit drug testing of more than a million federal employees, which one official said could cost as much as $50 million in 1987.

Reagan's comments came as White House officials expressed concern that news reports that the president might order mandatory testing for some federal employees could prevent the public from fo-

12

A SHORT HISTORY OF
DRUGS

Ad for French tonic wine, made with coca leaf extract.   It promised to help the user's digestion and disposition (c. 1896 by Charles Levy-Courtesy of the Estate of Timothy C. Ploughman).

U sing drugs to change our mental state is nothing new. As long as we, the highest order of life on Earth, have had to think, we've searched for ways to alter our state of consciousness. Whether we wanted to forget our harsh surroundings, come to grips with our mortality, alter our mood, explore feelings, promote social interaction, or enhance our senses, we felt a desire to tinker with reality. There are so many ways to change our perception of reality: we can seek religious experiences, we can push the body past its physical limits, we can immerse ourselves in our work, we can become insane, or we can take psychoactive drugs.

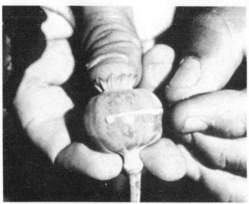

Opium poppy seed being slit to extract the gummy opium resin.

More than 4,000 years ago, the Sumerians, living in the area we now call Iran, cultivated the opium poppy. They named it, "the joy plant." The milky white fluid from the dried bulb was boiled to a sticky gum, then chewed, burned, inhaled, or mixed with fermented liquids and drunk. As with most potent and desired substances, the rulers and holy men tried to control its use to dominate their society.

500 years before the birth of Christ, the Scythians, whose territory ranged from the Danube to the Volga rivers in Eastern Europe, threw marijuana on hot stones placed in small tents, and in-

haled the vapors. The Greek writer Herodotus wrote, "No Grecian vapor bath can surpass the Scythian tent. The Scythians, transported with the vapor, shout aloud."

Ripe female marijuana plant (Cannabis sativa) almost ready for harvest.

Almost eight centuries ago in South America, high in the Andes Mountains, the Incan Emperor Manco Capac controlled use of the coca leaf, the raw ingredient for cocaine. "The right to chew the coca leaf was prized far above the richest presents of silver and gold." All the nobility carried their precious supply of coca leaves in ornate bags strapped to their wrists. A plentiful supply of the drug, which was considered divine, was buried with each mummified nobleman and noblewoman.

Peter Brughel the Elder's portrayal of peasants crushing grapes for wine (c. 1490).

The ancients looked on alcohol, particularly wine, as a gift from their gods: Osiris gave it to the Egyptians, Dionysus to the Greeks, and Noah to the Hebrews. In the Middle Ages, the monasteries cultivated wine grapes for use as a sacrament. As the hordes of invading barbarians, from the Goths to the Huns, swept through Europe, the oft-enslaved peasant found solace in this fermented beverage. Thus, the Dark Ages were somewhat lightened by hoisting a flagon or goblet.

Columbian stone head (c. 1400) depicting user's cheek stuffed with concada (coca leaf mixed with guano).

To the north of the Incan Empire, about the time Columbus arrived in the Americas, the Huichol, Cora, and Tarahumare Indians of Mexico were digging up the peyote cactus or psilocybin mushrooms and celebrating their hallucinogenic effects in sacred ceremonies. The Spanish conquistadors, on the other hand, considered peyote and other hallucinogenic drugs as instruments of the Devil.

A devil entices a Central American Indian to eat a Teonanacatl (psilocybin) mushroom (c. 16th century).

King George of England sent a proclamation to America in 1750 encouraging the planting of hemp (marijuana). Though the purpose was to establish an American textile and rope industry, the possibilities for smoking were not lost on our forefathers.

The British government grew opium in India to trade with China for tea. "The Wars for Free Trade" as the British called them, or the "Opium Wars," were fought in the mid 1800's to enforce the British right to sell opium to the war lords who in turn sold it to the peasants to help them forget harsh living conditions.

A Hankow, China opium den (c. 1900).

Since opium and its derivative morphine are pain killers as well as euphoriants, the widespread use in the U.S. Civil War to ease the suffering of the wounded created scores of "morphine eaters, drinkers, and shooters." Opium overuse was considered preferable to alcohol abuse since the user "wasn't as rambunctious or noisy and just sat in a corner dozing off."

A Civil War Pharmacist dispenses drugs (c. 1863).

Vin Mariani, a fine Bordeaux wine laced with coca leaf extracts, became quite popular in the 1890's, spurred on by the first celebrity endorsements from such luminaries as Thomas Alva Edison and President William McKinley.

Advertisement for Vin Mariani Wine (c. 1894)

Other over-the-counter medicines sold at the turn of the century had imaginative names such as Mrs. Winslow's Soothing Syrup and McMunn's Elixir of Opium, all loaded with opium, heroin, or cocaine.

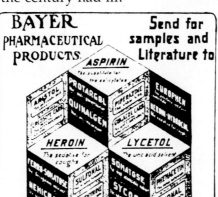

1888 Bayer Pharmaceutical ad promoting heroin and aspirin for that nasty cough.

Kit on sale at Macy's (c. 1902) included vials of cocaine, heroin, and a reusable syringe.

Heroin/cocaine kits were advertised in newspapers and sold in the best stores. Our ambivalence toward drug use reached its zenith at the start of the 20th century. The age of the average user at this point in our history was 42.

between 1905–1915

By 1914, the Pure Food and Drug Act, the Opium Exclusion Act, and the Harrison Narcotic Act eliminated the over-the-counter availability of opiates and cocaine. Unfortunately, the tight control of all supplies encouraged the development of the illicit drug trade which today, in the U.S., is estimated at 100 to 200 billion dollars a year.

ate it, drank it & shot d ?

In 1920, it took thirteen months to ratify the Eighteenth Amendment prohibiting the manufacture and sale of liquor. Thirteen years later it only took ten months to repeal that same amendment. We hadn't changed our feelings about the benefits of alcohol. We had simply found out that Prohibition didn't work.

During World War II, American, British, German, and Japanese army doctors routinely prescribed amphetamines (speed) to soldiers to fight fatigue, heighten endurance, and "elevate the fighting spirit." Uppers were as plentiful as chipped beef on toast and c-rations.

Calms the Tense, Nervous Patient
in anxiety and depression

Miltown ad, targeted for doctors, to help them convince their patients of the drug's value (c. 1955).

Barbiturates, first used at the turn of the century, came into their own in the frantic fifties. The prescribing of those drugs plus the development of Miltown and other "milder" tranquilizers made many believe in the slogan, "Better living through chemistry."

Dr. Timothy Leary encouraged the children of the 60's to "Turn on, tune in, and drop out." The guru of LSD spoke out for drug experimentation to "alter the mind." Psychedelics and stimulants (LSD, marijuana, and speed) were the most popular.

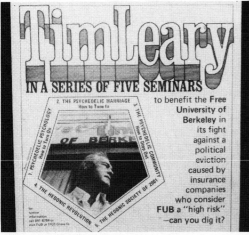

Dr. Leary traveled the lecture circuit to advocate psychedelic experimentation.

In the seventies, an unwanted war in Vietnam, along with the flood of opium from the Golden Triangle (Cambodia, Laos, and Thailand), encouraged the use of downers such as heroin.

The eighties have seen a surge in the use of smokable cocaine (freebase, rock, crack) and illicit methamphetamines. Along with this apparent wave of stimulant abuse, depending on which headline you read or what statistics you believe, the use of marijuana, PCP, Valium, heroin, synthetic opiates, and especially alcohol continues. The drugs of choice in the nineties and of succeeding generations may vary, but the basic reasons for reshaping our own realities and consciousness will stay the same. We can only say that psychoactive drugs have always been part of civilization and there's no reason to think this will change.

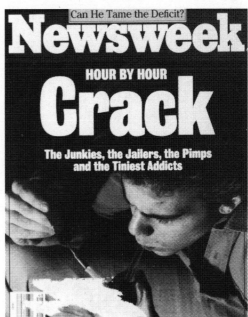

1893

MANIA FOR MORPHINE

Grave Charges That Have Been Made Against Physicians of Paris.

A SPECIALIST'S OPINIONS.

Fifty Thousand Persons in the Capital Use the Drug Every Day.

A TABLE OF THE "FIENDS."

Physicians and Their Wives Found To Be at the Top of the Heaviest Users.

A GRAVE charge has been brought against [illegible] cians, a charge so [illegible] that one would [illegible] to believe it [illegible] were not for the [illegible] that it has been [illegible] a man who is himself a famous physician [illegible] specialist [illegible] in proof of his [illegible] statements an array of statistics which certainly seem to be conclusive.

When Aubert was arrested in Paris the other day on the charge of [illegible] young philatelist, Delahaeff, it [illegible] apparent that he was a confirmed [illegible] fiend. During his trial he suffered [illegible] for lack of the deadly drug, and [illegible] public prosecutor, fearing that he [illegible] tarly collapse, instructed a physician to administer a timely injection. This [illegible] the prisoner being on trial, was a [illegible] able proceeding, but what surprised [illegible] no more than the fact that a poverty [illegible] fellow like Aubert should have [illegible] dicted to the use of such an expensive [illegible] as morphine. Hitherto the popular [illegible] has been that only the comparatively well-to-do could afford a luxury of this kind. [illegible]

1923

MARIHUANA MAKES FIENDS OF BOYS IN 30 DAYS: HASHEESH GOADS USERS TO BLOOD-LUST

Physicians Called On to Urge Harding Bid All Nations Meet to Throttle Dope At Its Source; United States Laws Too Lenient

"The Federal Government, operating under the Harrison Act, and the amending Jones-Miller bill, employs one hundred and seventy-three narcotic enforcement agents. For their year's labors Congress appropriates the sum of $750,000. The country is divided into thirteen districts under as many district chiefs, and their agents must cover the country. It is a feeble appropriation and a woefully light brigade."—Sidney Howard, in current issue of Hearst's International.

By ANNIE LAURIE

ARTICLE X.

Strange old story—the story of Medusa.

It's come such a long way down to us from the bright old days when "all the men were brave—and all the women beautiful."

Medusa, the beautiful woman, half mortal and half goddess, with the hair that was not hair at all, but a coiling mass of hissing serpents.

And he who followed the soft wooing of Medusa's voice and looked upon the twining serpents that were her hair was turned to stone—and never knew again the delight of human communication with human kind.

Medusa—if we believed in her existence today—we should call her the patron saint of "dope."

Morphine, cocaine, heroin, hasheesh, marihuana—these are the snakes that curl about the head of this modern Medusa.

Where is the Perseus to look with unblinking eyes at this horror and put an end to it once and for all?

COMES BY TONS.

By the tons it is coming into this country—the deadly, dreadful poison that racks and tears not only the body, but the very heart and soul of every human being who once becomes a slave to it in any of its cruel and devastating forms.

Which is the worst of [illegible] evils?

Who can say?

Marihuana is a short cu[t to the] insane asylum.

Smoke marihuana cigar[ettes for] a month and what was on[ce your] brain will be nothing but [a store]house of horrid specters.

Hasheesh makes a [murderer] who kills for the love of [it, out] of the wildest manner [ever a mani]ac ever laughed at the [illegible] [no] "habit" could ever get [illegible]

Morphine shrivels the [skin] and bone, atrophies [illegible] and turns a normal huma[n being in]to the sick shadow of [a man] who will sell his own f[lesh and] blood, no matter how yo[ung and] tender, to the horrible [illegible] of the streets to get his d[ope].

Cocaine stifles reason, [kills] all sense of responsibility [and] looses upon the world a da[ngerous] "Frankenstein" with neit[her rea]son nor conscience to [guide] him.

Heroin combines morph[ine and co]caine and is stronger a[nd more] deadly than either.

Every new "dope" slave means new money in his pocket.

Arrest such a man under the city ordinance in New York City and what can you do with him?

Try him for a misdemeanor—not for a crime—and send him to the island for a few days and make him pay a few dollars' fine, which means just about as much to him as one or two street car fares would mean to you or me.

PUNISH AS CRIME.

Change the city ordinances, make "dope" selling not a misdemeanor but a crime, and punish it as crimes are punished.

In some States the State laws make it about as serious to be caught selling "dope" as it is to be caught throwing a torn envelope into the street instead of into the corner trash box.

The Harrison narcotic law is a good law as Federal laws go, but it does not go far enough.

The Jones-Miller law, which was passed last May, is an excellent law. It makes the penalty for "dope" selling or "dope" buying or "dope" possession ten years in the penitentiary and $5,000 fine.

It gives the power to deport immediately any foreigner caught selling "dope," and it lays a fine upon any ship caught bringing "dope" into American ports.

1928

FEBRUARY 23, 1928

60 PER CENT OF ALL VIOLENT CRIMES TRACED TO COCAINE

Underworld's Pet Drug Makes Youths Into Thugs and Slayers; Stealthy Narcotic Most Noxious for Trapping Boys and Girls

By WINIFRED BLACK.

"SNOW." "Joy Powder." "Happy Dust." These are some of the names by which the Underworld calls cocaine, one of the most deadly drugs in existence.

The "dope" ring, the big distributers and the "dope" peddlers sometimes call it "the kid catcher."

They do that because cocaine is the one drug that boys and girls pick up first, and it is astonishing and horrifying to discover how many boys and girls there are in this country today who are "snow birds," as the police call them.

WINIFRED BLACK.

Do the police know cocaine? Do the police know murder? and robbery and kidnaping and all the kindred crimes? They have a name for these crimes in police circles.

"Coke stuff"—that's what they call gun plays, holdups, bold robbery, outrageous and maniacal murders.

All these things are tarred with the same unmistakable brush.

All these crimes, or nearly all of them, are committed by men who go for "sleigh rides," as they call a cocaine party in that strange, secret, whispering life we call the underworld.

The Underworld's Drug

Cocaine is as much a part of Underworld life as food and drink is a part of normal, healthy, human existence.

Cocaine begins in the Underworld and ends there—but it does not stay there all the time. There are cocaine parties that are nowhere near the slums and there are "snow birds" who move in the [illegible] n every city in [illegible] tomobile—these [illegible] changed the [illegible] of America.' [illegible] body had ever [illegible] ped car in a [illegible] tal, downtown [illegible] lul, commercial [illegible] see them as a [illegible] Do men need [illegible] they did years [illegible] by guards and [illegible] ficient—not so [illegible] ne as they [illegible] the reason of [illegible] e official you [illegible] ough at you. [illegible] or heroin, or [illegible] ut it's mostly [illegible] over 60 per [illegible] of violence in [illegible] gang that's [illegible] or hold up a [illegible] up on co- [illegible] lling and they [illegible] in a high- [illegible] motor car; [illegible] to crime in [illegible] def of police [illegible] n. [illegible] an Francisco [illegible] hicago. Ask [illegible] ork. It's the [illegible] "dope," that's [illegible] east the most [illegible] he answer to [illegible] tion.

Doped and Brutish!

Garhard Kuhne, chief of the bureau of criminal identification in the City of New York, says:

"The atrocious manner in which the victims of holdup men are abused and needlessly maimed shows conclusively that the gunmen while committing these crimes are not rational.

"I doubt if they would have the courage to attempt such crimes if they were not full of drugs at the time.

"This is verified by the fact that in all crimes of violence of recent years, where the offenders are apprehended, they are found to be drug addicts, and admit they were loaded with drugs when they committed the crime.

"The notorious Whittemore gang, who have all been recently con-

1985

A New Study Profiles Users Of Marijuana

Chicago

Marijuana users are characterized by a higher use of other drugs, psychiatric hospitalization and close association with other marijuana users, a study showed yesterday.

Denise B. Kandel, a researcher at Columbia University School of Public Health in New York, studied 1325 young adults.

Marijuana use reaches a peak between ages 20 and 22 — and declines at age 25, Kandel said in the American Medical Association's Archives of General Psychiatry.

"Involvement with marijuana-using friends and use by spouse or partner, as well as use of other illicit drugs, were important predictors of current marijuana involvement."

Users of marijuana are "quite different" from non-users in values and lifestyles, she said. Users exhibit a lower level of 'social achievement and psychological well-being, are involved in a social network of drug-using associates and use cigarets, alcohol and other drugs.

Men and women who used marijuana at least four times a week — compared to non-users — were two to three times as likely to have ever consulted a mental health professional and seven to eight times as likely to have been hospitalized for a psychiatric disorder.

United Press

1986

A Study Indicates Cocaine May Lead to Heart Attacks

By PETE THOMAS, *Times Staff Writer*

The recent sudden death of Len Bias, former University of Maryland basketball star, and the possibility that cocaine was a contributor, has put the spotlight on the relationship between cocaine and its effects on the heart.

Cardiologists Mark Estes and Jeffrey Isner of the New England Medical Center, which is affiliated with Tufts University near Boston, have released a study suggesting that cocaine affects the heart in a life-threatening manner.

The study, the largest of its kind, offered some answers in light of reports that Bias, the Boston Celtics' first-round draft pick, had used the drug shortly before his death last Thursday.

Seven patients, between 20 and 37, were part of the study, which was conducted in 1984-1985. All seven had used cocaine within six hours of being taken to the hospital with heart difficulties and none had shown previous signs of heart disease. Of the seven:

—Four patients had heart attacks and one of them died.

—One patient had severe scarring of the heart muscle, which improved after six months of medication and complete abstinence from cocaine.

—Two patients had ventricular arrhythmias - unstable heart rhythms resulting in rapid heartbeats and ineffective pumping of blood. One of those patients — a chronic user – was found dead.

"He was found dead in bed and had been using [cocaine] several times a week for at least two years," said Estes, director of the Cardiac Electrophysiology Laboratory at the hospital.

In light of the study, if Bias used cocaine just before his death, as preliminary reports indicate, his death can't be considered *altogether* surprising.

Declining to comment specifically on the Bias case, Estes nevertheless said: "In other young patients who had been free of heart disease, we clearly have seen serious heart problems that had been associated with the use of cocaine."

1987

New Form of Heroin Linked To Rise in Overdose Deaths

By JOEL BRINKLEY

Special to The New York Times

WASHINGTON, March 27 — An unusually potent and dangerous new form of Mexican heroin is being spread rapidly across the United States, Federal drug enforcement officials say. They assert that it has led to dozens, perhaps hundreds, of deaths by overdose, as well as to thousands of injuries in the last year.

The new heroin, which users call black tar because it resembles roofing tar in color and consistency, is increasingly dominating the nation's heroin markets. It is now sold in 27 states, up from four in 1983, according to officials of the Federal Drug Enforcement Administration.

It is blamed for causing the first general increase in overall heroin use in more than five years, in part because its low price has forced down other heroin prices.

The drug agency says black tar sells in some areas of the country for one-tenth the price of the heroin previously available, even though purity levels are as much as 40 times higher.

"It's a very serious problem and it's getting worse," John C. Lawn, head of the Drug Enforcement Administration, said in an interview. "Nineteen eighty-six is not going to be a good year for us."

The drug agency says the substance is manufactured and distributed by a new combination of amateur Mexican processors and smugglers, frustrating law-enforcement officials accustomed to investigating Mexico's more conventional drug-trafficking groups.

Simplified Process Used

Farmers in the states of Durango, Sinaloa and Sonora in northern Mexico are processing it themselves from their own opium poppy crops, using a simplified process that accounts for the new heroin's unusual appearance and high purity as well as its low price.

In the United States, black tar sells on the street for as little as $2.50 for an average-size single dose of about 10 milligrams. Conventional Mexican heroin sells for about $24 a dose.

The increasing availability of black tar is leading to a nationwide decline in prices for all types of heroin, according to a Drug Enforcement Agency report published earlier this week. "Some areas are reporting decreases of 25 to

Continued on Page 11, Column 2

THE GENERAL EFFECTS OF
PSYCHOACTIVE
DRUGS

What constitutes a psychoactive drug? If you talk to people who have used drugs, or are involved in drug abuse prevention, they will tell you.

Marijuana smoker: "Sinsemilla is the number one strength...and Thai sticks are second...and Columbian is the worst. And then there's always home-grown, backyard weed that everybody grows."

Inhalant user: "I like nitrous oxide a lot better than the other two things: isobutyl or amyl nitrite. You shouldn't stand up or walk around when you do them."

DEA officer: "You're looking at a marijuana plant that's 16 feet tall. You could probably get a good three pounds of buds off it."

Alcoholic: "I started drinking gin and tonic. And then after a while, about a month, I started drinking gin over ice. And then I switched to brandy."

LSD user: "Acid, in our heyday, was a lot stronger. One hit then, was the equivalent of 5 or 6 hits today."

Pill user: "A guy came up to me and asked if I wanted some Cibas, which are Doridens. I didn't know what they were but it got me real stoned. And this guy in the park would sell Seconal; three for a dollar."

Drug testing laboratory supervisor: "In this sample we have a moderate amount of cocaine, and we also have benzocaine, caffeine, cocaine, and some heroin. Heroin and cocaine mixed together are known as a speedball."

Valium user: "This doctor I went to started out giving me Nembutal, Darvon, a little phenobarbital, Valium, and Compazine. The drugstore delivered all at one time. My health insurance paid for them. I mean, luxury, right there."

PCP user: "Sometimes you can tell how strong it is by the taste, if it isn't rolled up with a mint. Usually you don't know what it is till you take it."

Heroin user: "I'd been using China White heroin, about 95% pure, for a year and a half. We ran out. I don't remember anything that happened for about 4 days. I do remember trying to drink alcohol to try to alleviate the pain."

Crack smoker: "If it's real pure, you get a real intense vibration, like waves of energy. Lots of times there's too much baking soda left in the rock."

Codeine user: "I used to use loads; codeine and Doriden. It was cheaper than using heroin."

CLASSIFICATION OF PSYCHOACTIVE DRUGS

Street names like "crack," "junk," "angel dust," "Shermans," "loads," "crank," "base," "window pane," "whack," "Adam," "hubba," "rock," "horse," "ecstasy," and "U4Euh" continue to evolve almost daily among drug users. Each commonly used and abused substance may have ten or more labels. Just as confusing is the continued synthesis of new psychoactive drugs with chemical names such as methylenedioxyamphetamine and alpha-methyl-fentanyl. Attempts at classifying psychoactive drugs based upon their street or chemical names have been as bewildering as the drugs themselves. Even lawmakers have to be careful when outlawing a drug. They must describe it exactly.

A more practical way of classifying these agents has come from drug users who distinguish these substances by their overall effects. Thus, **UPPERS, DOWNERS, ALL AROUNDERS**, and **INHALANTS** have been chosen to describe the most commonly abused psychoactive drugs.

When we talk about the effects of drugs, we mean the average effects of a moderate dose on an average person. Since effects can vary radically from person to person and even from dose to dose, our information about the action of drugs on the body should be used as a general guideline and not as an absolute. Later we will discuss the effects of large doses and prolonged use.

"Terminal" in this San Francisco drugstore sign referred to the nearby bus terminal, not the effects of their pharmaceuticals, tonics, and cough remedies.

UPPERS are central nervous system **stimulants:** cocaine (freebase, crack), amphetamines (speed, crank, ice), diet pills, "psychic energizers," "look alikes," nicotine, and caffeine.

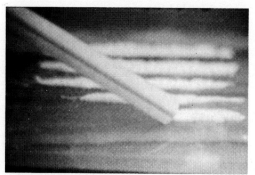

Lines of cocaine go up the straw and into the nose; the most common method of using cocaine hydrochloride.

Physical effects: The usual effect of a small to moderate dose is an over stimulation of the nervous system creating energized muscles, increased heart rate, increased blood pressure, and decreased appetite. It can cause heart, blood vessel, and seizure problems, particularly if large amounts are used or the user is extra sensitive. The stronger the stimulant, the greater the effects.

Mental effects: A moderate dose of the stronger stimulants can make one feel more confident, outgoing, eager to perform, and excited. It can also cause a certain euphoria depending on the physiology of the user and the specific drug. Larger doses or prolonged use of the stronger stimulants can cause anxiety, paranoia, and mental confusion.

DOWNERS are central nervous system **depressants.** The three main categories are

Opiates & opioids: opium, heroin, codeine, Percodan, methadone, Dilaudid, Demerol, Darvon, etc.

Sedative-hypnotics: barbiturates, Valium, Librium, Xanax, Quaalude, Doriden, Miltown, etc.

Alcohol: beer (and lite beer), wine (and wine coolers), hard liquors (and cute mixed drinks).

The home dispensary-prescription downers at your fingertips.

Physical effects: Small doses slow heart rate and respiration, decrease muscular coordination and energy, and dull the senses. Downers, opiates in particular, can also cause constipation, nausea, and sexual dysfunction.

Mental effects: Initially, small doses can act as stimulants because they lower inhibitions, but as more is taken, the overall depressant effect takes over, dulling the mind and slowing the body. Certain downers can also induce euphoria, or a sense of well being.

ALL AROUNDERS or **psyche-delics** are substances which can distort perceptions to induce delusions or hallucinations: LSD, PCP, psilocybin peyote, mescaline, MDA, MDMA, marijuana, etc.

Physical effects: Most hallucinogenic plants, particularly mushrooms and cacti, cause nausea and dizziness. Marijuana increases appetite and makes the eyes bloodshot. LSD raises the blood pressure and causes sweating. MDA, MDMA, and even LSD act like stimulants but generally, except for PCP which acts as an anesthetic, the physical effects are not as important as the mental effects.

Dried psilocybin mushrooms and capsules of street psilocybin.

Mental effects: Most often, psychedelics overload or distort messages to and from the brain stem, the sensory switchboard for the mind, so that many physical stimuli, particularly visual ones, are intensified or distorted. Imaginary messages can also be created by the brain, (i.e., hallucinations).

INHALANTS are gaseous or liquid substances, inhaled and absorbed through the lungs: organic solvents such as glue, gasoline, metallic paints; volatile nitrites such as amyl or butyl nitrite sold as Bolt, Rush, etc., and nitrous oxide (laughing gas).

Amyl nitrite is popped in the bag and snorted.

Physical effects: Most often there is central nervous system depression. Dizziness, slurred speech, unsteady gait, and drowsiness are seen early on. The solvents in particular can be quite toxic to lung, brain, liver, and kidney tissues. Some inhalants lower the blood pressure, causing the user to faint or lose balance.

Mental effects: With small amounts, impulsiveness, excitement, and irritability are common. Eventually, delirium with confusion, some hallucinations, drowsiness, and stupor can be found in inhalant abusers.

There are other drugs such as antihistamines and steroids which don't quite fit in any category, and these will also be discussed in other chapters.

PHYSICAL VS. EMOTIONAL EFFECTS

People take psychoactive drugs for a number of reasons.

Crack user: "I felt I wasn't a whole person without it. I needed the drug to become myself, especially dealing with my peers. I was more of an introvert when I was off the drug. When I had the drug, I'd be really outgoing."

Speed user: "Very high energy, as though I could walk for miles. I would clean my apartment; use brillo on the floor; just lots of energy. It also made me feel very euphoric."

Heroin user: "I'm always in pain. I have bad shoulders, arthritis, and all these things so it was my excuse cause I knew this stuff would get me high so I would take it. I would say, 'Oh, I'm just killing my pain."

Valium user: "It relieved certain anxieties. It alleviated depression which I had. Lots of depression. You tell the doctor, 'I'm depressed.' 'OK, take some Valium.' I had a heart attack at home and I called him and I said, 'I think I had a heart attack.' And he said, 'I don't think you did; it's nerves. I'll send over 100 Valium.'"

Barbiturate user: "I'd go into a bar, and I'd be all dressed up nice, and I'd have a few pills in my pocket, and my rap was pretty good, I thought. I thought I was Rudolph Valentino, or somebody like that."

Alcohol user: "Somebody walks in the room and what do you do, you offer them a drink. It's cordial. That's how you break the ice. You ask, 'Would you like a drink?' And I frankly don't know anyone who says no. I like to drink. Drink is good. It makes me happy. It makes everybody else I know happy. It's a social event."

Marijuana user: "It makes time go by fast, sometimes slow, depending on if you're watching the clock and if you're bored. If you're really enjoying yourself, it makes the time go by lots faster."

LSD user: "I was really into the literature of the time....The Politics of Ecstasy, or something like that, by Timothy Leary, High Priest of the LSD movement. It was more like an adventure, looking for things in it. I think people doing it at the time were trying to find out what it was like to have some sort of spiritual experience."

Inhalant user: "I was walking by St. Boniface church and here's this wino. He takes this little bottle of gasoline or paint thinner out and he pours it in this rag and he goes snort, snort, snort. He looked real bad...like death on a soda cracker."

High school football player: "I was 125 pounds. Not big enough for the team. I started taking steroids I got from a weightlifter friend so I could bulk up. By the way, there was also a little buzz off them."

If drugs did only what people wanted them to, then drugs wouldn't be much of a problem. But drugs not only create desired emotional **effects**, they create unwanted, even dangerous, physical and emotional **side effects.**

This competition between the emotional effects that users want, and the physical/emotional effects they don't want, is the main danger from psychoactive drugs.

For example, a psychoactive drug such as codeine (an opiate/downer) is prescribed by a physician to relieve pain, to suppress a cough, or to treat a bad case of diarrhea. It also acts as a sedative, gives a feeling of well being, and induces numbness and relaxation. So a user who self-prescribes codeine just for the feeling of well being will also get the pain, cough, and constipation. Users will also be subject to

- nausea and occasional vomiting because the drug is attracted to the nausea center in the brain
- pinpoint pupils because opiates affect the optic nerves and muscles
- slowed respiration, and pulse because the drug affects the part of the nervous system that controls those functions
- dry skin and itching
- slowed speech and movement.

And if users take **large quantities** of a drug to get desired emotional effects, they could

- suppress breathing to dangerous levels
- become lethargic and have drastically slowed reflexes
- slow the heart rate, lower the blood pressure, and become unconscious.

And if users wanted those emotional effects **over a long period of time** they could

- become severely constipated
- lose sexual desire
- become dependent on the drug
- cause addiction in a fetus.

Limits the high

So users have to learn how to use enough to get the emotional effects desired without damaging or even killing the body and mind. Unfortunately, each drug has certain properties which affect this emotional/physical balance and make it difficult to self-prescribe the drug. Factors such as disruption of the nervous system, tolerance, tissue dependence, and withdrawal have to be taken into account.

To understand these processes it's helpful to begin by examining the ways a drug enters the body.

HOW DRUGS ENTER THE BODY

There are five common ways that drugs may enter the body:

Orally
When someone swallows a codeine tablet, eats a peyote button, or drinks a beer, the drug passes through the esophagus and stomach to the small intestine where it is absorbed into the tiny blood vessels (capillaries) lining the walls. Drugs taken this way have to pass through mouth enzymes and stomach acids so the effects are delayed and weaker than with other routes of administration (20 to 30 minutes reaction time).

Contact
A tiny "window pane" of LSD made of gelatin can be dropped in the eye or on a moist part of the skin where it is absorbed. In hospices for terminally ill patients, morphine suppositories are used for patients too weak for an injection or oral dose of a painkiller. Drugs taken in this fashion act more quickly than with the oral route (5 to 10 minutes reaction time).

Snorting and Sublingual
Cocaine and heroin are often snorted into the nose and absorbed by the tiny blood vessels enmeshed in the mucous membranes lining the nasal passages. The effects are usually more intense and occur more quickly than with the oral route. Crushed coca leaves (mixed with ash) can also be placed on the gums and absorbed through the mucous membranes (3 to 5 minutes reaction time).

Inhaling
When an individual smokes a joint or inhales freebase cocaine, the vaporized drug enters the lungs and is rapidly absorbed through the tiny blood vessels lining the air sacs of the bronchi. From the lungs, the drug-laden blood is pumped back to the heart and then directly to the body and brain thus acting more quickly than any of the other methods (7 to 10 seconds reaction time).

Injection
Substances such as heroin, cocaine, speed, and barbiturates can be put directly into the body with a needle. Drugs may be injected into the bloodstream (I.V.), into a muscle mass (muscling), or under the skin (skin popping). I.V. use is a quick and potent way to absorb a drug (15 to 30 seconds reaction time in a vein; 3 to 5 minutes in a muscle or under the skin). It is also the most dangerous method, exposing the body to many potential health problems such as hepatitis, abcesses, septicemia, or AIDS.

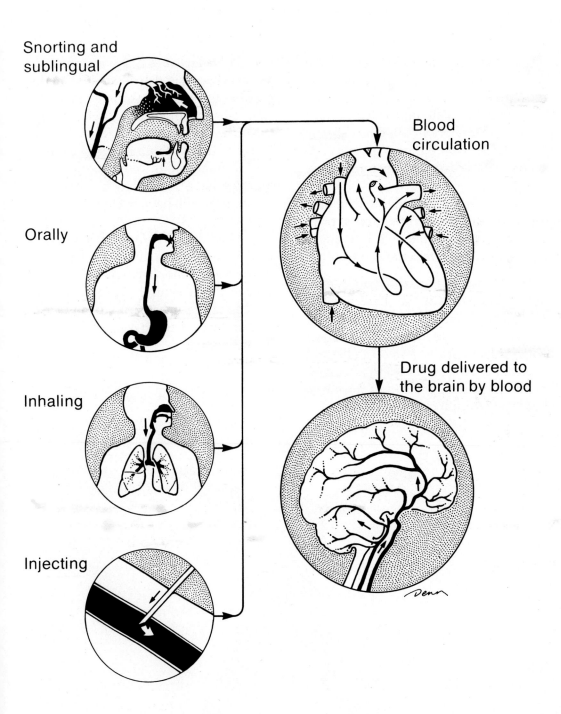

Snorting and
sublingual

Orally

Inhaling

Injecting

Blood
circulation

Drug delivered to
the brain by blood

The Effects
DRUG CIRCULATION

No matter how a drug enters the body, it eventually ends up in the bloodstream. The molecules of the drug then circulate and travel to and through every organ, fluid, and tissue in the body where they will either be ignored, absorbed, or transformed. *Liver*
Kr

In the bloodstream, the drug may be carried inside the blood cells, or in the plasma outside the cells, or it might hitch a ride on protein molecules.

The distribution of a drug within the body depends on the characteristics of the drug as well as on blood volume. As body size decreases, the blood volume decreases, so a small child of 12 might only have 3 to 4 quarts of blood to dilute the drug instead of the 6 to 8 quarts in an adult circulatory system.

The effect of a drug on a specific organ or tissue is also dependent on the number of blood vessels reaching that site. For example, veins and arteries saturate the heart muscles, so most drugs will pass through the heart and possibly affect it. Your bones and muscles have fewer blood vessels so most drugs will have less effect.

Most importantly, within only 10 to 15 seconds after entering the bloodstream, the drug reaches the approach to the central nervous system, the blood-brain barrier. On the other side of the barrier the drug will have its greatest effect.

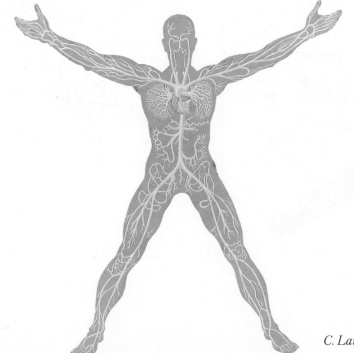

C. Laurel Schaubert

THE BLOOD-BRAIN BARRIER

The drug-laden blood flows through the internal carotid arteries toward the central nervous system (the brain and spinal cord, or the CNS). The structure of the blood vessels surrounding the nerve cells which make up the CNS is such that only certain substances can penetrate and affect the functioning of the nervous system. One class of drugs which can infiltrate this "blood-brain barrier" is psychoactive drugs (uppers, downers, all arounders, inhalants).

Note, however, that the brain is the most protective organ of the body. Thus, drugs that can penetrate its protective barrier inherently possess the ability to penetrate and affect all other organs of the body.

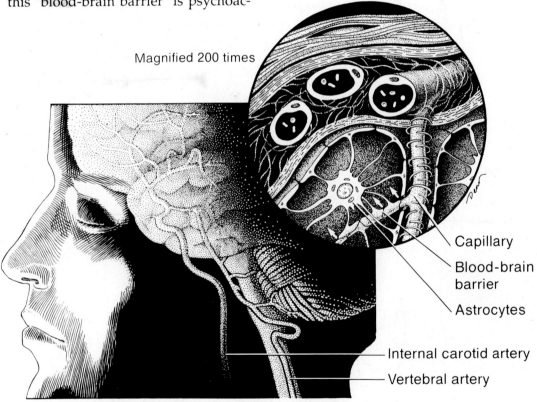

Magnified 200 times

Capillary

Blood-brain barrier

Astrocytes

Internal carotid artery

Vertebral artery

THE CENTRAL NERVOUS SYSTEM

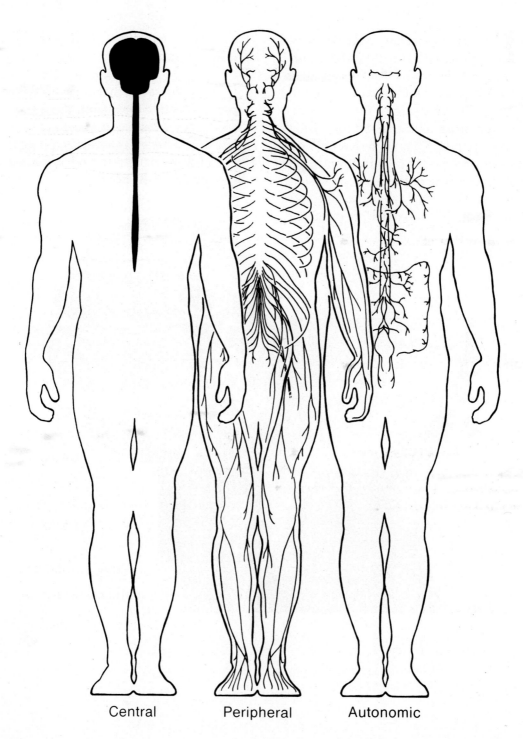

Central   Peripheral   Autonomic

Since the principal target of psychoactive drugs is the central nervous system (the brain and spinal cord), it is important to understand how this network of 100 billion nerve cells functions. The central nervous system is one third of the complete nervous system. The other two parts are the peripheral nervous system and the autonomic nervous system.

The **autonomic nervous system** controls involuntary functions such as circulation, digestion, respiration and reproduction. It automatically helps us breathe, pump blood, sweat, etc., to preserve a stable internal environment.

The **peripheral nervous system** transmits sensory messages between the central nervous system and our environment. (Our senses interpret the environment for the central nervous system.) The peripheral nervous system transmits instructions back to muscles and other organs or tissues from the central nervous system allowing us to react to that environment.

The **central nervous system** acts as a combination switchboard and computer, receiving messages from the peripheral and autonomic nervous systems, analyzing those messages, and then sending a response to the appropriate system of the body: muscular, skeletal, circulatory, nervous, respiratory, digestive, excretory, endocrine, and reproductive. It also enables us to reason and make judgments.

The **complete nervous system** helps us distinguish sensations such as light and dark, loud and soft, sweet and sour, pleasure and pain. It governs our emotions such as love, fear, and hate; it controls our physical movements such as walking, flinching, or kissing; it regulates our bodily functions; it lets us think.

A psychoactive drug, being an alien substance, alters information sent to our brain and disrupts messages sent back to the various parts of the body. A psychoactive drug disrupts our ability to think and reason. A psychoactive drug not only affects the nervous system, it affects the other eight systems of the body as well. It affects them directly while passing through the tissue or indirectly by manipulating the nerves of the central nervous system.

The Effects
NERVE CELLS

Understanding the precise way messages are sent by the nerves is crucial to understanding how psychoactive drugs affect us.

For example, if a dentist extracts the left molar, the damaged nerve endings send minute electrical pain signals towards the brain with a frequency of 1000 pulses a second and at speeds up to 200 miles per hour. The message is routed from one neuron to the next till it reaches its target in the brain.

At that point, the brain consults millions of other nerve cells, then reacts to the message and sends the appropriate signals back to that part of the body that needs to react. The brain might tell the patient's jaw to bite the dentist's finger.

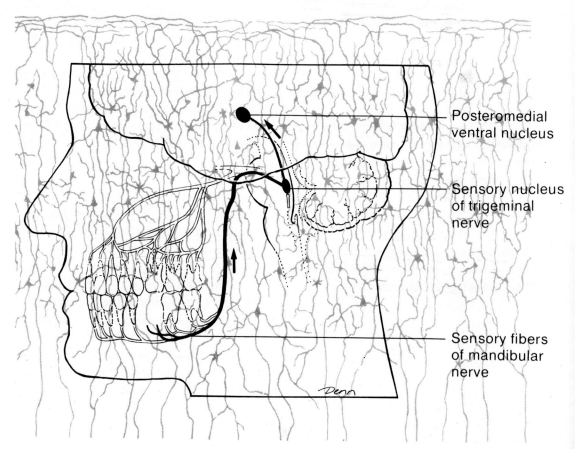

Posteromedial ventral nucleus

Sensory nucleus of trigeminal nerve

Sensory fibers of mandibular nerve

Cutaway view of the nerves that would transmit a message of pain from a left molar to the brain. The background drawing of a network of billions of nerve cells gives a magnified visual rendition of the complexity of the network that makes the nervous system function.

The building blocks of the nervous system, the nerve cells (neurons), have four essential parts: **dendrites** which receive signals from other nerve cells, the **cell body** which nourishes the organism and keeps it alive, the **axon** which carries the message from the dendrites and cell body to the **terminals** which then relay the message to the dendrites of the next nerve cell.

The length of a neuron is determined by the length of the axon which varies from a fraction of a millimeter between brain cells, to a foot between the tooth and brain, to several feet between the spinal cord and toe.

But here's the crucial part. Terminals of one nerve cell do not touch dendrites of the adjoining nerve cell because a gap, a tiny, tiny space exists between them.

The message jumps this **synaptic gap,** from the presynaptic terminal to the post-synaptic dendrite, not as an electrical signal but as microscopic bits of biochemicals. This biochemical signal completes the circuit. So, electrical and chemical signals alternate till the message reaches the appropriate section of the brain.

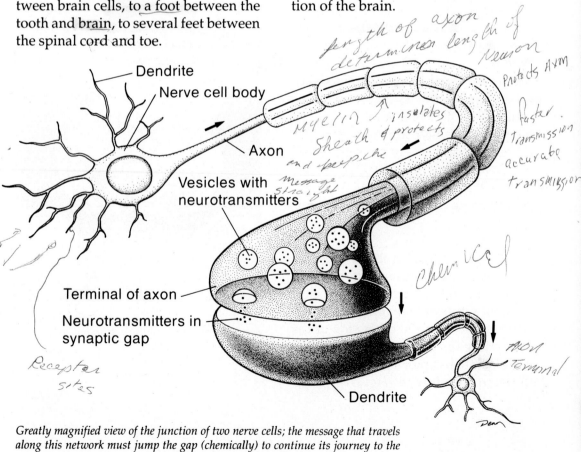

Dendrite

Nerve cell body

Axon

Vesicles with neurotransmitters

Terminal of axon

Neurotransmitters in synaptic gap

Dendrite

Greatly magnified view of the junction of two nerve cells; the message that travels along this network must jump the gap (chemically) to continue its journey to the brain and eventually back to muscles and organs throughout the body.

35

NEUROTRANSMITTERS I

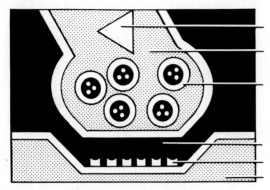

Nerve impulse

Presynaptic neuron

Vescicle with
neurotransmitters

Synaptic gap
Receptor site
Postsynaptic neuron

*Fig. 1: The electrical message arrives at the junction
of two nerve cells, the synaptic gap.*

The biochemicals that transmit messages across the nerve synapses are called **neurotransmitters** because they **transmit** information from one **neuron** to another. Their names sound exotic: dopamine, endorphin, enkephalin, seratonin, epinephrine, substance "P," acetylcholine, and at least 25 more. A single electrical message might release several types of neurotransmitters from several neurons. A pain message will release substance "P" at one synapse and enkephalin at another. *(Fig. 1)*

Normally, the electrical message will cause neurotransmitters to be released from tiny holding sacs (vesicles) and sent across the gap (magnified here 10,000 times). On the other side of the synaptic gap, the neurotransmitters will slot into receptor sites, retriggering the electrical message. *(Fig. 2)*

Psychoactive drugs disrupt the normal functioning of the neurotransmitters. **Sometimes the disruption is useful, sometimes desirable, and sometimes it is extremely dangerous.**

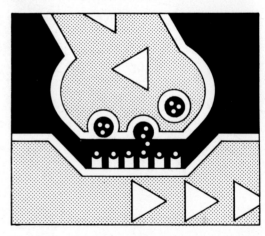

Fig. 2: The electrical message is retriggered in the postsynaptic neuron by neurotransmitters slotting into specialized receptors.

For example, an **upper** such as cocaine will force the release of large amounts of epinephrine and dopamine (without an electrical stimulus) thereby creating, stimulating, and exaggerating messages to and from the central nervous system. *(Fig. 3)*

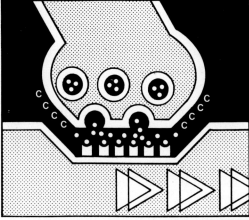

Fig. 3: Cocaine forces the release of extra neurotransmitters, triggering an exaggerated electrical signal in the post synaptic neuron.

A **downer** such as heroin, will inhibit the release of substance "P" by attaching itself to the sending nerve cell so the pain signal is dulled, dampened, and weakened. This is a useful effect. It will also attach itself to certain receptor sites in the emotional center of the brain inducing a sensation of pleasure or reward. This is a desired effect. It will also attach itself to the breathing center thereby depressing respiration. This is a dangerous effect. *(Fig. 4)*

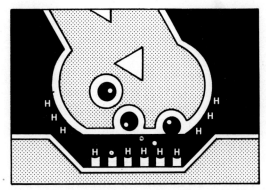

Fig. 4: Heroin inhibits the release of substance "P" and also helps block most of those neurotransmitters that do get through. So the electrical signal is greatly weakened in the postsynaptic neuron.

An **all arounder** such as LSD might stimulate neurotransmitters, but mostly it will confuse them, exaggerating some messages, distorting others, and even creating imaginary ones, particularly visual and auditory images. *(Fig. 5)*

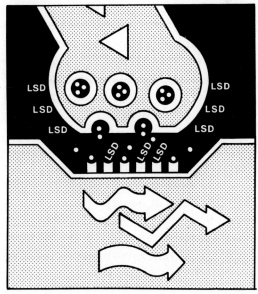

Fig. 5: LSD causes transmitted messages to become distorted or it simply creates its own messages.

37

NEUROTRANSMITTERS II

The discovery of naturally occuring hormones (neurotransmitters) with opiate-like activity (endorphins and enkephalins) was the most significant development in the understanding of how drugs work in the body and how they can cause addiction. For the first time, reaction and addiction to psychoactive drugs could be described in terms of the physical and genetic makeup of a person. As with other diseases like diabetes (a dysfunction of the insulin producing pancreas) or thyroid deficiencies, addiction to opiates was matched to a true biocellular and neurochemical disturbance.

Those who are born with low endorphin/enkephalin capacity have a genetic propensity for opiate and alcohol addiction. Even those born with normal capacities could disrupt and impair their ability to make those neurohormones through continuous excessive exposure to opiate drugs. This means though that like other illnesses, addictions are treatable and their progression can be arrested.

Once opiate-like neurotransmitters were discovered, the search for natural hormone correlates for other drugs began in earnest. Although it is clear that most psychoactive substances work through a variety of neurotransmitters, current investigations indicate some which are more specific to certain drugs.

These suspected psychoactive drug/neurotransmitter correlates include

Drug	Neurotransmitter
Alcohol	Met-enkephalin, gama amine butyric acid (GABA), serotonin
Valium and the benzodiazepines	GABA, glycine
Marijuana	Acetylcholine
LSD	Acetylcholine, dopamine, serotonin
Nicotine	Adrenalin, endorphin, acetylcholine
Cocaine & amphetamines	Adrenalin (epineph-, rine), noradrenalin (norepinephrine), serotonin, dopamine, acetylcholine
MDA, MDMA	Serotonin, dopamine, adrenalin
PCP	Dopamine, acetylcholine, alpha-endo-psychosin

There are more than 60 substances such as neurotransmitters and neuromodulators known to affect the central nervous system. It is estimated that eventually some 300 brain chemicals will be identified.

On the previous pages, we showed a simplified version of the synaptic gap and its biochemical activity. The figure below shows a more complex version of this crucial interface, and even this version is vastly simplified. We show it to give you a feeling of the incredible complexity of biocellular activity in the brain.

In the diagram (courtesy of Matrix Laboratories) (1) the precurser (which stimulates neurotransmitter production) is released in the nervous system; (2) the nerve cell absorbs the precursor; (3) the absorbed precurser synthesizes the neurotransmitter; (4) the neurotransmitters are stored in vesicles; (5). when needed, the vesicles move to the surface of the presynaptic neuron, and release the tiny bits of neurotransmitter; the neurotransmitters can slot into (6) receptor sites, to activate an electrical signal in the post-synaptic neuron; the released neurotransmitters can also be reabsorbed, by the (7) pre-synaptic neuron, or (8) be degraded biochemically, or (9) be flushed from the system, or (10) slot onto a monamine autoreceptor, or on to (11) an opioid autoreceptor in order to signal the cell to make fewer neurotransmitters.

NEUROTRANSMITTER DYNAMICS

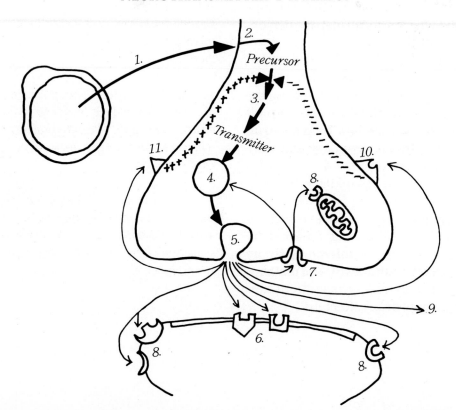

THE NATURE OF DRUGS

It is amazing to think of the control exerted by tiny neurotransmitters on our actions, feelings, and behavior. It is just as startling to realize the effect a tiny quantity of a psychoactive drug can have on these neurotransmitters and therefore on every system of our body.

One example might give a sense of proportion about the effects of psychoactive drugs on neurotransmitters. There exists a drug called carfentanyl, a synthetic opiate/downer that is 25,000 times more powerful than heroin. It is so powerful that a quantity of the drug the size of a grain of salt would be enough to kill 150 people. By contrast, it might take 2 quarts of chugalugged whiskey to kill just one person.

There are a variety of factors besides strength of the drug--i.e., purity, quantity, how, when, and where the drug is taken, physical and mental makeup of the user, how long the drug has been used, and even age and sex-- which must be considered when judging the effect a drug will have.

There are also various aspects of adaptability to the drug reflected by such phenomena as **tolerance, tissue dependence, withdrawal, and metabolism** which are also crucial to understanding how drugs affect us.

LSD user: "Everytime you took it, you were experimenting. 'Well, am I going to get up tight or am I going to freak out?'"

Marijuana smoker: "Sometimes you feel jumpy, ready to go; sometimes not. You just feel like sitting around relaxing, not doing a whole lot. Sometimes you're running around and playing soccer."

Speed user: "When I first started, I remember having a huge reaction to a small amount of it. Inside of a year, I could shoot a spoon of speed easily, which is a pretty fair amount, and it finally got to a point where I couldn't even sleep unless I'd done some ."

Codeine user: "I went to a party and I started drinking and using codeine, and I became drunk very fast. I didn't realize that mixing the two could cause a severe overdose.

Quaalude user: "They put some people to sleep. They have a tendency to keep me awake and happy. The only problem is that when I'm not taking them, I'm not so happy as usual."

Cocaine user: "When I took cocaine, there was a heavy beating, tachycardia, a sense of not being able to get my breath. The sensation of everything moving very quickly and intensely."

The Effects
TOLERANCE

The body regards any drug it takes as a poison. Various organs, especially the liver and kidney, try to eliminate the chemical before it does too much damage. But drug use over a long period of time forces the body to change and adapt.

For example, the body is so efficient in tolerating the effects of downers that the drug appears to weaken with each succeeding dose. More has to be taken just to achieve the same effect.

DOSE OF SECONAL NEEDED TO PRODUCE SLEEP OR EUPHORIA OVER TIME

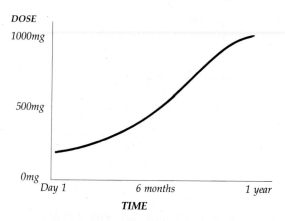

One tablet of Seconal on the first day, three on the 100th day, and nine on the 300th day might be needed to give the same sedation. A glass of whiskey on day one might give the same buzz as a quart on day 200. Two puffs of Persian Heroin on day one might produce the same high as six puffs on day 20.

There are different types of tolerance.

Dispositional tolerance: The body speeds up the breakdown or metabolism of the drug, particularly with barbiturates and alcohol.

Pharmacodynamic tolerance: The nerve cells become less sensitive to the effects of the drug and even produce an antidote or antagonist to the drug. With opiates, the brain will grow more opiate receptor sites and produce its own antagonist, cholecystokinin.

Behavioral tolerance: The brain learns to compensate for the effects of the drug by using parts of the brain not affected. An alcoholic will pass a sobriety test but a few minutes later he will be staggering again.

Inverse tolerance: The person becomes more sensitive to the effects of the drug as the brain chemistry changes. A marijuana or cocaine user, after months of getting a minimal effect from the drug, will all of a sudden get an intense reaction. *acute - unexpected*

Darvon user: "You know, my tolerance to Demerol, morphine, and things like that was tremendous. I had to have tons of the stuff. I went to have a local surgery and they were like, 'Okay, how's that?' And, I was 'Like what? Is this just a test or what?'"

✱ **Reverse tolerance:** Initially, you become less sensitive to the drug, but as it destroys certain tissues and/or as you become older, the trend is suddenly reversed and you become more sensitive. This is particularly true in alcoholics when, as the liver is destroyed, it loses its ability to metabolize the drug. A wino with cirhossis of the liver can stay drunk all day long on a pint of wine because the raw alcohol is passing through his body, time and again, unchanged. takes time - caused by damage

Alcohol user: "At first, I could drink so much, about 8 or 9 years. They'd say I finished 2 bottles in the bar but I'd never get drunk. I'd be pretty high, but I wouldn't fall, never passed out. Now, if I drink over about 4 drinks, I go into a blackout."

✱ **Acute tolerance:** In these cases, the body begins to adapt almost instantly to the damaging effects of the drug. With tobacco, for example, tolerance and adaptation begin to develop with the first puff. Someone who tries suicide with barbiturates can develop an instant tolerance and survive the attempt though he has twice the lethal dose in his system.

Sedative-hypnotic user: "For a long period of time, I would need about 3 or 4 Seconals or Tuinals to get me straight, just to make me feel normal. And, I would take maybe 9 or 10 of them at a time to get high."

Select tolerance: If increased quantities of a drug are taken to overcome this tolerance and to achieve a certain high, it's easy to forget that tolerance to the physical side effects also continue to escalate but not at the same rate, so the dose needed to achieve an emotional high comes closer and closer to the lethal physical dose of that drug.

DOSE OF SECONAL NEEDED TO PRODUCE EUPHORIA OR SLEEP VERSUS OVERDOSE

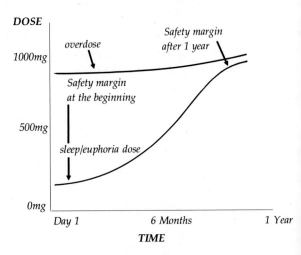

Barbiturate user: "As many pills as I had, I would take. I didn't really care about overdose which I did many times."

The Effects
TISSUE DEPENDENCE AND WITHDRAWAL

The biological adaptation of the body due to prolonged use of drugs is quite extensive, particularly with downers. In fact, the body can change so much that the tissues and organs come to depend on the drug just to stay normal.

Darvon user: "I would start to feel very abnormal after 2 or 3 hours and it was like trying to maintain until I could begin to feel normal. And that was the only kind of normal that I knew, Darvon induced normality."

For example, alcohol disrupts the release of certain neurotransmitters in the brain. It also increases the amount of cytocells and mitochondria in the liver that are available to neutralize the drug. The tissues have come to depend on the alcohol to maintain this new balance.

However, when the user stops taking the drug, the body is left with an altered chemistry. There might be an overabundance of one kind of enzyme and a lack of certain neurotransmitters. All of a sudden, the body tries to restore its balance. Usually, all the things the body was kept from doing while taking the drug, it does to excess.

For example, look at the withdrawal symptoms of a long time heroin user when he suddenly stops taking the drug compared to the usual effects he gets.

Effects		Withdrawal Effects
Numbness	*becomes*	*Pain*
Euphoria	"	*Anxiety*
Dryness of mouth	"	*Sweating, running nose, salivation*
Constipation	"	*Diarrhea*
Slow pulse	"	*Rapid pulse*
Low blood pressure	"	*High blood pressure*
Cough suppression	"	*Coughing*
Shallow breathing	"	*Rapid breathing*
Pinpoint pupil	"	*Dilated pupil*
Sluggish muscle tone	"	*Severe hyper-reflexes & cramps*

In fact, with many compulsive users, the fear of withdrawal is one reason they keep using. They don't want to go through the aches, pains, insomnia, vomiting, cramps, and occasional convulsions. Many treatment programs use mild drugs to soften these withdrawal symptoms.

Heroin user: "The rush I would get was, all of a sudden, my body would not be sick anymore. That was the high, that was the rush. I would get well."

Withdrawal from opiates, alcohol, many sedatives, and even nicotine seem to emanate from an area of the brain stem known as the locus cereleus. Drugs like Clonidine, Vasopressin, and Baclofen, which act at this part of the brain, block out the withdrawal symptoms of these drugs.

There are three distinct types of withdrawal symptoms: **non-purposive, purposive,** and **protracted.**

✗ **Non-purposive withdrawal** consists of objective physical signs that are directly observable upon cessation of drug use by an addict. These are seizures, sweating, goose bumps, vomiting, diarrhea, tremors, etc. These signs are a direct result of the tissue dependence that has developed.

Heroin user: "When I ran out, it was severe. I mean, body convulsions, long times of memory lapse, cramps that were just enough to...you couldn't stand them. And, it lasted for about 5 days; the actual convulsions, the cramps, and the pain and stuff. And then, it took another couple of weeks before I ever felt anywhere near normal."

✗ **Purposive withdrawal** results from either addict manipulation (hence the purposive or "with purpose"), or from a psychic conversion reaction from the expectation of the withdrawal process. For example, a common behavior of most addicts is manipulative behavior. In an effort to secure more drugs, sympathy, or money, addicts may claim to have very diverse and difficult to verify withdrawal symptoms i.e., "I'm so nervous that my nerves are in an uproar, so you've got to give me something, Doc!" It would be both dangerous and clinically unsound to respond to such manipulations.

Valium user: "The minute I went off pills, I went to another doctor, told him my problem with drugs, and he actually gave me a shot of Demerol knowing my problem with drugs. It's funny about these doctors, they can't help but give you a drug."

Heroin user: "It takes a doctor 30 minutes to say no but it only takes him 5 minutes to say yes. We used to share doctors that we could scam. We called them "croakers."

Within the past few decades, the portrayal of drug addiction by the media, books, movies, and television has resulted in another kind of purposive withdrawal. Younger, addiction-naive drug users expect to suffer withdrawal symptoms similar to those portrayed in the media, when they run out of drug. This expectation results in a neurotic condition whereby they experience a wide range of reactions even though their tissue dependence has not truly developed. There is much danger in overreacting to these symptoms.

Protracted Withdrawal: A major danger to both maintaining recovery and preventing a drug overdose during relapse is protracted withdrawal. This is a flashback or recurrence of the addiction withdrawal symptoms and heavy craving for the drug long after one has detoxified. The cause of this reaction is most likely a post-traumatic stress phenomena, where some sensory input (odor, sight, noise, etc.) stimulates the stressful memories experienced during drug withdrawal and evokes a reexperiencing of those symptoms by the addict. For instance, the odor of burnt matches or metal burning (smells that occur when cooking heroin), causes a heroin addict to reexperience withdrawal several months after detoxification. Any white powder causes the same reaction in a cocaine addict; the odor of hemp burning does it to a marijuana addict; a blue pill does it to a Valium addict; etc.

Cocaine user: "Walking down the street, you will smell it coming out of your lungs. You smell the ether. It's a psychological thing. You want to use again."

Heroin user: "After I've passed withdrawals, and I pass by areas like where I used to hang out, and I see other people nodding, in my mind, I start feeling like I'm sick again.

Protracted withdrawal often causes a user to try his drug again, leading possibly to a full relapse. Unfortunately, these slips are associated with a greater chance of drug overdose as users are prone to use the same dose they were using when they quit. They forget that their last dose was a high one they could handle because the body had changed and had developed a tolerance. They forget that their abstinence returned their body to a less tolerant state, unable to handle a high dose.

Heroin user: "We cleaned up because we didn't have any connections when we moved. We had about 15 Clonidine to help us through and I was drinking. Then we each did one bag, one $20 dollar bag of cut, and both of us were on the floor."

The use of psychoactive drugs which cause a milder tolerance can still create problems.

Marijuana smoker: "I was smoking two or three joints a day when I quit. Then I was at my girlfriend's house and she had a rolled joint passing from hand to hand. Two puffs and I was a staggering, babbling idiot. Before I quit, that amount would have barely made me yawn. I got picked up for drunk driving."

METABOLISM

Metabolism is defined as the body's mechanism for processing, using, and eventually eliminating foreign substances such as food or drugs. So, as a drug exerts its influence upon the body, it is gradually neutralized, usually by the liver or kidneys. It can also be metabolized by the blood, the lymph fluid, or most any body tissue that recognizes the drug as a foreign substance.

The liver, in particular, has the ability to break down or alter the chemical structure of drugs, making them less active or inert. The kidneys, on the other hand, filter the blood continuously and excrete toxic substances into the urine. Drugs can also be excreted out of the body by the lungs, in sweat, or in feces.

Think of the liver as a series of tiny chemical factories filled with active body chemicals called enzymes. For example, alcohol is ultimately converted to water, oxygen, and carbon dioxide, then passed from the body through the kidneys, sweat glands, and lungs. Valium, on the other hand, is transformed by the liver's enzymes into three or four compounds which are more active than the original drug.

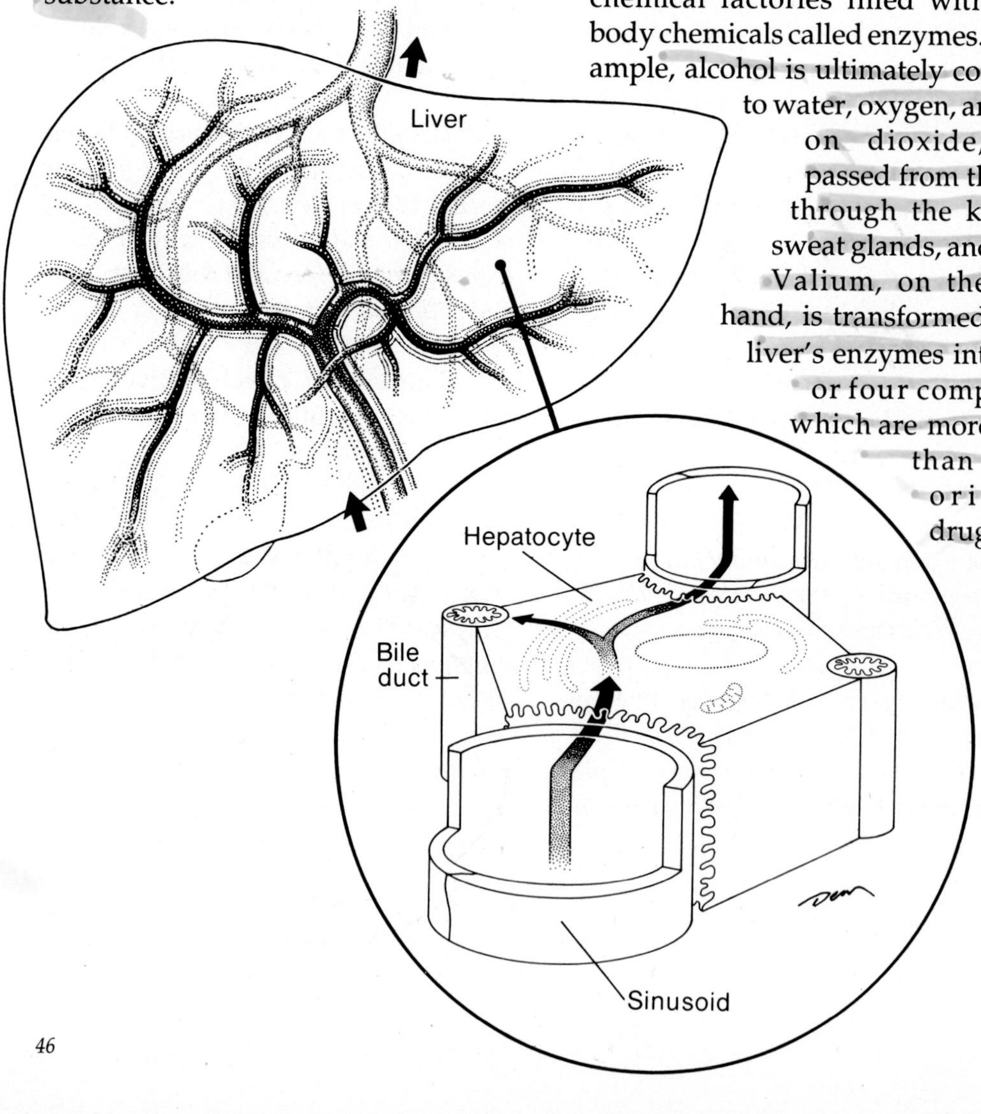

Liver

Hepatocyte

Bile duct

Sinusoid

If a drug is eliminated slowly, as with amphetamines or Valium, it can affect the body for hours, even days. If it is eliminated quickly, as with smokeable cocaine or nitrous oxide, the major reactions might last just a few minutes, though other subtle side effects last for days, even weeks.

Some other factors which affect the metabolism of drugs are

Age: After the age of 30 and with each subsequent year, the body produces fewer and fewer liver enzymes capable of metabolizing certain drugs so, the older the patient, the greater the effect. This is especially true with drugs like Valium and other benzodiazepines.

Race: Different ethnic groups have different levels of enzymes. Most Asians break down alcohol more slowly than do Caucasians. They generally suffer more side effects such as nausea and redness of the face. They will, in fact, get drunk on less alcohol.

Heredity: Individuals pass certain traits to their offspring that affect the metabolism of drugs. They might have a low level of enzymes that metabolize the drug; they might have more body fat which will store certain drugs like Valium or PCP; or they might have a high metabolic rate.

Sex: Males and females have different body chemistry. Drugs such as barbiturates, which are protein bound, generally have greater effects in women than in men.

Health: Certain medical conditions affect metabolism. Alcohol in a drinker with severe liver damage (cirrhosis) causes more problems than in a drinker with a healthy liver.

Emotional State: The emotional state of the drug user also has a major effect on the drug's action. LSD in someone with paranoia can be very dangerous.

Other Drugs: The presence of another drug can keep the body so busy that metabolism of a new drug is delayed. For example, the presence of alcohol keeps the liver so busy that a Seconal or Quaalude will remain in the body two or three times longer than normal.

In addition, such factors as weight of the user, the level of tolerance, and even the weather or time of day can affect the metabolism of a psychoactive drug.

REVIEW

1. The major classifications of psychoactive drugs are **uppers (stimulants), downers (depressants), all arounders (psychedelics),** and **inhalants.**

2. Drugs can enter the body through eating/drinking, inhaling (smoking), injection, contact, snorting.

3. Drugs travel in the bloodstream to reach the central nervous system (CNS). They must cross the blood-brain barrier to reach the nerve cells of the CNS.

4. Drugs which reach the cells of the central nervous system are called psychoactive drugs. These drugs affect the rest of the body either directly or by acting on the nerves of the central nervous system.

5. The central nervous system controls all body functions, thought processes, and emotions, so drugs that affect these nerve cells affect every system in the body.

6. Neurotransmitters are biochemicals found in all nerve cells. It is these biochemicals which are actually responsible for the transmission of nerve impulses.

7. Psychoactive drugs inhibit, stimulate, or distort the release of these chemicals. They can also stimulate or inhibit the actions of neurotransmitters.

8. The magnitude of the effects depends on the quantity and quality of the drug taken and how it is metabolized by the body. The liver is the principal organ for neutralizing drugs. The kidneys are the principal organs for filtering drugs from the blood.

9. The major problem with psychoactive drugs is that when people take them, they focus on the desired mental and emotional **effects** and forget the potentially damaging physical and mental **side effects** that can occur.

10. When a person takes certain drugs over a period of time, particularly depressants, the body becomes used to their effects so more is needed to achieve the same high. The user develops a tolerance to the drug.

11. The body tries to adapt to the increased quantities of drugs taken and so tissue dependence develops (in particular with downers). The user has to keep taking the drug just to stay in balance.

12. When a user stops taking a drug after tissue dependence has developed (mostly with opiates, alcohol, and sedative-hypnotics), the body experiences many of the sensations and physical changes it was kept from feeling while taking the drug. This backlash is known as withdrawal.

The Effects
QUESTIONS

1. Name the four major classifications of psychoactive drugs and list three drugs in each category.

2. Describe a physical and an emotional effect of heroin.

3. Describe the five ways a drug can be taken and how it reaches the bloodstream. List the five routes in order of speed of action.

4. Describe the route a drug takes when swallowed, from the mouth to the blood-brain barrier.

5. What is the function of the blood-brain barrier?

6. What are the three different parts of the complete nervous system and what are their functions?

7. What are the two parts of the central nervous system?

8. What is a synapse?

9. What are neurotransmitters?

10. How do the different classes of psychoactive drugs (uppers, downers, all arounders) affect neurotransmitters?

11. Name three different neurotransmitters.

12. What is tolerance?

13. What is tissue dependence?

14. Name five effects of codeine and their equivalent withdrawal rebound effects?

15. What organs of the body metabolize and/or filter out psychoactive drugs?

16. Name five factors such as age which govern the metabolism of a psychoactive drug.

1897

WHOLE TOWN MAD FOR COCAINE.

Most Prominent Residents of Manchester, Conn., Afflicted with the General Craze for the Drug.

WANT LEGISLATIVE ACTION.

Druggist Started the Habit a Year Ago by Preparing a Seductive Remedy for Asthma.

ALL MUST HAVE IT NOW.

Threaten Violence if Denied and Treat One Another to "Pinches" in Public Places.

[BY TELEGRAPH TO THE HERALD.]
HARTFORD, Conn., Dec. 27, 1896.—The cocaine habit has taken such a hold on the residents of Manchester that steps are being taken to obtain legislative restriction on the sale of the drug. The evil had its inception when a local druggist a year ago made a preparation of cocaine and menthol which could be used as a cure for asthma. It was intended as a specific for asthma, and now hundreds of persons have become slaves to the stuff.

NEW YORK HERALD, JANUARY 3, 1897.

TOWN AROUSED AGAINST A DRUG.

Beneficial Results of the Herald's Exposure of the Cocaine Habit in Manchester, Conn.

PARENTS DID NOT KNOW IT.

Interest Aroused in Medical Circles Over an Evil That Threatened a Community.

WHAT TO DO WITH "FIENDS."

[BY TELEGRAPH TO THE HERALD.]
HARTFORD, Conn., Jan. 2, 1897.—The town of Manchester never was so deeply stirred as it has been this week by the revelations in the HERALD concerning the cocaine habit that portion of the town known as South Manchester, really the business centre of the village...

DEMAND COCAINE AT ANY PRICE.

Condition of South Manchester, Conn., a Town Whose Residents Generally Are "Fiends."

WILL HAVE DRUG OR DIE.

More Common Than the Tobacco Habit, Its Victims Are Marked by Physical Decay.

PHYSICIANS ARE HELPLESS.

Druggists Are Determined Not to Replenish Their Stocks, but Fear the Results.

[BY TELEGRAPH TO THE HERALD.]
HARTFORD, Conn., Dec. 28, 1896.—The physicians of South Manchester are astonished at the spread of the cocaine habit in that village, as told in the HERALD yesterday, but they are powerless to stay it. A stranger going to the pretty little place on an electric car will first see the conductor or motorman take out a bottle, shake a white powder in the palm and then snuff it with intense satisfaction and a long drawn sigh of relief...

1927

COCAINE, BROUGHT TO U.S. AS BLESSING, SOON A CURSE

'Addict Army Here Grew Rapidly as "Glorious Discovery" of 35 Years Ago Was Bought for Base Uses and Became Ally of Crime

By WINIFRED BLACK.

SAN FRANCISCO, Feb. 22—Cocaine came into America about thirty-five years ago.

It was hailed as a glorious discovery and for a long time no one realized the insidious and cruel danger it brought with it.

Physicians, dentists and the makers of patent medicines, too, made immediate and very practical use of it.

All at once people who were taking new "catarrh cures" found themselves victims of the cocaine habit.

Force Behind Crime

What is behind the gunmen and his gun today? Nine times out of ten, cocaine.

What is behind the holdup and the brutal murders of bank cashiers and petty shopkeepers and payroll masters?

Cocaine—nine and a half times out of ten.

Take "Sleigh Rides"

When a "snow bird" is going out to a cocaine party, he says he's going for a "sleigh ride" and intimates to his associates that there's plenty of "bells" to decorate the excursion.

U.S. Full of Stuff

The annual consumption in the United States of cocaine amounts to over a million pounds.

Cost Runs High

It takes from three dollars to thirty dollars a day to keep a "coke fiend" supplied with "snow."

That's where the thieves come from. That's why young girls suddenly begin to forge their fathers' names on checks.

"Sniff the Snow"

1986

'Marijuana of the '80s

Cocaine — a Fact of Life in America

By LEE MAY,
Times Staff Writer

WASHINGTON—Panamanian diplomat Roberto Leyton took his family to the Fourth of July celebration near the Washington Monument last summer for fireworks and the Beach Boys concert, but he found a lot more.

"I couldn't believe what I saw," he said. "Everybody consuming drugs in front of the police, doing all type of stuff. People even came to our group and offered us drugs for us to give them ice."

For Leyton, who is Panama's special envoy to the United States on drug matters and its ambassador to the Organization of American States, the incident illustrates a profound strategic weakness in the...

The 'Plant of Plants'

Last in a series on Latin America's cocaine industry

ÜBER COCA.

UPPERS

The flowering coca shrub (Erythroxylon coca). 100 pounds of leaves will yield 1 to 2 pounds of cocaine.

GENERAL CLASSIFICATION

I n the United States, one to three million Americans use amphetamines (speed) for non-medical reasons; 10 to 20 million use cocaine (at least occasionally); 50 million smoke cigarettes; 100 million drink coffee; and most everyone has taken an over-the-counter medication containing caffeine. From a strong stimulant such as freebase cocaine to a mild one like a cola soft drink, uppers are an intimate part of our lives.

Drug Name	Trade Name	Street Name
COCAINE		
Cocaine HCL (hydrochloride)	None	Coke, blow, toot, snow, flake, girl, lady
Freebase cocaine	None	Base, rock, crack, pasta, hubba, bazooko, petillos, base
AMPHETAMINES		**CRANK, SPEED, ICE**
d, l amphetamine	Benzedrine, Obetrol, Biphetamine	Crosstops, black beauties, whites, bennies, cartwheels
Methamphetamine	Methadrine, Desoxyn	Crank, meth, crystal
Dextroamphetamine	Dexedrine, Eskatrol,	Dexies, Christmas trees, beans
Dextromethamphetamine		Ice, glass, batu, shabu, snot
DIET PILLS (AMPHETAMINE CONGENERS)		
Methylphenidate	Ritalin	Pellets
Phenmetrazine	Preludin	Pink hearts
Pemoline	Cylert	Popcorn coke
Phentermine HCL	Fastin, Adipex T-Diet, Phentercot	Robin's eggs, black and whites
Phentermine resin	Ionamin	
Phendimetrazine	Phenazine, Bontril, Plegine, Trimtabs, Melfiat, Pendiet, Statobex	
Diethylpropion	Tenuate, Tepanil	

LOOKALIKES

Alone or any combination of two or more of phenyl-propanolamine, ephedrine, or caffeine	Dexadiet, Dexatrim, etc.	Legal stimulants, legal speed, (also robin's eggs black beauties, pink hearts, etc.)

CAFFEINE

Over-The-Counter stimulants	No Doz, Alert, Vivarin, Tirend	
Coffee	Columbian, French roast, etc.	Java, Joe, mud
Colas (from cola nut)	Coca Cola, Pepsi, etc.	Coke
Tea	Lipton, Stash	
Chocolate (cocoa beans)	Hershey, Nestle, etc.	

NICOTINE

Pipe tobacco	Sir Walter Raleigh, etc.	
Cigarettes, cigars	Pall Mall, Marlboro	Cancer stick, smoke stogies, butts, toke
Snuff	Copenhagen, etc.	Dip
Chewing tobacco	Day's Work, etc.	Chaw

THE EFFECTS

Uppers are central nervous system stimulants.

Day in and day out the body produces a certain amount of energy chemicals, particularly adrenalin and noradrenalin. More of these chemicals might circulate at high noon while we are at work than at midnight while we are fast asleep, but the daily output is fairly consistent. These energy chemicals can increase heart rate, energize muscles, keep us alert, and help us function normally. In time they are metabolized and excreted from the body.

Sometimes, though, the body needs extra energy: when we exercise, are scared, have to fight, or are making love. At these moments, the nervous system releases extra amounts of adrenalin and other chemicals. Remember the surge of energy the body receives when frightened? This extra adrenalin is soon passed from the body or reabsorbed by certain nerve tissues.

The progression of events is

**The body demands
extra energy.**

$\downarrow$

**Cells release energy
chemicals.**

Enough chemicals are released to get the job done. The excess chemicals are then reabsorbed.

Uppers reverse the process.

Uppers force the release of the body's own natural stimulants without a demand from the body.

In addition, stronger stimulants such as cocaine or crack keep the chemicals circulating by blocking their reabsorption, so the effects are exaggerated. If this is continued for hours, even days, the body is infused with all this extra energy which has no place to go except if it's expended through increased muscular activity, hard work, hard partying, talkativeness, restlessness, combativeness, and irritability.

If we take stimulants occasionally, the body has time to return to its natural balance. But if we take stimulants over a long period of time or take large quantities, the energy supply becomes depleted and the body is left without reserves. We've squeezed it dry. Most systems must shut down in an attempt to replenish the body's energy supply.

Remember, the energy we receive from stimulants is not a free gift. It is a loan from the rest of the body and must be repaid.

With stronger stimulants, this withdrawal, collapse, and depression can last for days, weeks, even months, depending on the length of use, the strength of the drug, and the extent of biochemical disruption.

In addition, many stimulants constrict blood vessels, thus decreasing blood flow to many tissues, particularly the skin and extremities. At the same time they increase blood pressure so with stronger stimulants, a ruptured vessel (a stroke if it's in the brain) is possible.

The disruption of the body's neurotransmitters also disturbs our mental balance. Generally, stimulants increase our confidence, create a certain euphoria, and make us feel we can do anything. When we are overstimulated, or continually stimulated, these feelings can quickly turn to irritability, talkativeness, suspiciousness, restlessness, and insomnia.

Everything seems exaggerated under the influence of a stimulant: our problems; our suspicions; our irritability; our existing neuroses; our sense of loneliness. We need to do something, anything, to use up this extra stimulation.

"The Horrors of Cocaine." A movie poster from the late 1930's.

Rock of freebase cocaine made by the dirty basing method using baking soda.

COCAINE

Cocaine is extracted from the coca plant which grows on the slopes of the Andes Mountains in South America, in certain parts of the Amazon Jungle, and on the Island of Java in Indonesia.

Incan mask of cocaine chewer (c. 1750).

Native cultures have used coca leaves for thousands of years for social and religious occasions, to fight off fatigue, lessen hunger, and increase endurance. The South American Indians, the Incas in particular, either chewed the leaf for the juice or chopped it up and spooned it under the tongue so the active ingredients could be absorbed by the tiny blood vessels in the gums. This process requires the combination of coca leaf (containing 1 to 2 percent cocaine) with some alkalai substance like ash, soda lime, or guano. The alkalai enables the cocaine to leave the cells of the plant for absorption into the gums. The chewing of these coca leaf/alkalai preparations is called a concoda and even to this day remains one of the most popular ways of using cocaine in South America.

In 1860, cocaine was isolated from the other chemicals in the coca leaf and extracted as the hydrochloride salt, cocaine hydrochloride. Because this form of cocaine readily dissolves in water, by the 1880's, two new ways of using the drug had developed. These were the injection of cocaine directly into the veins and the drinking of cocaine, mixed in with soft drinks (Coca Cola, etc.) and wine (Vin Mariani, etc.)

Lithograph ad for a French tonic wine spiced with cocaine extract; by Alphonse Mucha, Paris, 1899. Courtesy of Sasha Runa, Chicago and the estate of Timothy C. Ploughman.

Injecting cocaine resulted in an intense rush within 15 to 30 seconds, while drinking it resulted in a mild yet longer lasting stimulation 30 to 45 minutes after ingestion. Both methods popularized the use of cocaine in the United States by the turn of the century.

Around 1914, a pharmaceutical company introduced cocaine cigarettes in America but the high temperature (198° C) needed to convert cocaine hydrochloride to smoke, resulted in destruction of much of the chemical and so the cigarettes never became very popular. Instead, the ban on cocaine limited its supply and gave rise to a popular new form of cocaine use, snorting of the chemical into the nostrils. Called tooting, blowing, or horning, this method gets the drug to the nasal

A bottle of rinse to soothe and clean the nasal passages irritated by cocaine snorting.

mucosa, not the lungs, allowing for absorption into the brain within 3 to 5 minutes.

Chewing, drinking, injecting, and snorting cocaine remained the principal routes of cocaine use until the mid 1970's. At that time, street chemists converted cocaine hydrochloride to cocaine free base in an effort to purify the street drug from its many cuts or dilutents. This new "free base" form of cocaine, now known as "rock," "crack," "hubba," "fry daddies," and various other names, ushered in a more powerful form of cocaine, smokable cocaine. Unlike the cocaine hydrochloride cigarettes, introduced in 1914, "free base" cocaine converted to smoke at a much lower temperature (89° C), enabling the drug to be smoked without destroying the psychoactive properties. Smoking gets the cocaine into the lungs, permitting greater absorption and the most rapid delivery of the drug to the brain. Via the lungs, cocaine reaches the brain within only 5 to 8 seconds compared to the 15 to 30 seconds via injection cocaine. "Baseballing" and "basing" cocaine has brought about a new cocaine epidemic to rival that witnessed during the late 1800's. New forms of cocaine like "pasta" and "báse;" a new plant source, the Erythroxylum coca variant ipadu plant; along with new methods of making free base cocaine like Boulya indicate a continuing evolution and abuse of this drug for many more years.

Physical and Mental Effects

Cocaine is not only a stimulant, it is also the only naturally occurring local anesthetic. It is used to numb the nasal passages when inserting breathing tubes in a patient, to numb the eye during surgery, and to deaden the pain of chronic sores. (This topical anesthetic effect numbs the nasal passages when the drug is snorted.) Cocaine will also stimulate the heart muscles directly before it reaches the central nervous system.

Cocaine snorter: "At first, when you put it in your nose, it starts a numbness, and you can feel a little drip going down your throat. And then you get hyperactive in 20 minutes. When you smoke it, it's an instantaneous rush."

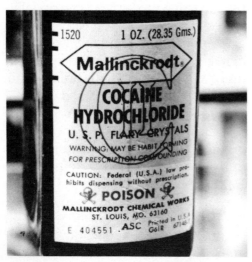

When sold legally in the U.S., one ounce, or 28 grams, costs about $60. In Columbia, one ounce of illicit cocaine would cost about $600 and on the streets of New York or Miami, about $2,700.

Most of the effects, however, occur when the drug disrupts the neurotransmitter balance in the central nervous system. Initially, this disruption and overstimulation of the body's chemical balance seems extremely pleasurable: increased confidence, a willingness to work (sometimes endlessly), a diminishing of life's problems, a euphoric rush.

Cocaine user: "I felt real ecstatic, very euphoric; it felt...my mind had a great deal of pleasure. I felt like a somebody. I felt like a super person. I could do anything."

The problem, of course, is that you can't be selective about which neurotransmitters you stimulate and how much you disrupt them. For example:

The greatly increased release of **epinephrine (adrenalin)** raises the blood pressure, increases the heart rate, causes rapid breathing, tenses muscles, and causes the jitters. It forces the release of excess amounts of these energy chemicals, ultimately depleting the supplies. But initially, the stimulation is intense.

Cocaine shooter: "It exaggerated almost everything that was going on for me. Initially, it exaggerated excitement or happiness or euphoria. It seemed positive. As it became negative, it became extremely negative. Everything seemed out of proportion to everything else.

Besides epinephrine (adrenalin), other disrupted neurotransmitters can cause additional problems. Unbalanced **dopamine** can overstimulate the brain's fright center causing paranoia. (Yes, there's a physical reason for this phenomenon.) Any shadow, movement, loud voice, etc., suddenly seem enormously threatening. We react in much the same way a deer in the woods reacts to the crack of a twig.

Cocaine I.V. user: "A person I know does a shot every 15 to 20 minutes. He fights sleep. He'll go through days without sleeping and he'll collapse. He looks for people hiding under matresses, behind door hinges, and in books. He asks why you're smiling."

Unbalanced **acetylcholine,** another common neurotransmitter, causes muscle tremors, memory lapses, mental confusion, and even hallucinations.

Cocaine snorter: "My perception of everything was such that I no longer had any clear picture of what was going on. The complete inability to really have any awareness of what was actually happening and having to live in a world where I could only feel what seemed to be happening was the most horrifying thing I ever experienced."

Serotonin helps us sleep and stabilizes our moods, but if depleted by excessive cocaine use, insomnia, agitation, and severe emotional depression result.

The lack of epinephrine, norepinephrine, serotonin, and dopamine also causes severe depression and extreme lethargy. Heavy cocaine abuse is associated with ahedonia (inability to feel pleasure) and anergia (a total lack of energy, motivation, and initiative).

Cocaine snorter: "I'd realize that I hadn't been outside of my house for a couple of days and hadn't called anybody. I wouldn't answer my mail for months at a time."

Cocaine I.V. user: "The opposite sex can do anything they want to you and you won't react. Your body doesn't react to it, to any kind of touch or emotion."

All these physical effects are very similar to the effects of other stimulants, e.g., amphetamines and Ritalin. The major differences with cocaine are the intensity of the initial rush (stronger), the price (about $100 a gram-or on a per dose basis, about 10 times as much as amphetamines), and the speed with which it is metabolized by the body (about 40 minutes compared to several hours for amphetamines).

Cocaine smoker: "After doing it for a while, you just don't want to stop till everything is gone, till all the money's gone, till you have no choice but to stop."

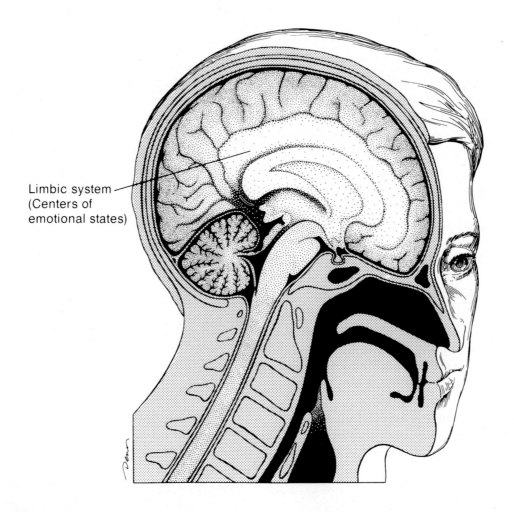

Limbic system
(Centers of
emotional states)

Reward / Pleasure Center: Cocaine disrupts our balance in one other important way. It stimulates our reward/pleasure center, that portion of the brain that tells us when we've done something good. For example, normally, this center gives us a surge of satisfaction when we've satisfied hunger, thirst, or sexual desire. When a drug such as cocaine stimulates this center, it fools us. It signals our brain that we're not hungry, though we've not eaten; that we're not thirsty though we've not drunk; that we're being sexually satisfied though we haven't had sex. This stimulation is perceived as an overall rush, an overall feeling of well being and pleasure. This rush diminishes over time but the memory lingers on.

Cocaine user: "When offered to me, the idea flashes through my head, 'Wow, how nice it was the first time. Maybe this time I can recapture that same experience I had the first time.' But it doesn't happen."

The Crash: The initial euphoria, the feeling of confidence, the sense of omnipotence, the satisfied feeling, disappears as suddenly as the mental and physical rush appeared, so the crash after using cocaine can be particularly depressing. It can be as crushing as the feeling we would have if we had just run a marathon or if a loved one had died. This depression can last anywhere from a few hours to days, even months. It depends on how much we have used, how badly we have depleted our energy supplies, and how severely we've disrupted our neurotransmitter balance.

Cocaine I.V. user: "I really did want to die, and I remember that as being way out of proportion to the actual events of my life although it seemed like my life was over."

Polydrug Use: One of the problems with cocaine is that the stimulation can be so intense that the user needs a downer to take the edge off or to get to sleep. The most common drugs used are alcohol, Valium, and heroin, though any downer will do in a pinch. Sometimes, the second drug can be more of a problem than the cocaine.

Cocaine snorter: "After the coke would be gone, you'd be all wired up and you couldn't sleep, so I'd always have a little bit of heroin on the side and it'd bring me down. And I wouldn't be all jittery all night and grinding my teeth."

Other Problems: Adulteration of cocaine involves dilution with such diverse products as baby laxatives, aspirin, sugar, tetracaine or procaine (both are topical anesthetics), even talcum powder. And as with the I.V. use of any drug, contaminated needles have spread hepatitis, blood and heart infections, and AIDS.

Overdose: An overdose of cocaine can be caused by as little as 1/50th of a gram or as much as 1.2 grams. The "caine reaction" is very intense and generally short in duration. Most often, it's not fatal. You only feel like you're going to die. However, in a small number of cases, death can occur within 40 minutes to 5 hours after exposure. It usually results from either the initial stimulatory phase of toxicity (seizures, hypertension, and tachycardia) or the later depression phase terminating in extreme respiratory depression and coma.

Cocaine smoker: "I did too much. My knees buckled; I fell on the toilet stool. I was shaking. If my buddy hadn't grabbed me and put me in the shower, I don't know what would have happened."

Cocaine I.V. user: "I have seen a friend go through overdose. His skin was grey green. His eyes rolled back, his heart stopped, and there was a gargling sound which is right at death. And I had to bring him back, and that's enough to put the fear of God in anybody."

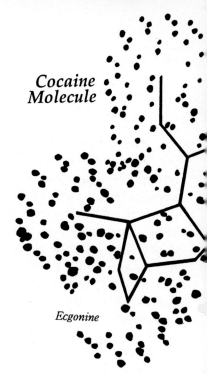

Cocaine Molecule

Ecgonine

Usually healthy people, even those who have used cocaine before, can get an exaggerated reaction, far beyond what might normally occur, or beyond what they have experienced in the past. This is partially due to the phenomenon already mentioned known as inverse tolerence or kindling. As people use cocaine, they get more sensitive to its toxic effects rather than less sensitive as one would expect. With large doses, cocaine can injure heart muscles and blood vessels, making permanent damage to those tissues more likely.

Problems associated with long term use: The elevations and drops in blood pressure caused by cocaine, plus some toxic effects to the vessels themselves, weaken blood capillaries, resulting in a greater risk of stroke. Strokes occur when a weakened blood vessel bursts, causing internal bleeding in the brain. Chronic cocaine use also causes a disorganization in the usual formation of heart muscles resulting in constriction bands on the heart. This makes users more likely to suffer a cocaine-induced heart attack.

Considering all the problems with cocaine--the expense, the dilution, the adulteration, the possibility of overdose, the illegality, the psychological dangers--two questions come to mind. **"Why do people use cocaine?"** and **"Why do they use it so compulsively?"**

Why do people use cocaine?

• We are drawn to cocaine because it **mimics natural body functions:** the adrenal energy rush, the confidence, the euphoria, the increased sensitivity, the stimulation of the reward/pleasure center. It is sometimes easier to get a chemical high instantly than a natural high over a period of time. A natural high is a stimulation of our energy supplies or our reward/pleasure center that comes from real deeds, i.e., the completion of a difficult physical or mental task, communion with God, or an emotionally fulfilling relationship. People also use because of peer pressure, curiosity, or availability.

Methyl-Alcohol

Why do people use cocaine so compulsively?

• The **initial rush** is extremely intense, and users try to recapture that feeling. Most find that it can't be done but that doesn't stop them from trying.

• The **down side** of the high is so intense that the user tries to keep going up to avoid that crash. In many cases, a user will shoot up or smoke every 20, or in some cases, 10 minutes.

• Coke lets some users **avoid life's problems** such as difficult relationships, lack of confidence, traumatic events, a hated job, or loneliness.

• The **memory becomes ingrained** with the pleasurable sensations of using the drug. Just as we come to remember a phone number after repeated dialing, so it becomes easier to remember that

cocaine high. Many seemingly innocuous sensory cues in our environment will trigger that memory and create a severe desire to use: seeing white powder, holding the freebase pipe, having money in the pocket.

• Cocaine is the **most compulsive drug** we know. In and of itself, the chemical will cause a user to keep shooting, snorting, or smoking until every last microgram is gone, until the user passes out, or overdoses. This hypnotizing effect is known as drug reinforcement.

• The final reason has to do with **heredity.** That is, certain people's natural neurotransmitter balance makes them react more intensely to a drug. They get more pleasure from it. They are in essence pre-sensitized to the drug. (*see Addictive Disease*).

Of the 40 million people who have experimented with cocaine, 5 million use it at least once a month and have had episodes where they find it hard to function. One to two million have severe problems with the drug.

Cocaine Called a Factor In Colorado Air Crash

Associated Press

Washington
Federal investigators yesterday for the first time blamed cocaine use by a pilot as a contributing factor in a commercial airline crash in which passengers were killed.

hol use has been blamed in so previous accidents.

Investigator Barry Strauch Silver had used cocaine betwe and 18 hours before the fligh said there was not enough evi to determine whether Silver

SMOKABLE COCAINE
Freebase, Crack, Rock, Etc.

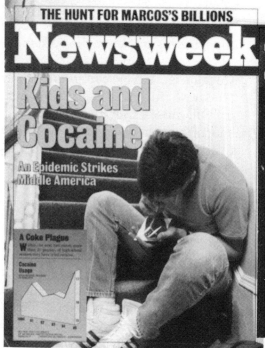

The words "**crack cocaine**" appeared on the streets and in the media in 1985, tentatively at first, as if society were trying out a new nickname. By 1986, there seemed to be a crack epidemic that crossed all social and economic barriers. The question is, "Was the spread of the so-called rich man's drug to the office, factory, school yard, ghetto, and barrio generated by media attention or by the actual properties of the substance?

An important clue to the answer is that crack is not an entirely new drug. It is freebase cocaine, and freebase is simply a chemically altered form of regular cocaine, cocaine hydrochloride. Freebase was developed in the mid seventies to make cocaine smokable. Freebase cocaine also known as smokable cocaine has been called "base," "báse," "rock," "hubba," "gravel," "Roxanne," "girl," "fry," "Boulya," and "crack." Perhaps next month another nickname will appear.

For example, the latest South American fad is "pasta" smoking. Pasta, a form of freebase nicknamed "bazooko" is an intermediate product of the cocaine refinement process. Being an intermediate product, it contains toxic chemicals such as kerosene and leaded gasoline. It is smoked, usually with marijuana or tobacco.

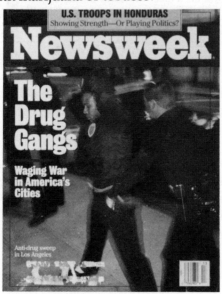

Whatever the name, freebase is still cocaine and when smoked, causes all the reactions expected from shooting, or snorting the drug, the differences being in the extra speed of delivery to the brain and the greater intensity of the effects.

There are two basic ways to make cocaine suitable for smoking.

The first method, developed about 1976, uses highly flammable or toxic chemicals such as ether, benzene, or even bleach along with ammonia or sodium hydroxide to convert cocaine hydrochloride, the refined form of the drug, to crystals of freebase cocaine. This creates a purer form of the drug since any additives are filtered out by the process. This method is called "basing" or "baseballing."

The other technique, developed in the early 80's, sometimes called "cheap basing" or "dirty basing," is to dissolve the cocaine in water, add baking soda or its equivalent, and heat the mixture till the cocaine base is crystallized into crack. This simpler method does not remove as many impurities as the basing technique. Residues such as talcum powder and, particularly, baking soda remain.

The converted freebase cocaine, made by either the basing method or the crack method, has two chemical properties sought by users.

First, it has a lower melting point than the powdered form so it can be heated easily in a water pipe and vaporized to form smoke at a lower temperature. Too high a temperature destroys most of the psychoactive properties of the drug. Since it enters the system directly through the lungs, smokeable cocaine reaches the brain faster than cocaine that is snorted.

Crack cocaine, rock cocaine, and freebase cocaine are much more intense, much more dramatic in their effects than snorting cocaine. They unbalance the brain chemicals more quickly, leaving the brain hormonal balance in disarray. Users react in their own way to the drug depending on how much is used, the purity of the drug, and how long they have been using.

Crack smoker: "You get heat energy, heat flashes that go all through your body. You get these pins and needles, depending on the cut of course."

25¢   THURSDAY, MAY 19, 1988   ★ MIDDAY EDITION

Teens, armed with guns, are foot soldiers in drug-dealing hierarchy

Kids' key role in S.F. crack trade

CRACK & KIDS

AN EXAMINER SPECIAL REPORT

By Lily Eng and John D. O'Connor
OF THE EXAMINER STAFF

Fast money and crack cocaine have lured a new generation of ruthless child entrepreneurs to San Francisco's street corners.

Rags packs a .22-caliber pistol for protection when he sells his crack. He is 14.

J. wants to become the biggest drug dealer in The City. He is 14.

Terence's ambition is to become a hit man in Los Angeles or New York. He is 17.

These child dealers, most of whom are too young to shave or to drive a car, talk dispassionately about the brutality and death they see on inner-city streets.

"I do what I have to do to protect myself and my operation," says Rags, a stocky boy with

anxious eyes. "The guys who stay in business the longest are the guys who protect themselves the best."

During a monthlong investigation, Examiner reporters found that Rags and many children like him play a major role in the crack cocaine trade. They peddle drugs on street corners and in housing projects from the Western Addition to Visitacion Valley.

Dozens of interviews with dealers and addicts, drug counselors and law enforcement officials revealed the attraction, and tragedy, of the crack cocaine epidemic among children.

In this two-part series, the children are identified by their first names, initials or street names. Their full names have been omitted at

— See CRACK, A-22

Next, it is more fat soluble than snorting cocaine and so is more readily absorbed by the fatty brain tissue causing a more intense reaction. Users are also able to get a much higher dose of cocaine in their system at one time because the very large surface area in the lungs, about the size of a football field, can absorb the drug instantaneously.

And since smoking cocaine causes more intense reactions than snorting, it makes sense that the side effects would also be more intense.

User (Crack smoker): "Physically you feel like you're dying, real depressed, like exhausted and wasted, burned out, you know? Like you need to do some more even to function, even to do anything at all."

Because a user inhales an extreme-ly harsh substance, smoking cocaine can also cause breathing problems.

Crack smoker (16 year-old boy): "I had a lot of coughing after using it and shortness of breath. I didn't really notice it at the time but if I went out to ride my bike or lift weights I would have really a hard time."

Crack smoker (16 year-old girl): "A friend was freebasing really heavy and he started going into convulsions and throw-ing up blood. It was real awful. I was real-ly scared, and I thought he was going to die myself. Me and my other friend, we just kept freebasing...and then when he came out of it, he started freebasing again."

Smokable cocaine is of particular danger to the fetus of a pregnant woman. When a pregnant woman smokes crack, within seconds her baby will also be exposed to the drug. The chances of miscarriage, stroke, and sud-den infant death are greatly increased. *(See Drugs in Pregnancy).*

The most frequent type of over-dose that people experience when smoking cocaine is on the mild side: very rapid heartbeat and hyperventila-tion. Going along with this is a feeling of impending death. Most people in fact don't die, but they get very sweaty and clammy and feel as if they're going to die anytime.

A collection of rocks of freebase cocaine, each made in a slightly diffeent manner. The various colors come from the impurities left in the "crack."

The intensive use of freebase in-creases the potential for the abuse of other drugs especially alcohol, heroin, and sedative hypnotics. Some smokers are putting rocks of freebase in marijuana joints in a combination called "champagne," "caviar," or "gremmies." In addition, users are even mixing PCP with crack in a nasty mixture called "space basing," or "whack." Further, there is the addition of freebase cocaine to smokable tar heroin to make a smok-able speedball called "hot rocks." Final-ly, crack or regular cocaine is being mixed in wine coolers for an oral speed-ball known as "crack coolers." When crack is not available, users have switched to shooting and even smoking methamphetamine (speed). A mixture of crank with crack smoked together has also appeared recently and is called "super crank."

Besides the reasons already mentioned for compulsive use of cocaine such as the search for the first intense rush, or avoidance of the down side, there are several other reasons for the compulsion associated with smoking cocaine.

First, smoking a drug is more socially acceptable than injecting or snorting it because cigarette, pipe, and cigar smoking are part of our culture (and legal).

Next, the economics of crack and rock cocaine have expanded the potential number of users, especially among teenagers. The reason is in the packaging. Crack is not cheaper than snorting cocaine; it is just sold in smaller units. A gram was the standard amount, going for about a hundred dollars. Now you can buy a twentieth of a gram that has been converted to crack or rock for 5 to 20 dollars, a manageable sum for teenagers and incidentally, about twice the price of snorting cocaine when figured on a per gram basis.

The economics of crack cocaine have created a lot more dealers and these people have a vested interest in keeping users using. Many housing projects in the inner city have become a haven for crack houses and dealers. Fifteen-year-old dealers are buying new cars, and drug gang homicides are expanding at an alarming rate. Gangs from other countries such as Jamaica and Columbia, have expanded to a number of American cities.

Unfortunately, this burgeoning drug market is making use of the best sales strategies of our free enterprise system: reduce the prices to increase sales; increase the size of the sales force to cover the territory more efficiently; encourage free trade to avoid tariffs and impounding; and create appealing packaging to make the product attractive to a wider segment of the population.

Our original question in this section was "Is it the media coverage or the actual properties of a drug that lead to an epidemic?" Well, our conclusion would be that the media can hype a drug all it wants but if the drug doesn't have inherently addicting qualities, then no amount of hype will lead to a sustained epidemic. Smokable cocaine has properties that lead to severe compulsive use. Those same properties will keep it around for decades to come. In fact, the majority of drug arrests in major cities is for cocaine possession and dealing.

AMPHETAMINES
(speed, meth, crank, crystal, ice, etc.)

Big Amphetamine Lab Raided in Richmond

Federal drug authorities followed a suspicious trail of chemical purchases to a Rich-~~...~~ ~~plant~~ this

Amphetamines, known variously as "speed," "meth," methamphetamines, "crank," "crystal," "ice," and "glass" are a class of synthetic, powerful stimulants, with effects very similar to cocaine but much longer lasting and cheaper to use. Amphetamines can be taken orally but shooting, snorting, and most recently smoking have gained in popularity.

There are several different types of amphetamines: amphetamine, methamphetamine, dextroamphetamine, and dextromethamphetamine. Their effects are almost indistinguishable from each other, the major differences being the method of manufacture and the strength (methamphetamine being the easiest to manufacture illegally). Currently, there has been an explosion of methamphetamine use in its various forms and a drastic increase in the number of "meth labs" raided by the authorities, particularly in Oregon, Texas, and California. Illicit methamphetamine manufacture is a risky busi-

ness. The fumes can be toxic and explosions can occur if the chemicals are handled improperly. Much of the street dealing in methamphetamines has been taken over by biker gangs because of the money involved and the partiality of bikers to the drug.

History

Amphetamines were discovered in the late 1800's but their medical applications weren't recognized till the 1930's when Benzedrine was marketed as a stimulant to counter low blood pressure. It was also used to dilate constricted bronchial passages, to help asthmatics breath. Later on, other amphetamines were used to treat narcolepsy and a form of epilepsy, and as a possible cure for depression. At the same time, the stimulant effects came to be appreciated by students cramming for exams, truckers on long hauls, any worker with extra long hours, and soldiers or pilots trying to stay awake for 48 straight hours.

Pharmaceutical companies in the 50's and 60's promoted the hunger-suppressing and mood-elevating qualities of amphetamines. This led to huge quantities of amphetamines such as Dexedrine, Methedrine, Dexamyl, and Benzedrine flooding the market. Unfortunately, weight watchers found that because of the rapid development of tolerance to this class of drugs, the appetite suppressing effects diminished after 4 to 6 months forcing the user to take ever increasing quantities to lose weight. Dangerous side effects started to outweigh the benefits.

Speed user: "Well, I almost never ate. And when I ate, I ate sugar; Coca Cola, Drake's Cakes; and that was all I ate. I mean, once in a while I'd go to Tab's Steak House and treat myself to a fabulous dollar-fifty-nine steak dinner. I weighed probably 90 pounds and I was anemic and weak but I always felt up and energized because I was always shooting speed."

The 60's were the peak of the speed craze but then the Controlled Substance Act of 1970 made it hard to buy amphetamines legally. A cap was put on the prescription use of these drugs. The street market, however, expanded to fill the need. Instead of buying legally manufactured amphetamines that had been diverted, people bought speed and crank that had been manufactured illegally.

Speed user: "I very seldom ran out in the beginning, in the 60's and 70's. It was cheap; people gave it away. It wasn't like using dope. You didn't have to get money together every day."

The late 1980's saw a resurgence in the availability and abuse of these illicit amphetamines particularly "crank" (methamphetamine sulfate) and "crystal" (methamphetamine hydrochloride-not to be confused with "Krystal" which is PCP). Once stymied by the tight control of chemicals needed to produce illegal amphetamines, clever street chemists now alter commonly available compounds and even use aluminum foil to produce "speed" products. However, a majority of street meth seems to be mostly look-alike drugs such as phenylpropanolamine (an antihistamine), ephedrine, or simply caffeine tablets.

As the 1990's begin, a new, highly potent, and smokable form of methamphetamine (dextromethamphetamine) called **"ice,"** "glass," "batu," or "shabu" has taken center stage to prolong the era of upper abuse.

The "traditional" types of amphetamines that were or are still diverted to street use or that are manufactured illegally, are: small tablets of amphetamine or methamphetamine ("crosstops," "whites"), originally made in Mexico; Biphetamines ("black beauties"), a combination of several amphetamine compounds; Dexadrine ("dexys," "beans"), a dextroamphetamine tablet; Benzedrine ("bennies"), one of the classic "stay awake" pills; and Methadrine, (or Ambar), a methamphetamine.

Routes of Administration

Because of the extremely bitter taste of amphetamines, they are usually put in a gelatin capsule or a piece of paper when taken orally. This route is popular because of the pain or danger of injecting or snorting the caustic drug.

Amphetamines usually cause pain in the blood vessels when used intravenously. Also, with injecting, you have all the attendant risks of contaminated needles. However, it does put large quantities of the drug directly into the bloodstream and causes a more intense "high" than snorting or swallowing.

IV meth user: "I'd already tasted that first high and wanted to get back to it but it was always different, each time I shot up. I started shooting when I was 13 and I was 20 before I learned you could get AIDS from it. I have it...I'm HIV positive."

Snorting "meth," done the same way as cocaine, is also not as popular as oral ingestion, because of extreme irritation it causes to the nasal mucosa.

Because of these limiting effects, users have taken to smoking "crank," "crystal", or "ice," a potentially more seductive method of use than the other ways. The technique of smoking "crank" or "ice" is similar to smoking freebase cocaine (in a pipe). Smoking gets the drug to the brain faster.

Whether swallowed, smoked, or shot..."crank," "crystal," "ice," and the other amphetamines offer a cheaper substitute for cocaine. Occasionally, they are mixed with cocaine ("supercrank") to prolong the effects. Amphetamines last 4 to 6 hours compared to only 40 minutes to one and a half hours for cocaine. "Ice," the newest form of methamphetamine, is alleged to last at least 8 hours, and some say up to 24 hours, after it is smoked.

Tolerance to amphetamines is pronounced. A long term user might need 20 times the initial dose to produce the same high.

Meth user: "When I first started off, I remember having a huge reaction to a small amount of it. And inside of probably a year, I could shoot a spoon of speed easily."

Effects

The effects of small to moderate doses include increased heart rate, respiration, and blood pressure, CNS stimulation, increased body temperature, and appetite suppression. Amphetamines can initially produce a mild euphoria and a feeling of well being, very similar to a cocaine high.

Meth user: "I would inject some speed and right after doing it, like you get an incredible...rush, which some people compare with sexual feelings. And your heart pounds, and I've seen people actually pass out from having too much speed. My heart would pound, and I would sweat, and the rush would pass, and then I would just be, you know, very high energy."

Because the effects last for hours, it means that energy supplies are being continually squeezed from the nerve cells and eventually metabolized. Amphetamines slow the metabolism of these newly released energy supplies, unlike cocaine. This slowed metabolism accounts for the longer duration of action of amphetamines. This still means, however, that extended use or the use of large quantities will severely deplete those energy supplies. Prolonged use of amphetamines as with prolonged use of cocaine can therefore ultimately lead to extreme depression and lethargy.

Speed user: "If I didn't have speed, if I ran out, I would become depressed; very anxiety ridden; I had suicidal thoughts; and I would sleep for long stretches of time till I had more speed. And then, I would start the whole process over again."

The neurotransmitters are also unbalanced by amphetamines, so prolonged use can induce extreme paranoia. The paranoia that occurs can result in homicidal and even suicidal ideations in many users. This paranoid schizophrenia and/or vegetative depression (more common with high dose IV use or heavy smoking) is usually not permanent. Upon cessation of use, the disturbed user will usually return to some semblance of normal, after the brain chemistry has been rebalanced. Unfortunately, this can take anywhere from a few months to a year or more.

Long term use can also cause hallucinations, sleep deprivation, heart and blood vessel toxicity, and severe malnutrition. If the user has not built up a tolerance or takes an unusually large dose, an overdose can occur.

Crank user: "I shot some speed once, and had a seizure immediately. Apparently my heart stopped beating and the person I was with was pounding on my chest; I was real sore and blue the next day."

Much like cocaine, amphetamines release neurotransmitters that mimic sexual gratification. Thus, they are used by those who are sexually active; prone toward multiple partners and prolonged sexual activity. The drug has also been used heavily in gay populations for these sexually enhancing effects. But again, because of the rapid development of tolerance, larger and larger quantities are needed to produce the same effects resulting in an actual decrease of sex drive and performance.

Because of their chemical properties and the feelings they create, amphetamines can be very seductive. Users go on binges or "runs," staying up for 3, 4, or even 10 days at a time, putting a severe strain on their bodies, particularly the cardiovascular and nervous systems. During these runs, people will try to use their excess energy anyway they can...cleaning the kitchen at midnight, taking apart a car, or painting the whole house.

Meth user: "If I ran out of stuff to do, I would dump out everything in the vacuum cleaner, and vacuum it back up. I didn't like to be outside too much because I would get paranoid; I felt uneasy."

Since withdrawal from prolonged amphetamine use is accompanied by physical and mental depression not life threatening or physically painful symptoms, the majority of patients who want to stop can be treated by encouraging abstinence, not drug substitution, and by intensive counseling. Users should avoid all stimulants, including caffeine and tobacco.

Meth user: "I think when you're using the drug, it's real easy to deny everything that's going on, and put everything on the shelf, and not cope with it. Your whole world becomes the acquiring of whatever drug you happen to be using. But when you stop, it's all there to meet you. And you have to deal with it, eventually."

When symptoms are severe and don't respond to counseling, a variety of medical treatments can be used. These include the use of antidepressant agents such as Tofranil, Norpramine, Elavil, Sinequan, or Desyrel. They rebalance seratonin, the neurotransmitter in the brain that deals with both depression and drug craving. Antipsychotic medications are also used such as Haldol, Thorazine, and others to buffer the effects of unbalanced dopamine, the neurotransmitter that moderates paranoia and pleasurable sensations (feeling sated for hunger, thirst, and sex). Sedatives such as Dalmane, chloral hydrate, Librium, phenobarbital, or even Valium are used on a short term basis to treat anxiety or sleep disturbance problems. Incidentally heavy users of amphetamines will self-medicate themselves with any downer to control the overstimulation of the amphetamine. This has led to a major polydrug problem called speedballing which in the past was the practice of injecting a combination of crank and heroin. Currently, speed balling has been extended to smoking a combination of these drugs, i.e. tar heroin mixed with crank or ice.

Though still being tested, many programs have started using nutritional approaches aimed at enhancing the production of those neurotransmitters which have been depleted by heavy speed use. This includes the use of amino acid proteins such as Tyrosine, which is a building block of dopamine in the brain; D-phenylalanine, which is used to make adrenaline, noradrenaline, and also increase the amount of enkephalin in the brain; lecithin, which is a building block of acetylcholine; glutamine, which is a building block of GABA, the natural inhibitory neurotransmitter affected by alcohol and many sedatives; and even the judicious use of tryptophane, a seratonin precursor. Note, high dose tryptophane has recently been implicated in the rare but dangerous blood disease, Eosinophilia Myalgia Syndrome.

Alarmingly, it seems that the current interest in crank, crystal, and ice abuse is concentrated among adolescents and older teenagers, particularly Caucasians and Asian-Americans. One of the reasons for this popularity of the drug is that initially, amphetamines induce qualities which we try to teach to our kids...alertness, motivation, self confidence, socialization, excitement, ability to work long hours, and trim bodies. Unfortunately, these desirable qualities quickly give way to the reverse effects; depression, antisocial behavior, and paranoia among others.

Ice, Glass, etc.

A prelude to the 90's decade was the spread and increase in "ice," "batu," "glass," "shabu," or "snot" (a reddish, liquid methamphetamine base) abuse from Hawaii to the Eastern States during the summer of 1989. Ice is dextromethamphetamine as opposed to methamphetamine. This form of methamphetamine stimulates the brain to a greater degree than the regular methamphetamine but stimulates the heart, blood vessels, and lungs to a lesser degree. Traditional street methamphetamine is therefore slightly less powerful mentally, but more dangerous physically than "ice." Further, "ice" is more smokable than "crank" or "crystal meth" and therefore may be more addictive. The decreased peripheral or heart and blood vessel effects of "ice" (stated to be up to 25% less than that of regular crank), is conducive to users smoking more resulting in a rapid imbalancing of their neurotransmitters. This means more "tweaking" or severe paranoid, hallucinatory, and hypervigilant thinking along with greater suicidal depression and addictive use.

Besides its smokability, greater strength, and longer duration of effects, "ice" is the newest **fad** in the stimulatory drug era. As with the spread of smokable cocaine ("crack," etc.), ice is being marketed as a "newer, better" amphetemine. The financial aspects of this new market (dealers charge up to 6 times as much as they do for traditional meth for a very minor chemical manipulation) will further push the spread of "ice."

DIET PILLS (Amphetamine Congeners)

With the legal supply of amphetamines severely limited because of federal legislation, pharmaceutical companies and physicians turned to amphetamine congeners, drugs which produce many of the same effects as amphetamines but which have a different chemical structure.

The most popular of these is Ritalin, prescribed as an anti-depressant. Ritalin has been used extensively as a treatment for hyperactive children. It works because all stimulants have the ability to focus attention. However, it is clear that it should be used very sparingly, and only after diet changes, counseling, and therapy have failed.

The other popular group of amphetamine congeners are the diet pills such as Preludin, Cylert, Fastin, and the like. The stimulation, the loss of appetite, and the mood elevation are similar to the effects of amphetamines with some of the same side effects: heart irregularities, occasional convulsions, restlessness, and irritability. Despite their widespread use to control appetite and shed weight, (there is significant weight loss in the first 4 to 6 months), users are soon back to and even above their starting weights.

Caught by Texas Computer Law

Diet Doctor's File Grew Fat on 'Speed' Prescriptions

By RONE TEMPEST, *Times Staff Writer*

NACOGDOCHES, Tex.—People in this old, narrow-laned Texas town knew something was wrong when crowds of slender people from the distant cities of Dallas and Houston began to show up outside Dr. John Hall Thomas' office every morning to be treated for obesity.

"It was just like people lining up to go to the movies," said Nacogdoches Police Chief Don Barlow.

"Everybody in town saw those long lines," said Dr. Robert Carroll, secretary of the Nacogdoches/St. Augustine Medical Society. "He was sticking out like a sore thumb down here."

Thomas, 38, a third-generation Texas physician, had turned his modest family practice into one of the biggest sources of "speed" drugs—Preludin, Ritalin and Desoxyn—in the history of the state. In a red-brick building here across the street from his turreted Victorian mansion and in a storefront "Texas Bariatric Clinic" in the slums of Dallas, Thomas wrote 5,065 prescriptions for powerful, dangerous drugs in five months.

Federal and state investigators were able to build a case against the doctor that resulted in his arrest, the loss of his medical license and, last week, a guilty plea in federal court to a charge of illegally dispensing a controlled substance. He faces up to five years in prison and a $15,000 fine.

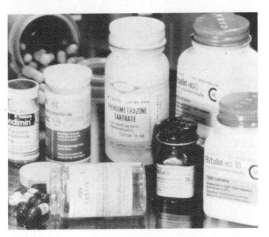

A collection of commonly used diet pills. Sometimes it's hard to tell whether decreased caloric intake or the psychoactive effects are what make you feel good while dieting.

LOOKALIKES

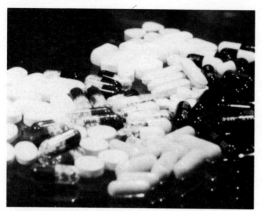

A collection of lookalike uppers sold on the street as the real thing, or through magazines as legal stimulants.

Giving credence to the idea that the 1980's are an era of upper abuse is the recent "lookalike" phenomenon. Taking advantage of the current interest in stimulant drugs, a few legitimate manufacturers began to make legal, over-the-counter products which looked identical to prescription stimulants.

Their products (ephedrine--an anti-asthmatic; phenylpropanolamine-a decongestant and a mild appetite suppressant; caffeine--a stimulant); are being combined, packaged, and sold as "legal stimulants" in a deliberate attempt to misrepresent the drugs. The same chemicals are also showing up as illicit amphetamine lookalikes such as street speed, cartwheels, and crank; and as cocaine lookalikes such as Super-caine, Super-toot, Snow. The cocaine lookalikes add benzocaine or procaine

to mimic the numbing effects of the actual drug.

The problem with the lookalike products is their toxicity (primarily on the heart and blood vessels), when taken in large quantities, and an amphetamine-like drug dependence in users who chronically abuse the drugs. The physical problems can be particularly severe since large amounts are required to get a speed, or cocaine-like high.

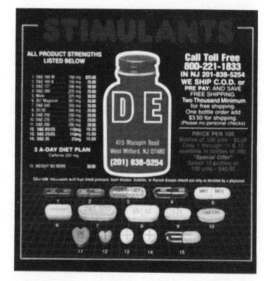

Ads for legal uppers run in magazines like "High Times."

CAFFEINE

Caffeine is the most popular stimulant in the world. It was first cultivated in Ethiopia, spread to Arabia about 800AD and finally to Europe by the 13th century. The drink was so stimulating that many cultures banned it as an intoxicating drug. The active ingredient, caffeine, was finally isolated in 1821 and discovered to be present in a number of plants including the cocoa bush (not coca) from which we get chocolate; in tea leaves; and in cola nuts.

Beverage or Food	Amount of Caffeine
1 cup freshly brewed American coffee	100 mg
1 demitasse espresso	200 mg
1 cup of instant coffee	70 mg
1 cup of tea	70 mg
12 ounce glass of Coca Cola	80 mg.
4 ounce bar of chocolate	80 mg
NO-DOZ tablet	100 mg

Caffeine, and particularly coffee, is a mild stimulant. In low doses it can make us more alert, dissipate drowsiness or fatigue, and help us think. It can also speed up the heart rate, raise blood pressure, and irritate the stomach. As with any drug, excessive use can cause other problems such as nervousness, mental confusion, irritability, muscle twitches, and insomnia.

Tolerance to the effects of caffeine does occur. We might eventually need three cups to "wake up" instead of our usual single cup with lots of cream and sugar. Also, withdrawal symptoms do occur after long term use or high dose use. These include headaches, fatigue, depression, sleep problems, and irritability but fortunately, most symptoms pass within a few days.

Coffee can become habit forming, but it is a much milder dependency than that found with amphetamines and cocaine.

Of the 100 million or so coffee drinkers in the United States, 20% to 30% consume 5 to 7 cups per day. At this dose, signs of caffeine toxicity--increased heart rate, palpitations, anxiety, high blood pressure, and insomnia--are readily apparent. Some women develop benign lumps in their breasts. Caffeine is lethal at about 10 grams (100 cups of coffee), but note that toxic effects start to appear after only 5 cups.

Coronary heart disease, ischemic heart disease, heart attacks, intestinal ulcers, diabetes, and some liver problems linked to caffeine, have been seen more often in countries with very high per capita caffeine consumption.

Uppers
TOBACCO (Nicotine)

The old peace pipe used tobacco, not marijuana, to promote friendship.

Tobacco is a psychoactive drug. It was used by Indians of the New World in religious rituals 2,000 years ago. It was banned by many European countries in the 16th and 17th centuries and in China in 1630 because it was so intoxicating. It is still considered evil by many religions. Curently, fifty-six million Americans smoke.

The active ingredient in tobacco, nicotine, disrupts neurotransmitter balance, stimulating some chemicals, disrupting the transmission of others, and increasing electrical activity in the brain in a manner very similar to, but not as intense as cocaine and amphetamines.

It also constricts blood vessels, raises the heart rate and blood pressure, decreases appetite, increases alertness, partially deadens the senses of taste and smell, and irritates the lungs.

Tolerance to the effects of nicotine, a strong poison, develops quite rapidly compared to other drugs.

A few hours of smoking is sufficient for tolerance to begin to develop. This rapidly induced tolerance is the key to understanding the addictive qualities of tobacco. Initially, tobacco causes significant mental and physical effects, including light-headedness and nausea. The body, in self-protection, immediately adapts to handle the toxins. Soon one comes to depend on smoking to stay "normal". The smoker wants to maintain the stimulation, and the altered body chemistry. Compare the dizziness and high from your first cigarette to the nagging cough and mild stimulation from your 30th cigarette of the day, one year later.

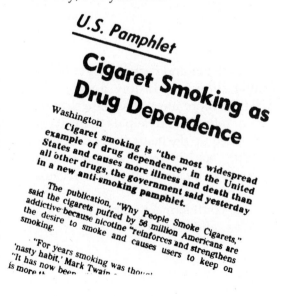

U.S. Pamphlet

Cigaret Smoking as Drug Dependence

Washington

Cigaret smoking is "the most widespread example of drug dependence" in the United States and causes more illness and death than all other drugs, the government said yesterday in a new anti-smoking pamphlet.

The publication, "Why People Smoke Cigarets," said the cigarets puffed by 56 million Americans are addictive because nicotine "reinforces and strengthens the desire to smoke and causes users to keep on smoking.

"For years smoking was thou... 'nasty habit,' Mark Twain ... "It has now been ... is more ...

Prolonged use of tobacco can cause lung damage, heart irregularities, and cancer. In fact, cigarettes cause more deaths than all other psychoactive drugs combined. Each year, 320,000 American deaths have been directly attributable to nicotine compared to only 6 to 7 thousand deaths from heroin and cocaine.

Withdrawal from a pack or 2 pack-a-day habit after prolonged use can cause headaches, severe irritability, inability to concentrate, nervousness, and sleep disturbances so it is not just an emotional addiction but a physical one as well. Recent research shows that nicotine works not only through neurotransmitters like adrenaline and noradrenaline but also through the opiate-like neurotransmitter, endorphin. This has led to a promising medical approach to the treatment of nicotine addiction, using Clonidine, which blocks opiate/opioid withdrawal.

Tobacco is the most addicting drug there is. Nicotine craving, in fact, may last a lifetime after withdrawal.

Warnings were first put on tobacco products in 1967 as a result of the Surgeon General's 1966 report on the dangers of smoking. Even though tobacco contains a number of cancer-causing chemicals (carcinogens), it is still sold legally. It is sold legally in spite of federal law which prohibits the sale of any product made for human consumption that is proven to cause cancer. The reason it is still legal is that a special law was passed exempting tobacco from the law. The speculation is that the exemption was passed because of pressure from the tobacco-growing states where it is a big cash crop.

The other reason for the exemption is the fact that 56 million Americans (and who knows how many in other countries) are addicted to tobacco and constitute a large voting block.

The battlefield in the 80's and 90's between smokers and non-smokers is being drawn over the issue of second-hand smoke. Numerous laws have been passed in many states and at the Federal level prohibiting the use of tobacco products in a variety of spaces and buildings (e.g., sections of restaurants, airplanes, some businesses, Federal buildings).

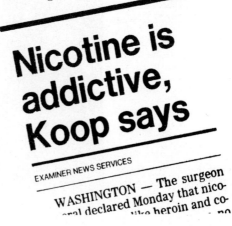

Nicotine is addictive, Koop says

EXAMINER NEWS SERVICES

WASHINGTON — The surgeon
eral declared Monday that nico-
like heroin and co-

The practice of placing snuff tobacco between the cheek and gum is called "dipping."

chewed till the nicotine in the juice is absorbed into the gums. Tobacco is somewhat less addicting in this form since it goes through several tissues instead of being sent directly to the brain via the lungs, but strangely enough, more of the nicotine reaches the bloodstream (heat destroys much of the psychoactive properties of tobacco) and the rush is somewhat more intense. Though the risk of lung cancer is reduced, oral or mouth cancer is more common among tobacco chewers.

Chewing tobacco has waxed and waned in its popularity over the years. Amazon Indians chop up tobacco and put it on their gums to allow absorption of the nicotine into the bloodstream. In more civilized societies it is packaged and sold in stores. In this form it is

In addition to chewing tobacco, **snuffs** called dip or chaw are put in the mouth and under the tongue for the nicotine effects. This has resulted in increased gum disease and mouth cancers.

NEW YORK'S NEW SMOKING FAD.

Picturesque Groups and Fighting Talk in the Rooms of the Men from Bagdad.

MANY DAINTY SMOKERS SEEN

A Fashionable Crush Early, and Later Young Men Who Talk Defiance.

GAMBLERS ALSO NUMEROUS.

Turks Have a King of Clubs of Their Own Now and Breathe Slaughter.

HE Turk and the Infidel have fun and trouble almost nightly now in a so-called Oriental smoking room in Broadway, near Thirtieth street. They also have the police.

As a matter of fact, it

NEW YORK HERALD, SUNDAY, APRIL 28, 1895.

A SCENE IN ONE OF THE RECENTLY OPENED TURKISH SMOKING PARLORS.

REVIEW

1. Uppers are central nervous system stimulants.

2. In general, uppers stimulate us by forcing the release of energy chemicals (particularly adrenalin), by increasing electrical activity in the brain, and by artificially stimulating our reward/pleasure center.

3. The basic effects of stimulants are increased energy, faster heart rate, higher blood pressure, quicker respiration, restlessness, dilated pupils, talkativeness, irritability, reduced appetite, or thirst, and variable euphoria depending on the strength of the stimulant.

4. Most problems with stimulants occur when we don't give the body time to recover from the stimulation and we deplete our energy supply.

5. Other problems with the stronger stimulants occur when we disrupt our neurotransmitter balance. We can become paranoid, have muscle tremors, become aggressive, and fall into a deep mental depression.

6. Another set of problems with the stronger stimulants comes when our stimulated reward/pleasure center tells us we don't need food, drink, or sexual stimulation. We can become malnourished, dehydrated, or unable to perform sexually.

7. A final set of problems with the stronger stimulants such as cocaine, comes from overdosing: using too much at one time, or having a severe reaction to a small dose. A "caine" or "speed" reaction can cause convulsions, uncontrolled heart rhythms, ultra-high blood pressure, heart attacks, strokes, dangerously high body temperatures, psychotic episodes, coma, and eventually death, if not handled quickly by trained or knowledgeable people.

8. The principal stimulants are cocaine, amphetamines (speed), diet pills, mood elevators, nicotine, caffeine and lookalike, over-the-counter stimulants.

9. Cocaine is the second most addicting stimulant (nicotine is first). It is noted for the intensity of its stimulation, the high price, and the speed with which it is metabolized from the body.

10. Cocaine can be snorted, injected, or smoked in a chemically treated form called crack, rock, freebase, or a dozen other names. Smoking is the fastest route to the brain, 7 to 10 seconds.

11. Cocaine's allure comes from the fact that it mimics natural body functions and highs. The comedown is also extremely intense, so the user keeps taking it to stay up. And finally, the brain becomes sensitized to the memory of the pleasurable effects.

12. An overdose of cocaine can be as little as 1/50th of a gram or as much as 1.2 grams or more. Most overdose reactions are not fatal but death can come from cardiac arrest, respiratory depression, and seizures.

13. Crack cocaine causes many problems because of the economics of the drug. It comes in smaller amounts, there's a large market for it, and the profits are great.

14. Amphetamines are very similar to cocaine, the main difference being that they are longer acting, take more time to metabolize, and are cheaper to buy.

15. Amphetamines were originally prescribed to fight exhaustion, depression, and obesity but were taken more often for their mood elevating and euphoric properties.

16. Prolonged use of crank and other amphetamines can induce paranoia, heart and blood vessel problems, increased body temperature, dehydration, and malnutrition.

17. Tolerance develops rapidly with amphetamines. Withdrawal after long term use causes physical and emotional depression, extreme irritability, and nervousness.

18. Many diet pills and mood elevators mimic the actions of amphetamines but are not quite as strong. They can still cause many of the problems found with amphetamines. Ritalin and Preludin can be as addicting as cocaine and speed.

19. Lookalike drugs were popularized to take advantage of the desire for the now hard-to-get amphetamines and cocaine. They are composed of over-the-counter stimulants. Heavy use can cause heart and blood vessel problems.

20. Caffeine, particularly coffee, is the most popular stimulant in the world. Tolerance can develop with caffeine and withdrawal symptoms such as headaches, depression, and irritability do occur, particularly if consumption is more than 5 cups a day.

21. Nicotine (tobacco) is the most addicting psychoactive drug. Fifty-six million people are addicted to cigarettes compared to 15 million addicted to alcohol. Nicotine causes more deaths than all the other psychoactive drugs combined.

QUESTIONS

1. What neurotransmitter is most responsible for the stimulation caused by uppers?

2. What are 3 major physical effects of most stimulants?

3. What are 3 major mental effects of stimulants?

4. Why do we lose our appetite when taking amphetamines, cocaine, or diet pills?

5. What are the major problems caused by
  a. Depletion of energy chemicals?
  b. Disruption of neurotransmitter balance?
  c. Stimulation of reward/pleasure center?

6. Name five kinds of stimulants.

7. What are the three most common ways to put cocaine into the body?

8. What are the major differences between amphetamines and cocaine?

9. What are the effects of an overdose of amphetamines or cocaine?

10. What are the main ingredients of lookalike stimulants?

11. What are the symptoms of caffeine withdrawal?

12. Which stimulant causes the most injuries and medical problems?

13. Which stimulant causes the most deaths?

1985

Allowed in 26 States

Drinking and Driving: a Legal Mix

By J. MICHAEL KENNEDY,
Times Staff Writer

HOUSTON—In this city of clogged highways, the evening drive from office to home can be as much as two beers long.

A trip to Dallas could easily be a six-packer, necessitating an ice chest to keep the road beers chilled for the five-hour drive.

In Texas, drinking and driving as common as the 7-Eleven st The state has no law against qu ing a Lone Star or sipping o Scotch and soda while crui down the interstate. Often, t here begin at the package store.

While that may seem odd inc to residents of California w such since legal statist Safet: senge the r Verm they a

3,70

If a
Key V
dian h

1921 Pharmacy Board Backs 3 Drastic Bills to Correct Law Weaknesses

First Offense for Peddling of Drugs Made Felony; Hospital on Island for Addicts Urged
JANUARY 4, 1921
BY WILLIAM H. JORDAN.
EXAMINER BUREAU
SACRAMENTO, Jan. 3.—The habit-forming drug traffic is to be attacked in the State Legislature.

Three measures, calculated to correct weaknesses in existing law and aimed at suppression of the business as well as to the care of the drug addict under proper State control and supervision, are to be presented to the Legislature with the sanction and approval of the State Board of Pharmacy.

A drastic tightening up of the penal law as to the unlawful sale of drugs and provision for an island isolation hospital for treatment of addicts are the two outstanding phases of legislation which will be asked for by the officials of the State board.
PROVISIONS OF BILLS.
The bills, which are being drafted, provide:

1—Making the first offense of

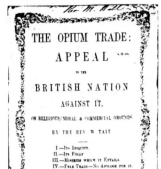

1856

THE OPIUM TRADE:
APPEAL
TO THE
BRITISH NATION
AGAINST IT,
ON RELIGIOUS/MORAL & COMMERCIAL GROUNDS
BY THE REV W TAIT
I.—ITS INIQUITY.
II.—ITS FOLLY
III.—MISERIES WHICH IT ENTAILS.
IV.—FREE TRADE—NO APOLOGY FOR IT.

1988

Nursing home patients still being over-drugged

By Celia Hooper

CHICAGO (UPI) — American nursing homes, largely ignoring persistent warnings that they are overmedicating most of their elderly patients, are giving them

"The irony is that these are the frailest people in the country, yet they are receiving the most intense medication with minimum physician involvement in surveillance" of effects and side effects, said Avorn

American Medical Association, published Thursday, they said about 220 residents were being given antipsychotic drugs, which reduce delusions in young patients with schizophrenia.

depressant drugs were not di ed as depressed, and one-fou these patients were given an tyline, the anti-depressant favored for geriatric pat because side-effects in iory problems, disorien tipation, difficulty urir ed vision and other probl rty percent of the patien criptions for tranquilizer ing pills — usually arly, rather than "as nee eliance on scheduled reg ychoactive medicines ind these drugs are not used y for periods of special ad this pattern of use is le with the concept of se iemical restraint,'" the r said.

1978 S.F. EXAMINER   Tues., Aug. 29, 1978

Opium smugglers help finance guerrilla insurrection in Burma

1913

By Robert Hollis
Examiner Staff Writer
(Second of four parts)

not taxed to support the Shan insurrection.

Freddie speaks American-accented English, having al Baptist missionaries. He has a wife i living in a frame house and he someday for a new life in Australia.

re never defeated by the British," he ver be defeated by the Burmese."

aion of the present military state of it for a moment and said, "It is a

WILL PULVERIZE THE RUM POWER

Senator James K. Vardaman Says He Is Going to Make It Unlawful to Sell or Give Away Liquor in District of Columbia---Negroes and Intemperance the Two Great Evils of Country.

STORY OF THE NEW SENATOR'S LIFE IS MOST EXCITING

Golden Triangle

all American boomtown. The smell of war is not far away.

The Shan agreed to become part of Burma when it gained its independence from Britain in 1947 only with the understanding that they would be guaranteed autonomy and home rule. In 1962, Gen. Ne Win overthrew the elected government and jailed a number of Shan leaders. Since that time, the rebel war against the Burmese has been constant.

Diplomatic sources dispute the Shan claim that the rebel Shan State Army (SSA) and other rebel groups are fighting only for independence.

"The Shans are just bandits, criminals capitalizing on political unrest to make millions," said one American diplomat who has served in Burma and Vietnam for nearly a decade.

The dirty streets are lined with small, family-operated stalls offering technically illegal consumer goods: Japanese radios, American and English whiskey, and, even the most rare of commodities, tires.

es-old status quo of the guerrilla war in northeast Burma may be slowly changing. Rumors have abounded in recent months that, after years of ignoring Burmese pleas, the Chinese government in Peking soon may yank the rug from beneath the Burmese Communists. The BCP's sole source of arms has been China. But with shifts in alliances occurring in Vietnam and Cambodia, diplomatic observers say China may need a stable Burma as its neighbor.

Should the BCP wither from lack of Chinese support, many Rangoon observers believe Ne Win could divert several thousand troops to the Shan state and surrounding border regions.

Recently, Burma and Thailand took the first tentative steps toward regional cooperation in anti-narcotics matters. Both governments agreed to pool drug suppression information.

The verbal pact — a first among governments in the Golden Triangle — has led to some cautious optimism among narcotics agents in Thailand that the booming opium business may one day be broken. No one, however, seems under the illusion that any changes will come quickly.

Tomorrow: The U.S. fights Asia's heroin kingpins

Research for this series was paid for in part by the Gannett Fellowships in Asian Studies for Journalists.

THE DRUGS
DOWNERS

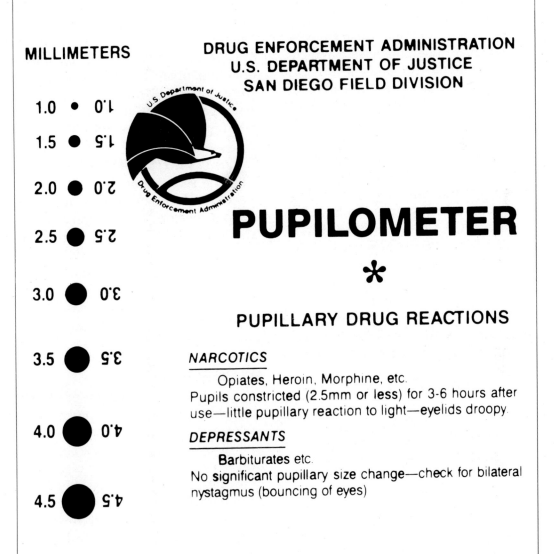

MILLIMETERS

1.0 •

1.5 ●

2.0 ●

2.5 ●

3.0 ●

3.5 ●

4.0 ●

4.5 ●

**DRUG ENFORCEMENT ADMINISTRATION
U.S. DEPARTMENT OF JUSTICE
SAN DIEGO FIELD DIVISION**

PUPILOMETER

*

PUPILLARY DRUG REACTIONS

NARCOTICS

Opiates, Heroin, Morphine, etc.
Pupils constricted (2.5mm or less) for 3-6 hours after use—little pupillary reaction to light—eyelids droopy.

DEPRESSANTS

Barbiturates etc.
No significant pupillary size change—check for bilateral nystagmus (bouncing of eyes)

A pupilometer is used to compare the size of pupils in a suspected drug user. Opiates and opioids contract pupils and are a strong indicator of drug use.

A GENERAL DESCRIPTION

Downers depress the overall functioning of the central nervous system to ultimately induce sedation, drowsiness, and even coma (if used to excess). Unlike uppers, which generally function through the release and enhancement of the body's natural stimulatory hormones, the diverse group of chemicals classed as downers induce sedating effects through a wide range of biochemical processes at different sites of the brain and spinal cord. Some mimic the actions of the body's natural sedating or inhibiting neurotransmitters (i.e. endorphins, enkephalins, GABA), while others directly suppress the stimulatory areas of the brain. Still others work in ways scientists haven't yet fully understood. Because of these variations, the depressants are grouped into a number of subclasses based upon their medical use, chemistry, and legal classification.

The main groups are:

OPIATES & OPIOIDS
SEDATIVE-HYPNOTICS
ALCOHOL

The minor groups are:

SKELETAL MUSCLE RELAXANTS
ANTIHISTAMINES
"LOOKALIKE" SEDATIVES
"OVER-THE-COUNTER"
   SEDATIVES

OPIATES & OPIOIDS

Opiates such as heroin, morphine, and codeine, are refined from the opium poppy. Opioids such as Demerol and Darvon are synthetic opiates, produced to mimic the effects of natural opiates. Opiates and opioids were developed for the treatment of acute pain. Most illicit users initially take them for the euphoric effects.

SEDATIVE-HYPNOTICS

The sedative-hypnotics represent a wide range of synthetic chemical substances developed to treat nervousness and insomnia. The first, a barbiturate, was created in 1864 by Dr. Adolph Von-Bayer. Since then, thousands of different sedative-hypnotics such as Valium and Quaalude have been created. All have toxic side effects or tissue dependence liability.

ALCOHOL

Alcohol, the natural by-product of fermented plant sugars, is probably the oldest and most widely used psychoactive drug in the world. It has been used for a tremendous number of medical remedies, from sterilizing wounds to stimulating sexuality. Alcohol is also the world's most devastating drug (second most in the U.S.) in terms of health and social consequences. In the United States alone, it is estimated that there are 15 million active alcoholics or problem drinkers.

SKELETAL MUSCLE RELAXANTS

Centrally acting skeletal muscle relaxants are actually synthetically developed central nervous system depressants aimed at areas of the brain responsible for muscular coordination and activity. They are used to treat muscle tension and pain. Though the current abuse of these products is rare, their overall downer effect on all parts of the central nervous system produces reactions similar to those caused by other abused downers.

ANTIHISTAMINES

Antihistamines are synthetic drugs, developed during the 1930's and 1940's for treatment of allergic reactions, ulcers, shock, rashes, motion sickness, and even Parkinson's Disease. In addition to blocking the release of histamine, these drugs cross the blood-brain barrier to induce the common and oftentimes very potent side effect of CNS depression resulting in drowsiness. Thus, even antihistamines are occasionally sought and abused for their depressant effects.

LOOKALIKE SEDATIVES

"Lookalike" sedatives were advertised along with lookalike stimulants in the early eighties. The great commercial success of the latter products encouraged shady drug manufacturers to sell products disguised as prescription downers. These companies took legally available antihistamines and packaged them in tablets and capsules so they resembled prescription downers; i.e., Quaalude, Valium, Seconal. As with the other antihistamines, lookalike sedatives cause drowsiness.

OVER-THE-COUNTER SEDATIVES

These are depressant drugs that are sold legally in stores, without the need for a prescription. Many have been marketed and used as sleep aids or sedatives for years. The bromides were, in fact, first used as depressants during the 1880's. Scopolamine in low doses, along with antihistamines, salicylates, salicylamide and even alcohol, constitute the active sedating components of these products. As with other downer drugs, these products are occasionally abused for their depressant effects.

OPIATES & OPIOIDS

A section of the San Francisco Sunday Examiner and Chronicle

1989

Africa wrestles with growing heroin problem

Region ill-prepared for fight, experts say

By Patrick Moser
UNITED PRESS INTERNATIONAL

NAIROBI, Kenya — Africa is faced with a new scourge it is ill prepared to fight: heroin.

Although virtually unknown a few years ago, a continent already wracked by droughts, diseases and civil war, heroin is slowly making its presence in African capitals.

A direct result of the increase of the "African connection" transit route between India...

1988

China opens center to fight drug abuse

BEIJING (UPI) — China, once plagued by rampant opium addiction, has admitted narcotics abuse is rising and announced it will open the nation's first treatment center in the country, health officials said today.

Jiang Zuoning, director of a Hospital in Beijing's northern outskirts, said a special medical unit for addicts will be established at the hospital.

The center will deal mainly with patients addicted to "licit, over counter drugs — for example, narcotics, sleeping pills," Jiang said in a telephone interview. He said most addictions result from poor monitoring by doctors.

When asked if he expected patients suffering from opiate or heroin addiction — major societal problems in pre-communist China — Jiang said, "We hope not. But maybe there will be such patients from other parts of the country."

Jiang told the official English-language China Daily that China remains officially drug-free except in some border areas, but that drug dependency is a growing problem.

Although Jiang downplayed the rise in drug addiction as "neither great nor epidemic," the opening of the clinic marks a rare admission by the communist government of the return of a problem it thought gone more than three decades ago.

Middle-Class Junkies

Heroin Now an Upscale Addiction

By MILES CORWIN,
Times Staff Writer

After a year of escalating cocaine use, Richard Chavez was snorting so many lines he was unable to enjoy the high anymore. Instead of the euphoric rush he once experienced, he was now anxious, paranoid and unable to sleep. A friend told Chavez that he knew of a way to salvage and prolong his cocaine high—heroin.

"I told him that I wasn't a junkie and I hated the needle," Chavez recalled. "But he showed me how to cut and sniff it. He was right. I got that coke rush, and before I could get too hyper I'd snort some heroin to mellow out. Pretty soon I gave up the cocaine and stayed with the heroin."

When Dallas Taylor bought his first ounce of heroin, he carefully rationed the supply. He only used it occasionally like "to take the edge off" after a cocaine binge.

"A month after I bought my first ounce I thought I had the habit licked," Taylor said. "But a doctor told me it wasn't the flu. I'd been using it and more heroin and had run out. I was kicking and didn't know it."

'Middle-Class Addicts'

Chavez, a sheet metal worker from El Monte, and Taylor, a Los Angeles drummer who has been on seven gold and two platinum albums—both of whom recently kicked heroin habits—are part of a new wave of addicts that is flooding hospitals and drug treatment programs. Called "middle-class addicts" by health professionals, they bear little resemblance to the stereotyped street junkie.

Most have jobs, families and health insurance. They began experimenting with the drug in their late 20s or early 30s, later...

1985

1923

AMERICA LEADS REST OF WORLD IN ADDICTION TO NARCOTICS

JANUARY 21, 1923.

1,000,000 to 4,000,000 Users of Dope Consumed 100,000,000 Ounces During the Year

TRAFFIC HAS U.S. HELPLESS

Like War, Evil Is Too Great to Be Faced by Anything Less Than Entire Population

By JAMES WHITTAKER

The United States has abandoned all lines of defense against the dope traffic.

It is defenseless against an evil that has already tainted two and a half million of its population and is vigorously ready immediately to multiply that number by six.

In the last five years dope has fought a great battle for evil and, in American law, won.

A six month survey, begun last July in this great land, extended since to include dope-stricken zones in every State in the Union, culminates to-day in the documental proof which permits the current issue of Hearst's International Magazine to make the cold statement:

The United States now uses more dope than all the...

Prosecutions of Those Who Supply Dope Fiends With Drugs.

1906

DRUGGISTS WHO SELL POISON TO BE ARRESTED

Charles B. Whilden, Secretary of the State Board of Pharmacy, and Miss Ethel Wigley, who has assisted in trapping many local druggists; and photograph of some of the evidence.

MISS ETHEL WIGLEY

Codeine Diversion Through 10 State Drugstores Charged

By ALLAN PARACHINI, *Times Staff Writer*

Failures in inventory control systems at the Bay Area warehouse of one of the nation's largest drug companies apparently led to the diversion of more than 16.7 million codeine tablets sold through just 10 California drugstores, federal agents say.

The apparent epidemic of what federal investigators called "excess" and "suspicious" orders was found to have occurred between early 1979 and sometime in 1982 at the Burlingame warehouse of Burroughs Wellcome Co. The facility supplies narcotics and other drugs to stores in the 13 Western states.

And release of the massive quantities of codeine was blamed by an assistant U.S. attorney in charge of the investigation in San Francisco for emergence in Southern California of a drug abuse fad called *loads*, in which users mix codeine and the sleeping pill Doriden as a substitute for heroin.

More Codeine Than Thrifty

U.S. Drug Enforcement Administration investigators say several small neighborhood drugstores involved in the apparent codeine diversion in Los Angeles, Oakland and San Diego each sold more codeine per year than the entire 131-store Thrifty chain.

First identified by drug treatment workers at Metropolitan State Hospital in Norwalk more than two years ago, *loads* was blamed in the deaths of 56 drug users in 1981 and 1982, according to the Los Angeles County Coroner's Office. For reasons that have never been fully explained by drug experts, codeine—a common narcotic pain reliever manufactured by many drug companies—apparently reacts in an unusually potent fashion when it is taken in combination with Doriden, a common though controversial sleeping pill.

widespread popularity so quickly. This uncertainty was expressed by doctors at Metropolitan State Hospital in Norwalk when they published the first reports in medical journals on the emergence of loads.

In March of 1982, however, DEA agents auditing records at the Burroughs Wellcome warehouse discovered that millions of codeine tablets were being shipped under questionable circumstances. Most of what investigators called "suspicious" and "excess" orders were bound for small drugstores in Los Angeles, one of which sold 3.1 million codeine pills between 1979 and 1982.

Addicts Resell Drug

The so-called diversion of the pills occurred, according to investigators, when drug abusers obtained quasi-legitimate prescriptions for narcotics from physicians or clinics and had the orders filled at the drugstores in question. Once they had obtained their prescription allotments, addicts commonly resold the drugs on the street to other users. The so-called diversion culture has been a bane of officials of Medicaid—called Medi-Cal in California—almost since it began in the mid-1960s. Many *loads* users turned out to be Medi-Cal recipients whose drugs were paid for by state funds.

Though the DEA and the U.S. Department of Justice said they have no reason to believe that executives at Burroughs Wellcome's headquarters in North Carolina were aware of the codeine diversion, the government has demanded nearly $1 million in civil penalties in quiet—but apparently unsuccessful—negotiations with the big drug maker that began late last year.

Frustrated in their efforts to obtain a consent decree—in which Burroughs Wellcome would...

1983

CLASSIFICATION

O ne of the oldest and best documented class of drugs, opiates and opioids have been the source of continual, and occasionally explosive, worldwide problems. Heroin gets the most publicity but there are many more opiates and opioids such as codeine and Demerol, which have created their own set of problems and their own group of compulsive users. Fortunately, recent developments in opiate and opioid research, following the discovery of the body's own natural painkillers, endorphins, represent the most significant change to the whole field of opiate and opioid abuse in this century. These developments, detailed in the Neurotransmitter section of the book, pages *(36 to 39)*, and later on in this section, give hope of a better understanding of opiate and opioid addiction.

Drug Name	Trade Name	Street Name
OPIATES (Opium Poppy Extracts or Modified Extracts)		
Opium	Pantopon, Paregoric Laudanum	"O", op, poppy
Codeine (usually combined w/aspirin or Tylenol)	Empirin w/codeine, Tylenol w/codeine	Number 4's (1 grain) Number 3's (1/2 grain) Codeine w/Doriden- loads, sets, 4's & doors
Morphine	Various	Murphy, morph, M, Miss Emma
Diacetyl morphine	**Heroin**	Smack, junk, horse, "H," Mexican brown, China White, Harry, skag, Rufus, tar, Perze
Hydrocodone	Hycodan, Vicodin	
Hydromorphone	**Dilaudid**	Dillies
Oxycodone	**Percodan,** Tylox	Percs
OPIOIDS (Synthetic Opiates)		
Methadone	Dolophine	Juice
Propoxyphene	**Darvon,** Darvocet-N	Pink ladies, pumpkin seeds
Meperidine	**Demerol**	
Fentanyl	Sublimaze	Derivatives are misrepre- sented as China White
Pentazocine	**Talwin**	Part of T's and blues
L acetyl alpha methadol	LAAM	LAM (long acting methadone)

HISTORY

The story of opiates starts with the opium poppy, the substances made from that plant such as heroin and codeine, and the effects of those drugs on our pain and pleasure centers.

Dried opium poppy capsule, drained of its psychoactive resin.

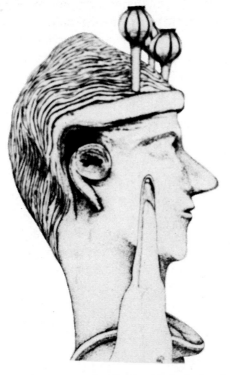

Sumerian crown, decorated with incised opium poppies (c. 3,000 BC).

History

The effects of the opium poppy were referred to 5,000 years ago by the Sumerians. They called it "The Joy Plant." The Egyptians were the first to record the dual nature of opium. Their ancient medical texts listed it as a cure for all illness and as a poison.

The opium poppy (papaver somniferum) was named after Somnis, the Roman God of Sleep, and though the drug was used extensively, the abuse potential was low because it had a bitter taste and was only taken by mouth. Orally, the drug has to go through the entire digestive system before it enters the blood stream and makes its way to the brain 20 or 30 minutes later.

It was the introduction of the pipe from North America to Europe and Asia that set the stage for the widespread non-medical abuse of opium. This is because smoking puts more of the active ingredients of the drug into the blood stream faster, via the lungs. The drug will reach the brain in as few as 7 seconds.

In 1806, a German pharmacist refined morphine from opium and found it to be 10 times stronger.

Next came the invention of the hypodermic needle which could put high concentrations of a drug directly into the blood stream. It takes 15 to 30 seconds for an injected opiate to affect the central nervous system. If the drug is injected just under the skin or in a muscle (skin popping or muscling), the effects are delayed 5 to 8 minutes.

Just before the turn of the century heroin was created from morphine in an attempt to find a more effective pain killer which didn't have addictive properties. Unfortunately, it also induced more euphoria, and so became more desirable, thus creating more abuse problems.

Elephant weights from S.E. Asia used to measure opium and heroin.

Opiates in their many forms became so popular that hundreds of tonics and medications came on the market, for everything from tired blood to toothaches, before the casual, non-medical use was declared illegal at the beginning of the 20th century.

Since then, growing, processing, and distributing opiates, especially heroin have become major sources of revenue for criminal organizations worldwide, i.e., the Chinese Triads, the Mafia, and the Columbian Cartel.

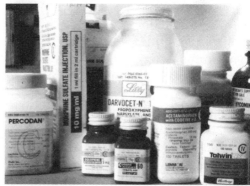

Collection of prescription opiates and opioids, still some of the most common prescription drugs.

In addition, diversion of legitimate prescription opiates and opioids like codeine and dilaudid, through theft, phoney purchases, and forged prescriptions has created an illegal, uncontrolled market of pills and injectibles.

There are an estimated 100,000 to 300,000 prescription opiate and opioid abusers in the U.S., compared to one half to one million heroin abusers.

The Effects

To understand opiates and opioids, it's important to understand pain and its connection to the nervous system. Pain, such as the pain of burned skin, is a warning signal. It tells us if we are being damaged physically. It sends a message to our brain which in turn tells the rest of the body to protect itself, to stop the damage. The pain message is transmitted by a neurotransmitter called substance "P."

If the pain is too intense, the body tries to protect itself by softening the pain signals. It does this by flooding the brain and spinal cord with special neurotransmitters, called endorphins. These endorphins attach themselves to the membrane of the sending nerve cell telling it not to send substance "P."

However, many signals still get through. If the pain is still unbearable, opiates and opioids can be used. These drugs are effective because they act like endorphins. They not only prevent too much substance "P" from being released, they also block what little does get through to the receiving neuron.

The effects of opiates and opioids are similar. The differences have to do with how long the drug lasts, how strong it is per gram, and how toxic it is to the body.

For example heroin, codeine, and Darvon will affect the user for 4 to 6 hours. A heroin user might shoot up 4 times a day. Fentanyl, on the other hand, will barely last an hour.

Heroin user: "Codeine just stops the pain and stops your nose from running. It just gets you able to function to go get you some heroin."

Medically, physicians prescribe opiates and opioids to deaden pain, stop coughing, and control diarrhea. Non-medically, users self prescribe opiates and opioids for the euphoria, to drown out their emotional pain, or to try to feel normal.

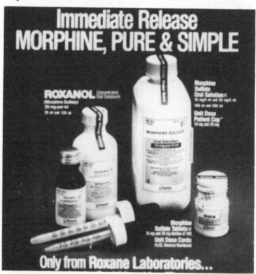

Prescription morphine is still the most effective treatment for acute and severe pain.

The other major effect of opiates and opioids has to do with pleasure. Just as pain is a warning signal to keep us from damaging ourselves, so pleasure is a signal to encourage us to do something that is good for the body and mind. And just as endorphins are released naturally, to block pain in the corpus striatum (a part of the brain), so they are released to activate what is called the reward/pleasure center in the limbic system, the emotional center of the brain.

For example, if we succeed at a task, we feel an extra surge of pleasure because our reward center is triggered saying, "Well done." It encourages us to keep on doing well. It is activated by the release of endorphins. If the reward/pleasure center is not being activated or if there are not enough endorphins in the system to do the job, we don't feel good, don't feel rewarded, and don't feel pleasure. Instead, we feel empty and depressed.

So some people searching for relief or a high try opiates or opioids because these drugs, particularly the stronger ones, artificially activate this reward center directly. They do this by slotting into the receptor sites on the receiving neurons meant for the endorphins. They send out false signals of pleasure.

It seems that opiates and opioids are a class of drugs that block pain and

induce pleasure just like the body's own natural biochemicals. That perception is false. This is because opiates, unlike the body's own endorphins, affect other organs and tissues besides the pain and pleasure centers.

They affect the heart, the breathing, the reproductive system, the digestion, the excretion, the thinking, the cough and nausea centers, the eyes, the voice box, the muscles, the immune system, in fact, every part of the body.

Some of the effects of opiates and opioids are mild but quite identifiable in the heavier user, particularly if the drug is heroin. The drug's ability to relax muscles causes eyelids to droop, the head to nod, and speech to become slurred and slowed. The walking gait is also slowed. The pupils become pinpoint and do not react to light; the skin dries out; itching increases.

Some of the effects of opiates and opioids are less obvious. The cough trigger is suppressed, making codeine-based cough medicine the most widely used prescription drug. Opiates and opioids also affect the nausea center.

Young heroin user: "It hit from the feet going up to the head. I was yelling at him to take the needle out and I was on the toilet seat. I mean, I hugged that toilet bowl for hours."

Other effects of opiates and opioids are more severe. They cause chronic constipation by numbing the intestinal muscles. They also depress the hormones. A women's period is delayed and a man produces less testosterone. Sexual desire is dulled, sometimes to the point of indifference.

28 year-old heroin user: "Lots of times I don't want to be bothered by anybody, or anyone touching me, like my girlfriend. Like if she wants to hug me, kiss me, I just say, 'Don't touch me.'"

24 year-old female heroin user: "You start to look more masculine. You feel out of your skin. You can't really feel yourself anymore. The same sort of people you really loved aren't attracted to you anymore."

Turn-of-the-century ad, naivly promoting heroin as a cough remedy, unaware of the addiction liability of the drug.

Because opiates and opioids cross the placental barrier between the fetus and the mother, pregnant users have a greater risk of miscarriage, placental separations, premature labor, breech births, stillbirths, and seizures. When a baby is born to an addicted mother, the child is also addicted and much smaller than normal.

Then the baby has to suffer through withdrawal from the drug. These symptoms can last 5 to 8 weeks, and unlike adults, babies in withdrawal can die.

Other effects of opiates in older users can also be life threatening. One reason this occurs is that opiates depress those parts of the nervous system that control automatic body functions. Breathing and heart beat are slowed; blood pressure and body temperature are lowered.

Some of the problems associated with opiates are fatal. The worst is a deadly overdose or transmission of the AIDS virus by a shared needle.

I.V. Heroin user: "As I used drugs more and started putting needles in my arms and smoking heroin instead of sniffing heroin, the clientele went down, the friends I associated with became more criminal-like, and they became people who went to jail more often, and I went to jail more often."

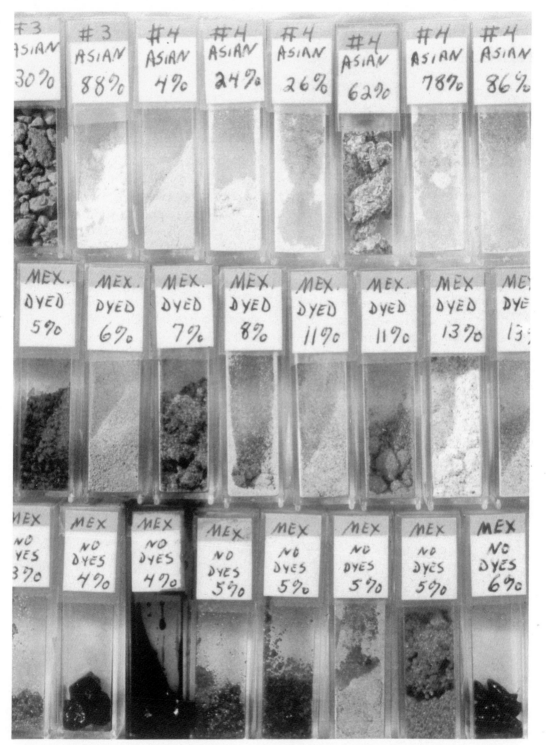

Samples of heroin seized by the Drug Enforcement Administration on the West Coast of the United States. Note that many highly diluted samples are dyed to make them appear a purer form of the drug, i.e., Mexican brown or tar. (Courtesy of Robert Sager, DEA)

HEROIN

Since the 1930's, heroin has captured more headlines than any of the other opiates. In fact, there are 5 to 10 million heroin users worldwide. A dozen countries are battling the growth, use, and exportation of heroin and other opiates on their own soil.

The area of Southeast Asia known as the Golden Triangle: Burma, Northern Thailand, and Laos, is the largest producer and exporter of heroin. It is also one of the largest users. Thailand alone has close to half a million addicts. Golden Triangle heroin, known as China White in its exportable form, can be up to 99% pure. Other Southeast Asian types of heroin are Indian, Cambodian, and Malaysian or Sri Lankan pink heroin (usually around 50% pure).

A small sample of Mexican tar heroin, the most common type of heroin sold in the U.S.

Since the 1940's, Mexico has been the major supplier of heroin to the United States. A relatively new form of Mexican heroin, known as tar or black tar, has taken over most of the market. It is extremely potent, 40 to 80 percent pure, and also has more plant impurities than the Asian form of the drug.

Dealer/user: "You throw up a lot more with tar. Tar really makes me sick to my stomach where as white dope doesn't. It's cleaner."

The region where there has been a major increase in the production and abuse of heroin is Southwest Asia. From Afghanistan, Iran, Pakistan, Turkey, and Lebanon comes a product that is known as Persian brown or Perze, which can be more than 90% pure. Much of it is smuggled via Italy. Several of these countries also have exploding addict populations.

Heroin smoker: "Persian heroin is simply raw processed morphine. The process to take raw morphine and turn it into number 4 white is a very expensive and lengthy chemical process which takes experts. So they're just giving you less quality for ridiculous prices."

smoking - persian
Brown

In addition, several countries have major refining facilities or are major trans-shipment points for heroin: The Netherlands; Canada; West Africa (the latter also grows its own).

There has also been a recent increase in home grown opium. However, a few criminal organizations still control most of the trade. The largest are the ones we mentioned: the Sicilian Mafia, the Chinese Triads, the Columbian Cartel, and the Mexican gangs.

For example, with the conversion of Hong Kong to the People's Republic of China in 1997, many of the Triads (Chinese criminal organizations) that were based there have decided that their headquarters would be wiped out if they stayed, so they have increased their presence in other countries and have tried to expand their market and the number of users.

They reportedly try to disguise some of their China White as Mexican Brown or tar so the authorities won't be as alarmed about their increased presence in the United States. They and the Mafia have also increased the importation of cheaper smokable heroin to encourage many young crack users to try it in their pipes to create a new market much the same way that crack cocaine expanded the number of cocaine users.

At the present time, injection is the preferred means of abusing heroin in the west. Occasionally it is snorted. In most Asian and Middle Eastern countries it is smoked.

Viet vet: "Snorting it, you have to snort more and then you have to wait to take it in your system and it might take you 10-15 minutes to get loaded. When you're snorting it and you get sick, your nose runs uncontrollably and you get stomach cramps."

Heroin can be smoked in a water or air pipe, be mixed in a regular cigarette or marijuana joint, or be heated on foil and the smoke inhaled with a straw. This last method is known as "Chasing the Dragon's Tail."

Heroin smoker: "If anybody has the delusion that it's all that much different than shooting heroin, they're in for a big surprise . It's just as easy to get addicted smoking heroin as it is shooting heroin."

"Chasing the dragon's tail." Tar heroin being heated on aluminum foil. The column of psychoactive smoke (the dragon's tail) is inhaled through a straw.

OTHERS

OPIUM

The term opiate refers to certain alkaloids or chemical compounds found in the opium poppy plant, Papaver Somniferum. There are over 25 known alkaloids in the poppy, but the two most important are morphine and codeine. Opium comes from the dried milky fluid of the unripe seedpod. Although a small amount of opium is used to make antidiarrheal preparations such as paregoric, virtually all the opium coming into this country is refined into its alkaloid constituents, principally morphine and codeine. At the turn of the century, it was used extensively in patent medicines..i.e., Mrs. Winslow's Soothing Syrup and Ayer's Cherry Pectoral. These kinds of tonics were available over-the-counter until 1914.

Syrup of opium; used to calm the crying baby, sooth edgy nerves, stop a bad cough, treat diarrhea.

CODEINE

One to 2.5% of the opium extract contains codeine. It can also be refined from morphine. Codeine is not as strong as morphine and is generally used for the relief of minor pain (aspirin plus codeine or Tylenol plus codeine), or to control severe coughs (Robitussin AC, Cheracol). Codeine is the most widely used, legal opiate or opioid. It is also the most widely abused prescription drug.

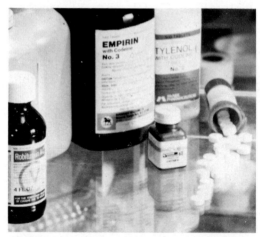

A collection of codeine bottles, mixed with Tylenol or aspirin.

Codeine is often abused in combination with Doriden, a sleeping pill. This combination knows as "loads," "sets," or "set ups," is taken orally and results in a heroin-like high. The combination has a great overdose potential because it depresses respiration and prolongs the effects.

MORPHINE

Four to twenty one percent of the gummy pure opium is morphine. It is usually processed into white crystal hypodermic tablets and injectable solutions. It may be administered into a vein, into a muscle, or under the skin. Morphine is one of the most effective drugs for the relief of pain.

Turn-of-the-century ad promoting a cure for morphine addicton. Morphine itself was once brought to China by the Jesuits to treat opium addiction. It was known as "Jesus' opium."

DILAUDID

A short acting, semi-synthetic, opioid, Dilaudid can be taken orally or injected. Once morphine is extracted from opium, a simple chemical process changes it to Dilaudid which is much stronger and shorter acting than morphine. Dilaudid is used as an alternative to morphine for the treatment of severe pain. Illegally diverted Dilaudid is becoming increasingly attractive to cocaine users for use in "speedballs."

PERCODAN

Also used for the relief of pain, Percodan is most often taken orally. By this route, it usually takes about 30 minutes before the effects appear and these effects last from four to six hours.

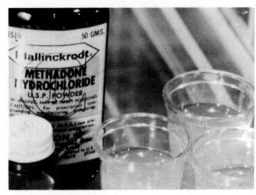

Methadone is mixed with fruit juice, ready to be drunk by heroin addicts.

METHADONE

Methadone and some of the illicit fentanyl derivatives are long-acting opioids. Methadone is usually taken orally causing depressant effects that can last 4 to 6 hours. It also reduces drug craving and blocks withdrawal symptoms for 24 to 72 hours. It is the only legally authorized opiate to treat heroin addiction, and despite heavy regulation, it is still abused and results in a number of overdoses a year. Like heroin, it too is addicting and must be monitored closely to prevent diversion. Much controversy has always swirled around the concept of opiate/opioid substitution. (see Opiate and Opioid Tolerance)

DEMEROL

A short acting opioid, Demerol is most often injected. It is a fairly strong analgesic (pain reliever) and is the abused drug of choice for many in the medical community.

TALWIN

Talwin comes in tablets or liquid for injection and possesses weak narcotic antagonist effects as well as opioid agonist effects. This drug was frequently combined and injected with an antihistamine drug (T's and blues). Increased vigilance and reformulation of Talwin by its manufacturer has almost stopped this problem although some abusers still take the combination orally or abuse Talwin by itself.

DARVON

Prescribed for the relief of minor pain, Darvon is often prescribed by dentists for pain. It is taken orally with the effects lasting 4-6 hours. It too can cause a serious overdose or addiction.

fentanyl & Demerol

DESIGNER HEROIN

These street versions of fentanyl (alpha, 3-methyl, and others) and Demerol (MPPP, MPTP, and others) are extremely potent, causing drug overdoses and even a Parkinson's disease-like syndrome. Sold as "China white," these drugs bear witness to a growing sophistication of street chemists who now can bypass the traditional smuggling and trafficking routes of heroin. Since these are street drugs made without controls, the "designer drugs" represent a tremendous health threat to the opiate abusing community.

NALOXONE & NALTREXONE

These are opiate or opioid antagonists or antidotes. They do not have much effect on the body except for their ability to block the effects of other opiate drugs and prevent them from working. Naloxone is effective in treating heroin or opiate overdose while Naltrexone is used to prevent addiction. While taking Naltrexone daily, one cannot feel the effects of heroin or any other opiate or opioid.

THE NATURE OF OPIATES & OPIOIDS

With opiates and opioids, direct physical side effects aren't the only problem. The other factors mentioned in an earlier chapter having to do with the nature of psychoactive drugs are particularly applicable to opiates and opioids.

Tolerance

The body is so efficient in tolerating the effects of opiates and opioids, that the drug appears to weaken with each succeeding dose. More has to be taken just to achieve the same effect. The body tries to neutralize the drug by first, speeding up the metabolism; second, desensitizing the nerve cells to the drug's effects; and finally, by altering the brain chemistry so it can compensate for the effects of the drug.

Young mother: "I used drugs for so long, to cover all the feelings I had...the hurt and such that one day they didn't work."

Users, initially, might only be able to tolerate 5 milligrams of heroin, but they would need 50 milligrams, or 10 times the amount to get the same effect after a month of steady use.

Tolerance extends to all opiates and opioids. That is, if users build a tolerance to heroin, they will also have a tolerance for morphine or codeine. This cross tolerance is the basis for one method of treating heroin addiction called methadone maintenance.

Methadone, a totally synthetic opioid, is not as intense as heroin and will not produce withdrawal symptoms for one to three days compared to heroin which will cause withdrawal symptoms in a few hours. So, the user avoids the roller-coaster of highs and lows, and the pain of withdrawal. The theory is that the user doesn't have to hustle for money to pay for a habit or get drugs and needles on the street, and therefore be exposed to a high risk lifestyle.

Tissue Dependence & Withdrawal

The biological adaptation of the body due to its tolerance to opiates and opioids is quite extensive. In fact, the body changes so much that the tissues and organs come to depend on the drug in a relatively short period of time just to stay normal. It usually takes two to three weeks of continuous use before an abrupt cessation will cause withdrawal symptoms. In general, short-acting drugs like heroin, morphine, and Dilaudid result in more severe yet short- lived (5 to 7 days) major withdrawal symptoms. Long-acting opioids like Methadone will delay the symptoms from 24 to 72 hours, but once they occur, these symptoms can last for weeks and are milder than those seen with short-acting opiates or opioids. Other opiates and opioids such as codeine, Percodan, and Darvon have withdrawal phenomena somewhere in between those two extremes.

Heroin user: "You get deep, deep muscle and bone pains. There's no way to get comfortable, and you fluctuate between being chilly and sweating a lot. You can either be constipated or have diarrhea. You're in total body agony that nothing relieves. It's real uncomfortable. I have actually, this is not a figure of speech, I have been going through withdrawal where I said I wish I was dead."

It is important to remember that although opiate withdrawal feels like an incredibly bad case of the flu, it is almost never life threatening as is withdrawal from alcohol or sedative-hypnotics.

Darvon user: "After 7 years of doing Darvon, I started having withdrawals after three or four hours of the last pill that I had taken, so I was addicted to my watch."

Overdose

Overdose occurs when so much of the drug enters the brain that the nervous system is shut down. The blood pressure drops and the heart beats too weakly to circulate blood. The lungs labor and fill with fluid. The person passes out and, unless quickly revived, will slip into a coma and die.

Dilution & Adulteration

One of the reasons an overdose occurs is that street drugs can vary radically in strength. Street heroin varies from zero to 99 percent pure. So if a user is expecting 3% heroin and gets 30%, the results could be fatal. Dilution of an expensive item like heroin with a cheap substitute like powered milk, sugar, baby laxative, aspirin, ajax, quinine, or talcum powder is the rule and not the exception.

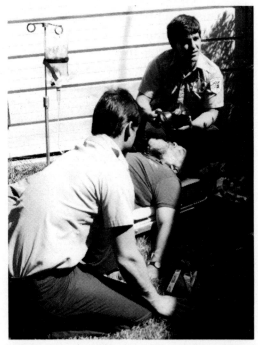

Emergency personnel prepare to inject Narcan to an overdosed heroin addict to neutralize the effects of the opiate.

Viet vet: "The first China White I got came from Vietnam and it looked like a 20 hitter. I know that if I was shooting up then I probably would have OD'd. A 20 hitter means that you could take like one gram and throw 19 grams of cut on it, and it'd still be good, it'd still get you off. With the tar that's going around now, the most you're going to get is basically a 6 hitter."

If a user knows the strength of his supply, then he is less likely to overdose because unlike barbiturates and other sedative hypnotics, there is a wide range between the amount of the drug needed to get high and a lethal dose.

Dealer/heroin user: "When I first got out here on the West Coast, I found out that it (China White) wasn't white dope at all, it was fentanyl and it wasn't even pharmaceutical fentanyl. It was bath tub fentanyl and people were dying and freezing up on it."

Street fentanyl can be up to three thousand times stronger than regular heroin. A dose the size of a grain of salt is powerful enough to kill 30 people.

As mentioned, street Demerol can and has contained a chemical, MPTP, which destroys brain cells, freezes the addict, and destroys most of the voluntary muscular movement by inducing the degenerative nerve condition known as Parkinson's disease.

Dirty & Shared Needles

The most dangerous problem with opiates, and the one that causes the most illness and death, is dirty or shared needles. Needles are used because they put a large amount of the drug in the blood stream at one time. Needles can also inject powdered milk, procaine, Ajax, or dangerous bacteria and viruses, including the AIDS virus. It is estimated that 50% to 80% of all needle using heroin addicts in the New York area test positive for the AIDS virus. (see Drugs in the Environment-Needle Use)

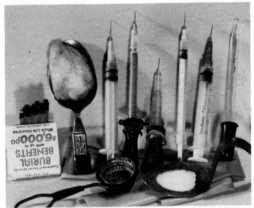

Addicts will use diabetic's syringes, eyedroppers, veterinary needles, almost anything to inject their drug

Older AIDS victim: "I watched someone who refused to wash the syringe out after I had it, and I said,'I have ARC (AIDS related complex), I'm positive, I have the disease.' And he said, 'I really don't care.' He didn't wash it out and you could see the syringe had blood in it, and he shot it up. I mean, I hope the man's alive."

THE ECONOMICS OF HEROIN TRAFFICKING

Representative selling prices for the equivalent of one kilogram of Southwest Asian heroin (60%-90% purity) at successive stages of trafficking (1980, Courtesy of the Drug Enforcement Administration).

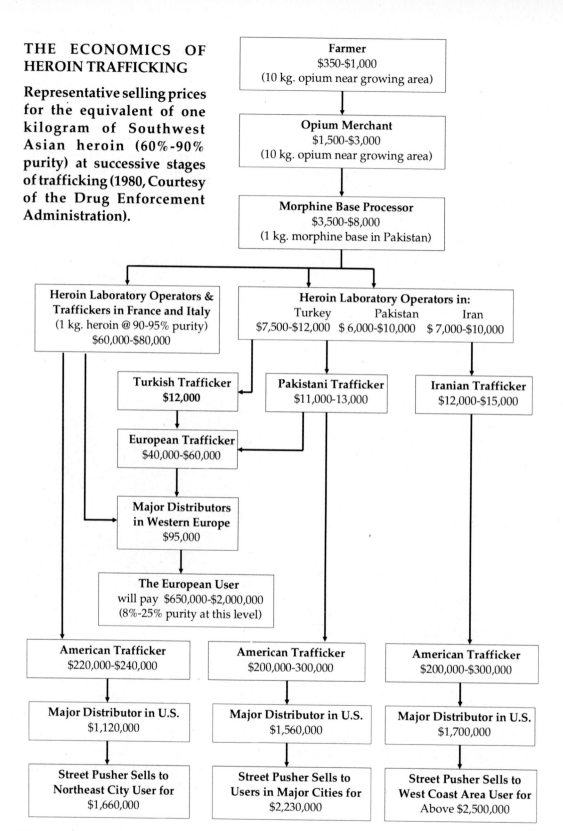

Farmer
$350-$1,000
(10 kg. opium near growing area)

Opium Merchant
$1,500-$3,000
(10 kg. opium near growing area)

Morphine Base Processor
$3,500-$8,000
(1 kg. morphine base in Pakistan)

Heroin Laboratory Operators & Traffickers in France and Italy
(1 kg. heroin @ 90-95% purity)
$60,000-$80,000

Heroin Laboratory Operators in:
Turkey   Pakistan   Iran
$7,500-$12,000 $6,000-$10,000 $7,000-$10,000

Turkish Trafficker
$12,000

Pakistani Trafficker
$11,000-13,000

Iranian Trafficker
$12,000-$15,000

European Trafficker
$40,000-$60,000

Major Distributors in Western Europe
$95,000

The European User
will pay $650,000-$2,000,000
(8%-25% purity at this level)

American Trafficker
$220,000-$240,000

American Trafficker
$200,000-300,000

American Trafficker
$200,000-$300,000

Major Distributor in U.S.
$1,120,000

Major Distributor in U.S.
$1,560,000

Major Distributor in U.S.
$1,700,000

Street Pusher Sells to Northeast City User for
$1,660,000

Street Pusher Sells to Users in Major Cities for
$2,230,000

Street Pusher Sells to West Coast Area User for
Above $2,500,000

Cost

For those who become compulsive opiate or opioid users (particularly heroin), cost becomes an overwhelming factor.

Viet vet: "Our habit, just to take care of it, was maybe a hundred and sixty a day and most of the time we were doing more, plus the coke on the side."

Contrary to popular belief, a majority of heroin users are gainfully employed, but they still have to turn to illegal methods to pay for their habit.

#3 heroin from SE Asia, generally less refined and more dilute than #4 shooting heroin.

Heroin user: "I had two other friends and one was blackmailing a pharmacist. We'd get outdated drugs they were supposed to throw away. We'd pick them up in the alley and we'd get gallons and gallons of cough syrup and any other narcotics pills."

Darvon user: "Since I worked in the medical field, writing my own prescriptions was no problem except that I committed a felony every time I did it, once a week. I never got caught, but I always lived in morbid fear that they would get me."

The number of crimes that heroin addicts commit is so great that when police in certain cities swept the streets of heroin abusers and sent them to treatment centers, the number of burglaries fell in half. In addition, many addicts get into dealing at one time or another to pay for their dope.

Wave of Killings Marks Return Of Sicilian Mafia to Drug Trade

By Roberto Suro
New York Times

Palermo, Sicily
The Sicilian Mafia is on the offensive again. Having survived a judicial crackdown, resurgent criminal families are conducting a campaign of terror against the state while striking underworld rivals in a series of daylight killings.

Eighteen people have been slain over the past two weeks in attacks linked to the Mafia. The mounting crime wave, which follows three years of relative peace, caught authorities just as they were anxiously trying to repair divisions and weaknesses in anti-Mafia forces.

The Mafia offensive and the government's disarray alarm both Italian and U.S. officials, who suspect that the Mafia's heroin trade to the New York area is passing unimpeded through new conduits and that Sicilian drug traffickers are forming a potentially dangerous alliance with Colombia's cocaine lords.

The sudden outbreak comes only 10 months after a jury convicted 338 people of Mafia crimes in a mass trial in Palermo. This triumph of law enforcement was followed by public feuding among magistrates over prosecuting tactics, which reached a climax last month amid

The police are working on a variety of hypotheses to explain the apparent onset of a new Mafia war. Perhaps a new alliance built around the Corleone clans has already split, or perhaps old quarrels have merely been reignited.

Further complicating the law enforcement effort is the emergence of new drug trafficking patterns.

Direct Route to New York

Both Italian and U.S. officials confirmed that Sicilian clans are now buying refined heroin in Southeast Asia and are shipping it to the New York area through channels that do not pass through Sicily and that the police have yet to uncover.

In addition, drug profits are being sent directly to banks in the Caribbean and in Switzerland, thus denying the Sicilian police another investigative trail.

Equally worrying are signs that the Sicilian Mafia, through its alliance with the Neapolitan underworld, is moving into the booming European trade in cocaine.

A senior U.S. law enforcement official in Italy expressed concern that this trade would reinforce Colombia's drug lords by providing them with a new source of guns and money.

"This is a very decisive and dangerous moment in terms of the Mafia's ability to intimidate the state

ace of the Eagles, the windows in some of the Baroque salons were fitted with thick bulletproof glass this week.

In the garden of a Jesuit study center that is home to priests who lead a prominent citizens' group, young policemen armed with submachine guns began standing among the fragrant jasmine vines.

Those killed in the past 14 days include a retired prosecutor and an anti-drug campaigner as well as people convicted of having Mafia links.

One crime in particular has convinced the police that the Mafia is once again taking aim at the public figures who dare oppose it. The killing on September 25 of Judge Antonio Saetta, a senior appellate court judge in Palermo, violated what had been considered a Sicilian taboo. The Mafia had never killed a sitting judge before.

'Major Act of Intimidation'

At the funeral, Archbishop Luigi Bommarito of Catania looked down from his pulpit at the assembled dignitaries and asked, "Mr. President of the Republic, Ministers, who will be the next victim?"

The question was rhetorical but not fanciful. A senior police commander here said: "This was a major act of intimidation, the kind of killing that is usually followed by others as the Mafia tries to undermine the state by creating a climate of fear and uncertainty."

Heroin I.V. user: "Dealing was a break for me. It helped me cut down on the fear and the terror and the pressure. But then I had to worry about other dope fiends ripping me off."

Polydrug Use

Another danger that comes with opiate or opioid use is combining these drugs with other drugs. For example, if another depressant such as alcohol or a barbiturate is used at the same time as a shot of heroin or a tablet of codeine, the effects are much greater than one would expect.

Heroin user: "I'd be waiting and waiting, and during the time that I was waiting, I'd be getting drunk. By the time I got around to doing my shot, I was already drunk. I'd hit up and boom, I'd be on the floor."

Drug users also combine drugs to enhance the effect of the opiate/opioid.

Heroin user: "I was using a lot of heroin and the heroin wasn't working. I wasn't staying loaded long enough, so I'd make doctors for barbiturates in order to enhance the heroin."

Finally, people use another drug to counter the effects of the opiate or opioid.

Young heroin user: "As one person said, "I like going up on speed; and I like taking heroin to come down; and I take cocaine to mellow out."

In fact most users in a treatment program have problems with more than just their drug of choice.

Heroin user: "I had a parole officer who told me 'Leave those other drugs alone. Drinking is OK, or smoking a little pot now and then,' but I have come to believe that I can't take any mood altering chemical into my body today and still remain in recovery."

COMPULSION & TREATMENT

If there are so many problems with the non-medical use of opiates, why do people get involved with these drugs? As with other drugs, people start using for the euphoria, to block emotional pain, or just to experiment, usually as a result of peer pressure or curiosity.

Dealer/user: "I just kind of got into little pills and the LSD, and one day someone said, 'Hey, I've got some heroin.'"

Heroin user: "My girlfriend was an addict and I didn't know she was an addict till a year later; and I seen that she was using large quantities of it and it was hurting me to see her use that much; so I'd take some away from her to use that rather than have her use that amount; and I didn't realize what I was getting into."

People continue using opiates because they keep wanting that rush, and they keep wanting to block out their emotional pain.

They continue using because their bodies are deficient in endorphins and have become dependent on the drug to stay normal and prevent withdrawal symptoms.

Heroin user: "I'd wake up in the morning and before I'd go to work, when I was working, I'd have to do a hit of dope just to function. I'd have do a hit of dope just to get out of bed. I'd have to do a hit of dope to go to the bathroom, and it wasn't a matter of getting high anymore. It was a matter of getting functional."

Dealer/user: "At a point when we were really strung out, we were spending 150 to 200 dollars a day to feel normal. It's one thing to spend that kind of money and get loaded but when you're spending that kind of money to just function as a human being, it's pitiful. That's when you say, 'Okay, time to clean up, the joke's over.'"

Most important, they continue to use because their bodies, body chemistry, and minds have changed under the influence of the opiate and they now have the condition or as others say, the disease of addiction.

Heroin user: "All I could see was the need to get high and the ways and means to get more , and I lived to use and I used to live. There's no in between. There's nothing in between that. The only thing I could think about was the obsession of shooting dope. I didn't think about anything else."

As with the abuse of other psychoactive drugs, there are several kinds of people who are subject to compulsion. There are some users who do not have enough endorphins in their system. They are more sensitive to physical and emotional pain. These people's neurotransmitters are disrupted from birth. They inherit the deficit.

Heroin user: "It was such a great feeling. I loved it so much that I ended up staying away from it for 10 years because I knew, I would become a raging addict."

They are much more likely to abuse opiates and opioids because they are closer to the edge. They like the sensations too much.

Viet vet: "The first time I tried it and got high I said ' I think I want to use some of this for the rest of my life if I could afford it."

The rest of the people who get into the abuse of opiates and opioids push their neurotransmitters into this unbalanced state instead of inheriting it at birth.

*I.V. heroin user: "As my drug of choice changed, things started changing drastically. When I was smoking pot and drinking beer, I **seemed** to function fairly well out there, and then as the disease progressed, I changed too."*

Users keep straining their system to neutralize the drug. Their use of opiates and opioids blocks the normal production of endorphins.

Darvon user: "I had a test to see if my brain was releasing any endorphins, you know, the natural ability to deal with pain. My brain was like zilch, zero. After the drugs took over to deal with that, I had no more ability to deal with pain.

Soon, the chemical system of a drug user resembles that of someone born with the problem. Now both groups are in the same "fix." Both have developed an opiate addiction and both are at risk for the rest of their lives to fall back easily into a pattern of abuse.

European Journal of Pharmacology, 44 (1977) 25—33
© Elsevier/North-Holland Biomedical Press

BRAIN SEROTONIN TURNOVER AND MORPHINE TOLERANCE-DEPENDENCE INDUCED
BY MULTIPLE INJECTIONS IN THE RAT

HEMENDRA N. BHARGAVA * and GEORGE A. MATWYSHYN

Department of Pharmacognosy and Pharmacology, College of Pharmacy,
University of Illinois at the Medical Center, Chicago, Illinois 60612, U.S.A.

Received 8 December 1976, revised MS received 4 February 1977, accepted 8 March 1977

H.N. BHARGAVA and G.A. MATWYSHYN, Brain serotonin turnover and morphine tolerance-dependence induced by multiple injections in the rat, European J. Pharmacol. 44 (1977) 25—33. Tolerance to and physical dependence on morphine in the rat was induced by injecting increasing doses of morphine sulfate (M.S.) administered i.p. twice daily for 14 days. The last dose of M.S. was 200 mg/kg. This procedure produced a 4-fold tolerance to morphine as evidenced by the increased dose of morphine required to produce analgesia. The degree of dependence was quantified by determining the naloxone ED50 for the stereotyped withdrawal jumping response. Body weight loss and hypothermic responses during abrupt and naloxone-induced withdrawal were also measured. The degree of tolerance and dependence produced by multiple injection procedure was comparable to that produced by 2 pellets containing 75 mg of morphine base implanted for 3 days. The level and turnover of brain serotonin, determined 6 or 12 h after the last morphine sulfate injection did not differ significantly from that of saline injected control animals. These data indicate that multiple injection technique produces a mild degree of tolerance to, and physical dependence on, morphine which was not related to changes in brain serotonin level or turnover.

Morphine tolerance and dependence   Multiple injections   Naloxone   Brain
Serotonin turnover   Hypothermia

The desire, or urge, to use, is always there with both groups. But this gives us a clue to controlling patterns of opiate abuse.

First, users have to clean the drug out of their systems to give their body chemistry a chance to return to a semblance of normal, to give their judgment and reasoning centers a chance to think clearly.

Talt Malone (counselor): "People can stop cocaine and their withdrawal is not nearly as bad as withdrawal from opiates. So most people that are going to kick any kind of opiate are going to be involved in some kind of program, whether they be in one like this one, a methadone program, or some kind of program to stop you from being sick."

Most programs use medications, including mild opiates like Darvon, to detoxify and taper the habit. This allows addicts to have less fear and pain of their withdrawal, thus engaging them in the treatment process.

An alternative to this treatment is Clonidine. It quiets the part of the brain that gets hyperactive when one goes through withdrawal. It also suppresses withdrawal symptoms.

Talt Malone (counselor): "The physical part of the detox is only a tiny portion. It's what happens after you get off, after you

detox that's important. Everyone around you is using, and in a lot of cases you may have financial problems. You may not even have a place to stay. There are other kinds of things that build up and cause you to use again."

After the withdrawal symptoms are controlled, the user needs help controlling the desire to use again. Long lasting opiate antagonists such as Naltrexone, which dull the stimulation of the reward/pleasure center, can help the user stay clean.

Old turn-of-the-century ads for morphine addiction cures.

Manuel Sanchez (counselor), to a heroin addict in a counseling session: *"You can stay clean for a while. Is that what you want? You want to stay clean for a while or for the rest of your life?"*

Addict: "I want to stay clean permanently."

Counselor: "Permanently drug free?

Addict: "But I can do it without attending those meetings."

Counselor: "All by yourself?"

Addict: "I mean with the medication that I take."

Counselor: "But the medications only are going to last you 21 days. Medications are only going to help you for a little while with the withdrawal of getting off heroin. What are you going to do when the urges come up?"

Addict: "I guess I'll deal with that when the time comes."

Counselor: "So you're just going to wait for it. You're going to wait for the urges to come on and start using then?"

Addict: "Nah, I can deal with it."

Counselor: "You're being highly uncooperative. As a matter of fact, we're going to stop the medications today because we can't have you using on the program."

Addict: "I need those medications."

Counselor: "What for? It's just another drug. What you're doing is using it like another drug. I'd like for you to come back to get into that group meeting we have at 3 o'clock."

Counselor: "Also, I want you to go to an NA (Narcotics Anonymous) meeting every day. I want you to go to these meetings and participate. Talk every opportunity you can. And also what I want you to do is bring back the signed thing that you attended. I want you to do that. That's just part of the requirement of being in the program. See, I'm going to assume that you want to stop using drugs."

An opium den in New York city (c. 1895).

Addict: "Why can't I just get the drugs?"

Counselor: "Because we're not just a medication program. It's a counseling program too. And I also want you to not be working for the next three months."

Addict: "But I can't quit my job."

Counselor: "You're working all right?"

Addict: "Well, it's part time."

Counselor: "I want you to quit that job."

Addict: *"But I need my job to be able to pay for my room and board."*

Counselor: *"Well, it seems to me right now what you're doing with the work you have, you're using the money for drugs. You're behind on your rent. You haven't paid in the last two months because you've been using it on drugs. What's the use of working?"*

Addict: *"But I got to eat. That's where most of my money is going."*

Counselor: *"Oh is it? I thought it was for drugs. You're using almost half a gram a day."*

Addict: *"Once in a while. I'm still trying to clean up though."*

Talt Malone (counselor): *"You aren't ever going to find anything as interesting as dope. That's not the idea. The idea is that you can't do it again. What are you going to fill up your life with when you stop. A lot of people work, so it may not be work. It may simply be learning how to deal with stress, with frustrations. Each person has to develop his or her own support system. For some people it may be NA or a 12-step program, and for others it's having someone they can talk to at 2:00 in the morning on a Saturday night and say, 'Look, I'm going to go out and use unless I talk.'"*

Sensationalist tabloid warned the working girl of the dangers of opium (New York c.1885).

Heroin user: *"The greatest junkie lines, and I've used them, everybody's used them...'I'm gonna quit forever... tomorrow.' 'I'm not a junkie because I only use it on weekends.' 'I only use it every now and then.' 'I've only been doing it for a week.' Don't kid yourself. Don't start it off. Do yourself a favor."*

SEDATIVE-HYPNOTICS

1985

Los Angeles Times
8 Part III/Tuesday, March 5, 1985★

Newswire

Ex-Clemson Coaches Indicted for Dispensing Prescription Drugs

A grand jury in Pickens, S.C., indicted former Clemson University track coaches Sam Colson and Stan Narewski and former Clemson assistant football coach Jack Harkness Monday on misdemeanor charges of dispensing prescription drugs to athletes.

The indictments came just three days after Clemson President Bill Atchley resigned and Athletic Director Bill McLellan asked to be reassigned. The two track coaches have admitted giving the muscle-relaxing drug phenylbutazone to several members of the track team. Three Tiger football players also say they received steroids from Colson, who doubled as the school's football strength coach. An investigation was prompted by the mysterious death last October of Clemson track star Augustinius Jaspers.

Quintin Dailey's agent, Bob Woolf, said the Chicago Bulls guard will rejoin the team after his two-day suspension, despite Dailey's squabble with Coach Kevin Loughery.

Dailey, suspended for late arrivals at a game and a practice, told the Chicago Sun-Times: "If he (Loughery) stays, I'm gone. . . . I'm tired of the personal vendetta part of it. You can see it. I'm not going to ... Kevin Loughery Jr. I'm ... Quintin ...

Unl [illegible] ... quar... beco... Na... pr... ...phomore ...an

off deciding on a pro career for at least two weeks.

If Kosar decides to turn pro, he must declare his intentions no later than April 16, two weeks before the draft. Kosar can become eligible because he is within a few credits of graduation. The Minnesota Vikings, holding the No. 3 pick, say they will select Kosar if he decides to turn pro.

"Blood boosting," the practice of enhancing performance with blood transfusions, will be banned by the International Olympic Committee before the 1988 Winter Games in Calgary, Prince Alexandre deMerode said.

The level of caffeine permitted ... also likely to be lowered

In an atmosphere of increasing urgency, negotiations between baseball management and players for a new collective bargaining agreement resume today.

Commissioner Peter Ueberroth has said he would order owners to open their books if the negotiators for both sides agreed it would help them reach a settlement. Lee MacPhail, the owners' negotiator, presented details of Ueberroth's move to the union at their last meeting in New York a week ago and asked the players for help in solving what he said were the game's severe economic problems. In Tampa Saturday, players voted to use income from licensing fees to fund any possible examination of management's books.

South Korea will organize a highly trained security force, consisting of 1,830 policemen, for the upcoming Asian Games and 1988 Olympics at Seoul. The policemen will be organized into 10 army-sized companies for deployment at Seoul and other provincial areas where games of the two international meets will be held, the officials said.

The team, specializing in anti-terrorist operations, will protect sports facilities as well as foreign delegations participating in the Seoul competition, the officials said. Officials fear that North Korea will attempt to infiltrate armed agents and disrupt the games.

Charlie Heard, a former All-American wrestler at Tennessee-Chattanooga and an alternate on the 1984 U.S. Olympic team, has been charged with felonious assault in Chattanooga in a stabbing prompted by an altercation involving his ex-girlfriend.

Heard was taken into custody Sunday night after Charles A. Griffith, 22, of Chattanooga, was stabbed in the left side of his chest. Griffith was reported in critical but stable condition Monday at Erlanger Medical Center.

Names in the News

Baseball Commissioner **Peter Ueberroth** ruled that the Chicago **Cubs** did not violate tampering rules when their radio and television station rights-holder signed former Houston Astros' broadcaster **Dewayne Staats.**

1989

Death linked to prescription drugs

TALENT — A registered nurse who had lived in town about two months apparently took her own life Monday night.

Judith Ann Schultz, 52, was found dead in her home at 232 Talent Ave., No. 24, by her husband at about 4 a.m. today. Police believe she took six different types of prescription drugs between 6 p.m. Monday and the time her husband found her.

She reportedly left a note that merely listed the types of drugs she had taken. She was pronounced dead at the scene.

1984

Why Penna. leads in prescription-drug use

By Edward Colimore
Inquirer Staff Writer

Pennsylvania is a state hooked on drugs. Powdered opium, methadone, amphetamines and barbiturates — thousands of residents here have an insatiable need for them. And some in the medical community, for whatever reason, seem willing to feed that need.

The state's 35,400 doctors prescribed or dispensed at least 15 million tablets of amphetamine and the depressant secobarbital two years ago — more than any other state per capita and more than twice the national average.

Pennsylvania also was among the top 10 states in 1983 in the per-capita use of 10 other prescription drugs, according to recent statistics compiled by the U.S. Drug Enforcement Administration (DEA).

Preliminary figures show that the same was true last year.

"I am genuinely concerned that a segment of our population . . . is consuming a disproportionate amount of legally dispensed controlled drugs," said Dr. H. Arnold Muller, state secretary of health. "I am incensed that a relatively small number of physicians and pharmacists are violating their trust and making the drugs available to abusers."

The result has been a predictable toll: 4,553 residents were treated in state programs for amphetamine dependence in 1984 and 3,782 in 1983. An additional 2,589 people underwent treatment for dependence on depressants and opiates in 1984; 2,622 received care the year before. And an undetermined number were treated at hospitals for addiction and overdoses of these and other prescription drugs.

"Many of these people are your next-door neighbors," said Bill Shepherd, a state Health Department spokesman. "They are community people — not town drunks. They are people who go to work and hold responsible positions. They are housewives who take care of children while the husbands work. They are your business colleagues."

The problem is puzzling to state officials. Why are so many more drugs prescribed and dispensed in Pennsylvania than in other states? Why are neighbors such as New Jersey, Delaware, New York and Maryland so far down the DEA list for use of the same drugs? Why are even California and Florida, states with the image of serious drug problems, well below Pennsylvania in prescription drug use?

"Either Pennsylvania is very ill, or there is abuse," said Jack B. Ogun, director of the Division of Drugs, Devices and Cosmetics for the state Health Department. "And I don't

(See DRUGS on 10-A)

A GENERAL CLASSIFICATION

More than 150 million prescriptions are written for sedative-hypnotics each year in the U. S. These drugs are usually prescribed as a sedative to diminish the possibility of neurotic reactions in unstable patients, to control anxiety, to induce sleep in chronic insomniacs, and to control hypertension and epilepsy. They are also used as mild tranquilizers and muscle relaxants. The effects of sedative-hypnotics are generally similar to the effects of alcohol. The basic difference between the two depressants is the concentration of the drug involved; sedative-hypnotics come in a more concentrated form than alcohol. Sedative-hypnotic withdrawal symptoms are also more serious than opiate/opioid withdrawal symptoms.

Name	Trade Name	Street Name
BARBITURATES		
Secobarbital	**Seconal**	Reds, red devils, seccies, F-40's, Mexican Reds
Pentobarbital	**Nembutal**	Yellows, yellow jackets, yellow bullets, nebbies
Equal parts secobarbital & pentobarbital	Tuinal	Rainbows, tuies, double trouble
Phenobarbital	(Generic)	Phenos
Amobarbital	Amytal	Blue heavens, blue dolls, blues
Hexobarbital	Sombulex	
Thiopental	Pentothal	
BENZODIAZEPINES		
Diazepam	**Valium**	Vals
Chlordiazepoxide	**Librium,** Libritabs	Libs
Flurazepam	Dalmane	
Chlorazepate	Tranxene	
Oxazepam	Serax	
Triazolam	Halcion	
Alprazolam	**Xanax**	
Lorazepam	Ativan	
Clonazepam	Clonopin	
Temazepam	Restoril	
Halazepam	Paxipam	
Prazepam	Centrax	

NON-BARBITURATE SEDATIVE-HYPNOTICS

Glutethimide	**Doriden**	Goofballs, goofers
Gluthemide & codeine	Doriden & codeine	Loads, sets, setups
Methaqualone	**Quaalude,** Sopor	
	Parest, Optimil,	Ludes, sopes, soapers, Q's
	Somnafac	
Ethchlovynol	Placidyl	Green weenies
Chloral hydrate	Noctec, Somnos	Jelly beans, Miki's,
		knockout drops
Methaprylon	Noludar	Noodlelars
Meprobamate	Equinil, Miltown,	
	Meprotabs	

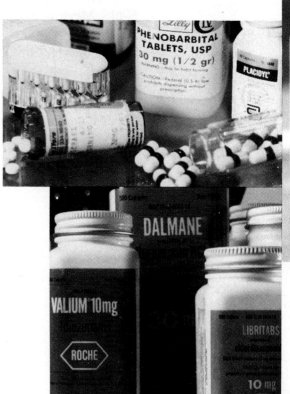
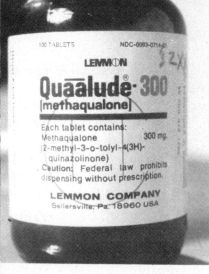

There seems to be an endless number of sedative-hypnotics on a drugstore's shelf, each with a slightly different set of properties and effects. Note that Quaalude was voluntarily taken off the market in the mid-80's. Only counterfeit or lookalike Quaalude are now available.

GENERAL EFFECTS & METABOLISM

Sedative-hypnotics are quite specific to those sections of the central nervous system they affect. The hypnotics such as barbiturates work on the brainstem, bringing on sleep along with depression of most body functions such as breathing, and muscular coordination. Sedatives such as Doriden, Quaalude, Miltown, and Valium are calming drugs. They work on a number of sites in the brain. Benzodiazepines, for example, act on the neurotransmitter GABA to help control anxiety and restlessness. Sedatives are capable of producing relaxation, lowered inhibitions, reduced intensity of physical sensations, drowsiness, body heat loss, and reduced muscular coordination in speech, movement, and manual dexterity.

Tolerance develops rapidly with sedative-hypnotics. However, tolerance to the mental and physical effects develops at a different rate. This means that when users increase daily intake to recapture a mental high, they might not be aware that tolerance to the physical effects such as respiratory depression, develop at a slower rate. Thus, the daily dose taken for the mental effects comes close to the lethal dose and any mistake can send the user under. The user's intake might reach 10 to 20 times the original dose. *Liver cells*

Withdrawal from sedative-hypnotics, after tolerance has developed, can be extremely dangerous. Within 6 to 8 hours after the last dose, withdrawal symptoms such as anxiety, agitation, loss of appetite, nausea, vomiting, increased heart rate, excessive sweating, abdominal cramps, and tremulousness will occur, peaking on the second or third day after withdrawal with short-acting drugs like most barbiturates. With long-acting barbiturates and tranquilizers such as Valium or Librium, the peak may not be reached until the second or third week, and the onset of symptoms can be delayed for several days. Severe withdrawal symptoms include seizures, delirium, uncontrolled heart beat, and death.

Overdosing with sedative-hypnotics might include cold, clammy skin, a weak and rapid pulse, and a slow to rapid, but shallow, breathing. Death will follow if the low blood pressure and slowed respiration are not treated. It is particularly dangerous to combine alcohol and any sedative-hypnotic because these combinations can cause an exaggerated depression of the respiratory center in the brain and therefore, a greater risk of death.

BARBITURATES

Though barbituric acid was first synthesized in 1868, it remained a medical curiosity for 40 years till it was chemically modified to enter the central nervous system, thus becoming psychoactive. Since then, more than 2,500 compounds have been created.

- The slow acting barbiturates such as phenobarbital, last 12 to 24 hours and are used mostly as daytime sedatives or to control epileptic seizures.

- The shorter acting compounds such as Seconal (reds), and Nembutal (yellows), last 4 to 6 hours and are used to induce sleep. They can induce pleasant feelings along with the sedation (at least initially). So they are more likely to be abused.

- The very short acting barbiturates such as pentothal, used mostly for anesthesia, can cause immediate unconsciousness. The extremely high potency of these barbiturates make them extremely dangerous if abused.

Temporary stimulation and eventual sedating effects are very similar to those of alcohol. And as with alcohol, excessive or long term use can lead to changes in personality and emotion (mood swings, depression, irritability, obnoxious behavior, and manipulation).

Tolerance to barbiturates develops in a variety of ways. The most dramatic tolerance, drug dispositional tolerance, results from the physiologic change of liver cells to more efficient cells which metabolize or destroy barbiturates more quickly. This results in the need to take more barbiturates to reach or maintain the same psychoactive effects.

Physical dependence to barbiturates occurs when 8 to 10 times the normal dose is taken daily for 30 days. Withdrawal symptoms resulting from this dependence are very dangerous and can result in convulsions within 12 hours to one week from the last dose.

VALIUM, XANAX & THE BENZODIAZEPINES

This class of drugs was developed in the 1950's, came into wide clinical use in the 60's, and by the 70's accounted for more than half the prescriptions written for sedative-hypnotics. The drugs were an innovation in the treatment of anxious disorders, replacing barbiturates, bromides, opiates and opioids, and even alcohol which were too toxic and had too many side effects. Benzodiazepines have a fairly safe therapeutic index, meaning that the amount of chemical needed to induce sedation is much lower than the amount that would cause an overdose. The problem was that while everyone

was hailing the new drugs and raving about patient acceptance, they overlooked its peculiarities: the length of time it lasts in the body, the ability to induce addiction at low levels of use, and the severity of withdrawal from the drug.

Tolerance develops because the liver becomes more efficient in processing the drug, so more is needed to achieve the same effects. However, age-dependent tolerance also occurs with these drugs, meaning that a younger person can tolerate much more of these drugs than someone older. The effect of a dose on a 50 year old first time user can be five or ten times stronger than the same dose on a 16 year-old.

THE BIOTRANSFORMATION (METABOLISM) OF VALIUM IN THE LIVER.

Valium is unique in that the liver metabolizes the drug into five other psychoactive drugs, some stronger than the original drug. These drugs can persist in the body for days or weeks.

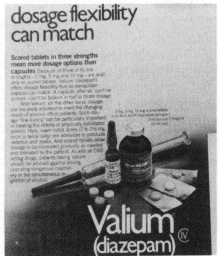

Patents on drugs are granted for 17 years with possible 7 year renewals. The drug patent on Valium ran out in the mid 80's paving the way for generic copies of the drug.

Physical addiction to the benzodiazepines can develop if the patient takes 10 to 20 times the normal dose for a couple of months, or takes a normal dose for a year or more. The recently discovered phenomenon of low-dose long-term physical addiction needs much more study. In addition, the pleasant mental effects and "hypnotizing" aspects of the drugs (reinforcement) can result in a mental or psychological dependence.

Withdrawal from the benzodiazepines after high dose, continuous use of about two months, or lower dose use for a year or more, can be extremely severe. In fact, more people have died from Valium withdrawal than Valium overdose.

The drug is long lasting so the symptoms will be delayed 24 to 72 hours. First, there will be a craving for the drug, then more anxiety, sleep disturbances, pacing the floor, tremulous movements, and even hallucinations. Some people even develop a temporary loss of vision, hearing, or smell. The symptoms continue and peak in the first to third weeks. These can include multiple seizures and convulsions. The severe symptoms will occur in 80-90% of the users who stop taking the drug after physical addiction has occurred.

Due to the huge financial success of Valium (it was the #1 prescribed drug in America at one time), many drug companies have jumped on the band wagon by selling other benzodiazepines.

Overdose symptoms include drowsiness, loss of consciousness, depressed breathing, coma, and death if left untreated, but it might take 50 or a hundred pills to cause an overdose. Unfortunately, street versions of the drug misrepresented and sold as Quaaludes, were so strong that only five or ten pills could cause really bad reactions. The relative safety of benzodiazepines does not extend to mixing them with alcohol or other depressants. People do die from just a few pills and and a modest amount of alcohol.

It is very important to note that despite their use as "tranquilizers" or sleeping pills, almost all benzodiazepines have an extremely long presence or "halflife" in the body. Thus, though taken only at bedtime or once every four to six hours, the drugs can accumulate in the body resulting in dependence and other subtly developing problems.

PLASMA HALF LIFE OF BENZODIAZEPINES

Trade name	Chemical name	Half life
Very long acting		
Dalmane	Flurazepam	90-200 hours
Paxipam	Halazepam	30-200 hours
Verstran, Centrax	Prazepam	30-200 hours
Intermediate acting		
Librium	Chlordiazepoxide	7-46 hours
Valium	Diazepam	14-90 hours
Clonopin	Clonazepam	18-50 hours
Short acting		
Restoril	Temazepam	5-20 hours
Xanax	Alprazolam	6-20 hours
Serax	Oxazepam	6-24 hours
Ativan	Lorazepam	9-22 hours
Very short acting		
Halcion	Triazolam	2-6 hours

(Modified from THE JOURNAL OF PSYCHOACTIVE DRUGS 15: 1-2. pg 43, 1-6/1983)

The long persistence of these drugs in the body from low or regular doses taken over a long period of time, results not only in withdrawal symptoms but in symptoms that erratically come and go in cycles separated by 2 to 10 days. These symptoms, described previously, are sometimes bizarre, sometimes life-threatening, and all complicated by the cyclical nature of the severity. Short-acting barbiturates, on the other hand, follow a fairly predictable course where the symptoms come, and then go, and don't return.

The benzodiazepines have been shown to exert their sedative effects by interacting with or acting like a naturally occurring neurotransmitter in the brain called gama aminobutyric acid, or GABA for short. GABA is recognized to be the most important inhibitory neurotransmitter. Drugs, like Valium, greatly increase the actions of GABA and also influence other sedating neurotransmitters such as serotonin and dopamine.

BENZODIAZEPINE WITHDRAWAL VS. SHORT-ACTING BARBITURATE WITHDRAWAL

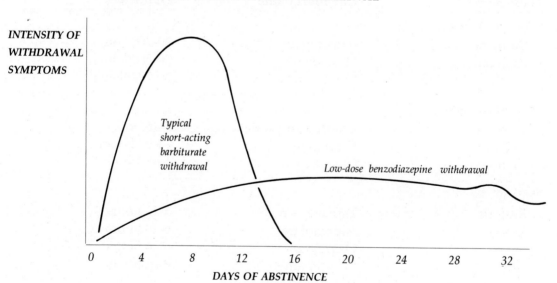

(fR. JOURNAL OF PSYCHOACTIVE DRUGS 15: 1-2, PG 89, 1-6/1983)

OTHER SEDATIVE-HYPNOTICS

QUAALUDE

Although widely used at one time as a sleep aid, the heavy abuse of Quaaludes led to the withdrawal of this product from the legitimate market. This led to a tremendous increase in the illicit production of Quaalude, known as bootleg ludes, which look identical to the original prescription drug. The actual chemical in Quaaludes, methaquaalone, is being manufactured by street chemists or smuggled from Europe or Columbia. However, there is no guarantee that the street version contains actual methaqualone, and even when it does, the dosage may vary dramatically, making an overdose more likely. The street samples analyzed have contained everything from PCP to Benadryl (an antihistamine), to Valium. Many of the substitute drugs are more harmful than the Quaalude itself.

The reasons for the popularity of methaquaalone are its overall sedative effect and the prolonged period of mild euphoria caused by suppression of inhibitions. This disinhibitory effect is similar to that caused by alcohol.

DORIDEN

Though widely available and somewhat abused in the 50's, it wasn't till the 70's and 80's that Doriden became popular on the street in a polydrug combination (Doriden and codeine), variously known as loads, sets, setups, four by fours, fours and doors, etc. The effect of this combination is prolonged drowsiness, relaxation, and euphoria over a period of 6 to 8 hours. The combination has led to a double addiction, a sedative-hypnotic and an opiate. An additional danger with Doriden is that the drug is pulled out of the blood by the liver, concentrated in the gall bladder, released back into the intestine, and then back into the blood, causing extended relapse, toxic effects, and a greater chance of harm.

PLACIDYL

Called green weenies, Placidyl is one of the older sedative hypnotics. It is still a prescription drug and is subject to limited abuse. It is about the equivalent of Doriden in potency, with similar toxic and addictive effects but is shorter acting.

MILTOWN

Miltown (meprobamate), first popularized in the 1950's, led to the first modern recognition of prescription abuse whereby a legal drug, used legally by prescription, can lead to addiction. The drug was both prescribed excessively and misused in larger than prescribed amounts. It was also the forerunner of a downer cycle dominated by sedative-hypnotics.

Budweiser and other brewers and distillers welcomed the end of prohibition and the end of an experiment in controlling substance abuse by controlling the availability of the substance. Once repealed, alcoholism rose quickly to overwhelm 4% to 5% of our total population, and has remained endemic in that proportion ever since.

Alcohol

Alcohol is the oldest psychoactive drug known to man. It was probably discovered by accident when some fruit, perhaps grapes or plums, was left to stand in a warm place allowing the fruit sugar to ferment into alcohol. Later it was found that the starch in potatoes, rice, corn, and grains could also be fermented, first to sugar, then to alcohol. The concentration of alcohol in each kind of beverage depends on the length of fermentation, the type of fruit or vegetable used, the percent of additives used, and the amount of distillation.

WINE
Red, white, rosé, champagne	12%
Sherry	20%
Vermouth	18%
Wine cooler	6%

BEER
Light lager or dark ale	6%
Malt or stout	8%
Light beer	4%

LIQUORS & WHISKEYS
Bourbon, whiskey, scotch, vodka, rum, gin, brandy	43% –60%
Tequila, cognac, drambui	40%
Amaretto, kahlua, etc.	28%
Everclear	95%

60 – 90 proof

(Note: 100% alcohol = 200 proof)

EFFECTS: Used in limited quantities, alcohol has been credited with reducing tension, lowering the risk of heart attacks, and even helping people to cope.

"Social" drinker: "Drinking is a way of life here. Somebody comes up and you offer them a drink. It's cordial. That's how you break the ice, I like to drink. Drinking is good. It makes me happy."

The reason for alcohol's disinhibiting effect is its action on the higher centers of the brain's cortex. It disrupts the chemical balance controlling reasoning and judgment. Then it acts on the lower centers of the limbic system that rule mood and emotion.

"Social" drinker: "If I'm down, it picks me up. If I'm hyper, it calms me down. I could get the same thing from meditation except meditation doesn't taste so good."

The suppression of our inhibitions can fool us because along with this apparent emotional stimulation comes a physical depression. The more alcohol that is drunk, the freer the user feels but, the blood pressure is lowered, motor reflexes are slowed, digestion becomes poor, body heat is lost, and sexual excitement is diminished.

"Social" drinker: "I don't take drugs. I have an aspirin once a month. I don't do drugs and I really don't like to be around anyone who does. To me, drugs are bad. I only drink."

Alcohol ranks third behind heart disease and cancer as this country's biggest health problem. According to a report by the Surgeon General, released in 1988, 125,000 people in the U.S. die each year from alcohol. The causes of death vary from cirrhosis of the liver to heart attacks and strokes. The number also includes 25,000 who die in alcohol-related automobile accidents. It includes half of all murders (particularly family violence) and a fourth of all suicides. It doesn't include an additional 4,000 who die from the combination of alcohol and other drugs.

30%

Alcohol abuser: "Well, you don't hear of any heroin addicts running their cars into people or getting in fights and cuttin' up people just from not knowing what they're doing. And when you're drunk, you do crazy things, get violent, and you get self-destructive."

Alcohol is one of the few drugs that the body metabolizes at a defined, continuous rate, based upon a person's body weight, amount of alcohol drunk, the time that has passed since the last drink, and to a lesser extent the tolerance to alcohol that has come from years of drinking. Thus, we can usually predict the amount of alcohol that will be circulating through the body and brain, and how long it will take to be metabolized by the liver and eliminated via urination, sweating, and breathing.

The amount of alcohol needed for a 175 lb. man to achieve legal intoxication (.10, to be drunk within one hour).

Wine	*Four 4-oz glasses*
Beer	*Five 12-oz cans*
Distilled whiskey.	*Five 1-oz shots*

ADULTS PATTERNS OF ALCOHOL USE

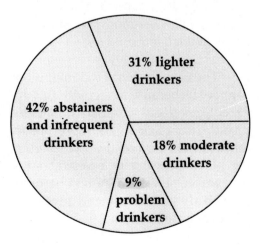

31% lighter drinkers

42% abstainers and infrequent drinkers

18% moderate drinkers

9% problem drinkers

The ability to tolerate alcohol depends mostly on the liver. Thus, as we drink over a period of time, the liver adapts and changes. It creates more enzymes to handle the protoplasmic

HOW AGING AND HEAVY DRINKING AFFECT LIVER'S ABILITY TO HANDLE ALCOHOL

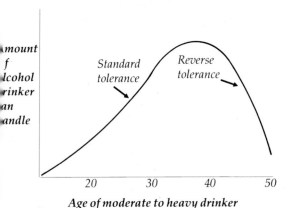

Age of moderate to heavy drinker

poison, alcohol. Unfortunately, since liver cells are also being destroyed by the drinking and by the natural aging process, the liver eventually becomes less able to handle the alcohol. A condition known as reverse tolerance occurs. So, a drinker who could handle two fifths of whiskey at the age of 30 will get drunk on half a pint of wine at the age of 40.

"Social" drinker: "I don't consider myself an alcoholic. I drink a lot. I have five drinks a day...and that's an average. It's hardly ever less than three. But, it's never interfered with my work. It's never interfered with my health."

90% of all high school seniors have tried alcohol and over 40% admit to a pattern of binge drinking or TGIFing, i.e., 5 shots or more of wine or booze on Friday, Saturday, or Sunday.

"Social drinker: "Being under the influence is like, you feel good and your spirits are lifted a little. Being drunk is when your words are slurred or you stagger. You shouldn't drive when you're like that. I've never had a ticket...and I mean I've driven when I shouldn't have. Who hasn't?"

The disinhibiting stimulant effect of alcohol soon becomes physical depression with continued use (c. 1890)

One Biological Model for the Disease of Alcoholism

Research during the late 1970's and early 1980's revealed that alcohol and opiates slotted into met-enkephalin receptor sites in the mid-brain. Met-enkephalin, a natural neurotransmitter, moderates stress and gives us a feeling of well being. Further, alcohol produces TIQ, in the liver which saturates met-enkephalin receptor sites. One theory states that the abnormal presence in the brain of alcohol, opiates/opioids, and TIQ all cause a decreased synthesis and lower concentration of natural met-en- kephalin. This makes a user crave more alcohol and opiates/opioids, forcing one to become more dependent on these drugs to deal with life's daily stresses. Researchers have found that those genetically prone to alcoholism, produce more TIQ in their liver when they drink. In addition to met-enkephalin, low brain levels of GABA and serotonin are also implicated in the disease of alcoholism.

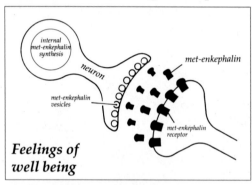

MET-ENKEPHALIN ADEQUACY

In a normal person, sufficient quantities of met-enkephalins are produced to give feelings of well being.

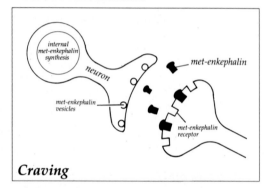

MET-ENKEPHALIN DEFICIENCY

Some people are born with a natural deficiency of met-enkephalins.. They are more likely to fall into a pattern of alcohol or opiate/opioid abuse.

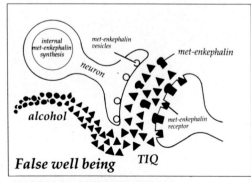

ALCOHOL SUBSTITUTION

In a drinker, alcohol and TIQ's replace natural met-enkephalins thereby inducing a false sense of well being. The body therefore produces fewer and fewer of its own (note: there are fewer vesicles).

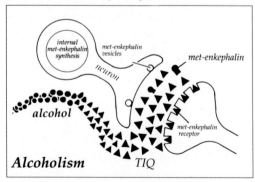

ALCOHOL THE DESTROYER

With long term use of alcohol, the body's ability to produce met-enkephalins is greatly impaired. The alcoholic needs alcohol to get any sense of well being. His body won't produce this feeling on its own anymore.

Courtesy of the Matrix Corporation (Michael Trachtenberg, PhD, Kenneth Blum, PhD.)

Physiological Effects

Alcohol is a protoplasmic poison. It can kill liver, brain, kidney, and other tissues on contact. It affects all systems in the body.

Skeletal system: Skeletal muscular coordination decreases.

Muscular system: Normal muscular coordination is impaired.

Circulatory system: The pulse rate increases and blood vessels dilate causing increased heat loss from the body. With large doses, full cardiac and vascular depression can occur.

Respiratory system: Small doses initially stimulate the respiratory rate, but increased doses cause a dramatic decrease.

Nervous system: An initial relaxation and lowered inhibitions at low doses are followed by mental confusion and uncontrolled mood swings at higher doses. Severe depression of the central nervous system can lead to coma.

Digestive system: There is an increase in digestive secretions causing irritation of the stomach and an greater accumulation of fat deposits in the liver. Chronic use can cause hepatitis and hepatic cirrhosis (liver scarring).

Excretory system: Depression of small and large intestine functions can cause constipation and diarrhea. Urine production and urination increase.

Endocrine (hormone) system: Increased secretions of various hormones also increase urination, raise, then lower blood sugar levels, dilates pupils, and raise blood pressure.

Reproductive system: Alcohol overuse during pregnancy causes more miscarriages, more infant deaths, smaller, weaker newborns, and more problem pregnancies. Specific toxic effects of alcohol on the developing fetus. known as the fetal alcohol syndrome, (FAS),are described in a separate section (*Drugs in Our Environment*).

Alcohol abuser: If I was drinking a quart a day and had a heroin habit, I would be more afraid of quitting alcohol, cause with drinking, you go into convulsions and you are really sick. I thought I was going to die from the pain in my stomach.., the throwing up, the sweating, the diarrhea. You don't have any energy, and you know if you just took a drink you'd feel better. And with heroin, you get some muscle cramps and you throw up and you get a little diarrhea but you're not going to get convulsions. You're not going to die. You can die from kicking alcohol.

38% of Victims Had Been Drinking Before They Died

Study Suggests Alcohol Has Role in Homicides

By LEE SIEGEL, Associated Press

A study showing that 38% of Los Angeles homicide victims had alcohol in their blood suggests that drinking alcoholic beverages raises the risk of being killed but does not prove it, researchers say.

Because researchers did not study blood-alcohol levels of people who weren't killed, "we can't really tell . . . if alcohol use increases the risk of becoming a homicide victim," said James Mercy, assistant chief of the Violence Epidemiology Branch at the Centers for Disease Control in Atlanta.

However, the results of the study suggest that the risk is increased, Mercy said recently.

"At this point, it's not scientific to conclude [that] there is a direct cause-and-effect relationship," said the study's principal author, Dr. Richard Goodman, a CDC epidemiologist and former assistant professor at UCLA's School of Public Health.

The CDC-UCLA study of all Los Angeles homicides in the 1970s also showed that a quarter of the victims were legally drunk when they were killed and that alcohol was found most commonly in homicide victims who were male, young and Latino.

"Alcohol was also detected most commonly in victims killed during weekends, when homicides occurred in bars or restaurants, when homicides resulted from physical fights or verbal arguments, when victims were friends or acquaintances of offenders, and when homicides resulted from stabbings," the study said.

Alcohol "could increase the likelihood of risk-taking and provocative behavior by some

homicide," the study said. It was published in last month's American Journal of Public Health.

The study examined police and coroner's files of all 4,950 homicides in Los Angeles from 1970-79. Blood-alcohol content was determined at autopsy for 4,092.

The other 858 victims' blood-alcohol was not determined because they were elderly or children, too much time had elapsed since the deaths, decomposition was too advanced or the

> 'It may very well be that the role alcohol plays is more important in terms of its effect in causing people to commit homicides.'
>
> — James Mercy

cases were not classified as homicides at time of autopsy.

Of the 4,092 victims tested, 46% had alcohol their blood, and 30% exceeded the level of legal intoxication for drivers in most states. 0.10 blood alcohol. Out of the 4,950 victims, 38% alcohol in their blood and 25% were legally drunk.

An unpublished companion study showed the

Angeles from 1970-79, mostly commonly in victims who were female, young and black, Goodman said.

The alcohol study's findings are consistent with previous research showing alcohol among large percentages of homicide victims in Philadelphia, Chicago, New York City, Pennsylvania's Allegheny County and South Africa's Cape Peninsula. But the latest study "was based on a larger number of cases over a longer period of time," Mercy said.

He said the study was part of a recently publicized larger research project that found that young black and Latino men are the most likely victims of homicide in Los Angeles.

The alcohol-homicide study did not examine alcohol use by killers, which would be difficult to measure. But "it may very well be that the role alcohol plays is more important in terms of its effect in causing people to commit homicides," Mercy said.

The study found that 51% of tested male victims had alcohol in their blood, compared to

Thursday, September 15, 1988

Drunk Driver Can Face Trial For Murder, High Court Says

By Perry Lang

A Shasta County man, accused of getting drunk and driving twice the speed li before becoming involved an accident in which people were killed, can charged with murder, the C

yesterday.

Justice Frank J. Richardson wrote the 5-to-2 decision reversing

torney's office had asked the California attorney general's appellate division to appeal the ruling before prosecuting Robert Lee Watson of

UCSF Study

First Genetic Clue To Alcoholism

By David Perlman
Chronicle Science Editor

The first direct evidence of a strong genetic link in severe alcoholics was reported yesterday by researchers at the University of California in San Francisco.

The scientists have tracked sensitivity to alcohol in generation after generation of human cells cultured in the laboratory and are launching similar studies in the families and offspring of alcoholic patients.

For many years, experts on alcoholism have known that the dis-

alcoholics proved to be chemically different from the progeny of cells taken from non-drinkers and were nearly 60 percent more sensitive to the effects of alcohol when they were exposed to it for the first time.

As is true of many drugs, virtually anyone can become addicted to alcohol if forced to drink enough of it, Diamond said. But some heavy drinkers find it relatively easier to quit than others, and the genetic factor may well be a powerful element in the "hard-core" addicts, Diamond said.

Scientists Find Clue to Alcoholic Genes

Proportion of Traffic Deaths Tied to Alcohol Drops to 51%

ATLANTA, Dec. 15 (AP) — Although more than 23,000 people were killed last year in alcohol-related traffic accidents in the United States, the proportion of fatal crashes involving alcohol

The Atlanta-based agency, in its weekly report, noted that alcohol-related traffic accidents last year robbed their victims of more than 780,000 years of "potential life" they would

San Francisco Chronicle

Friday, November 4, 1988

Many Live Productive Lives

Liver Transplants in Alcoholics Defended

Chronicle Wire Services

Chicago

Challenging ethical objections, doctors said yesterday that alcoholics have been good recipients of liver transplants, ending long, productive and alcohol-free lives after surgery.

The study, led by transplant pioneer Dr. Thomas Starzl, showed that 66 percent of patients with alcohol-damaged livers who received transplants at a busy transplant center in the past seven years are still alive.

More than 73 percent of the 41 patients survived more than a year after getting a new liver. Starzl, a surgeon at the University Health Center of Pittsburgh, attempted the world's first liver transplant in 1963 and was successful in 1967.

The team of 10 researchers re-

ported in today's issue of the Journal of the American Medical Association that all but two of the patients who survived for more than six months stopped abusing alcohol after their operations.

Study Links Drinks And Accidents

People who consume five or more alcoholic drinks on any given occasion are almost twice as likely to suffer fatal injuries as those who consume only one or two, says a new study.

People who usually consumed five to eight drinks per occasion were almost twice as likely to die of an injury as nondrinkers or those who consumed one or two, the researchers said in the study published in the Journal of the American Medical Association.

People who consumed nine or

more drinks per occasion had more than triple the risk of the low-consumption groups, they said.

The important finding in this study is that what people tell about us about alcohol use related strongly to their future risk of dying from an injury," said Dr. Robert F. Anda, co-author of the study and a researcher at the national Centers for Disease Control in Atlanta.

Doctors Eschew Personal Physicians

Medical doctors are less likely than college professors to have a personal physician, see a doctor regularly and have clinical procedures performed, a new study suggested yesterday.

A re-examination of a 1983 survey of physicians' attitudes toward medical care revealed that 44 per-

cent of the doctors surveyed had personal physicians compared to 74 percent of the Ph.Ds who also responded to the questionnaire.

"This does not imply that physicians are less healthy," said Dr. Katherine Kahn, a UCLA internist and chief investigator of the study reported in the current issue of the Archives of Internal Medicine.

"But the implication is that a substantial number of M.D.'s and Ph.D's do not have a personal physician and that they are less likely to receive good health maintenance and screening."

Kahn and her colleagues found that doctors who failed to see personal physicians were less likely to have such routine health maintenance tests as blood pressure examinations, cholesterol testing, rectal examinations for the presence of colon abnormalities and breast and pelvic exams for women.

DRUG SYNERGISM

If more than one depressant drug is used, the combination can cause a much greater reaction than simply the sum of the effects. One of the reasons for this synergistic effect lies in the chemistry of the liver.

For example, if alcohol and Valium are taken together, the liver becomes busy metabolizing the alcohol so the sedative-hypnotic passes through the body at full strength. Alcohol also dissolves the Valium more readily than stomach fluids allowing more Valium to be absorbed rapidly into the body. Valium exerts its depressant effects on different parts of the brain than the ones alcohol acts on. Thus, combined together, they cause more problems than if they were taken at different times.

The exaggerated respiratory depression is the biggest danger with the use of alcohol and another depressant. That combination also cause more blackouts.

Drug user: "I took my little medication with me and one night I went out drinking in the bar; played some pool. And that's all I remember. This was on a Sunday. When I woke up, it was Wednesday".

The synergistic effect causes 4,000 deaths a year. In addition, almost 50,000 people are treated in emergency rooms because of adverse reactions to multiple drug use.

THE SYNERGISTIC EFFECTS WHEN COMBINING ALCOHOL AND A SEDATIVE-HYPNOTIC

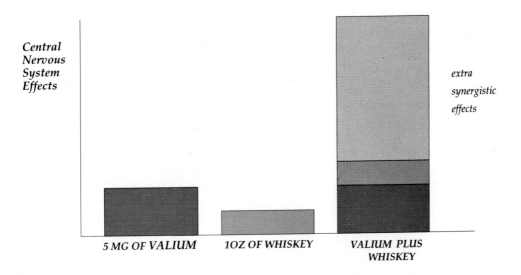

Central Nervous System Effects

extra synergistic effects

5 MG OF VALIUM   1OZ OF WHISKEY   VALIUM PLUS WHISKEY

CROSS TOLERANCE, CROSS DEPENDENCE

Depressant drugs also exhibit cross tolerance and cross dependence between different as well as similar chemical drug classes. Further, some depressants even exhibit these characteristics with stimulant, psychedelic and non-psychoactive drugs.

Cross tolerance is the development of tolerance to other drugs by the continued exposure to a particular drug. For example, a barbiturate addict who develops a tolerance to a high dose of Seconal is also tolerant to and can withstand high doses of Nembutal, Phenobarbital, anesthetics, opiates, alcohol, Valium, and even blood thinner medication. One explanation of cross tolerance lies in the fact that many drugs are metabolized or broken down by the same body enzymes. As one continues to take barbiturates, the liver creates more enzymes to rid the body of this foreign toxin. The unusually high levels of these enzymes result in tolerance to all barbiturates as well as other drugs also metabolized by those same enzymes.

Cross dependence occurs as an individual becomes addicted or tissue dependent on one drug resulting in biochemical and cellular changes that support an addiction to other drugs. A heroin addict for example has altered body chemistry such that he or she is also likely to be addicted to an opioid (Dilaudid, Demerol, morphine, codeine, methadone or Darvon). As with this example, cross dependence most often occurs with different drugs in the same chemical family. A Valium addict is also tissue dependent on Librium, Dalmane, and Ativan. A heavy Seconal user is also tissue dependent on Nembutal, Tuinal, and phenobarbital. Cross dependence has also been documented to some extent with opiates/opioids and alcohol; cocaine and alcohol; and Valium and alcohol.

REVIEW

1. Downers are central nervous system depressants.

2. The three main groups of downers are opiates/opioids, sedative-hypnotics and alcohol.

3. Other downers are skeletal muscle relaxants, antihistamines, lookalike sedatives, and over-the-counter sedatives.

4. Opiates (from the opium poppy) and opioids (synthetic versions of opiates) were developed for the treatment of acute pain.

5. Opiates include opium, heroin, codeine, morphine, Dilaudid and Percodan. Opioids include methadone, Darvon, Demerol, Talwin, and fentanyl.

6. Opiates and Opioids work by mimicking the body's own natural painkillers, endorphins, and enkephalins. They block the transmission of pain messages to the brain.

7. Opiates and opioids can also cause euphoria, increase nausea, depress respiration and heart rate, depress muscular coordination, and suppress the cough mechanism.

8. A physical tolerance to opiates and opioids develops rapidly, increasing the speed with which the body becomes dependent on the drug.

9. Withdrawal from opiates is like an extreme case of the flu. People do not usually die from opiate withdrawal. They can die from an overdose. However, newborn addicted babies can die in opiate withdrawal.

10. Heroin can be injected, smoked or snorted. The concentration of street heroin is generally 3% to 4% pure although much higher percentages have been seen recently.

11. Codeine is the most abused opiate prescription.

12. Recently, synthetic heroin (fentanyl and Demerol derivatives) have appeared on the street. The danger is that one by-product of street Demerol, MPTP, can cause Parkinson's disease, an irreversible nervous system disorder. Fentanyl derivatives are so potent that overdose occurs more frequently.

13. Sedative-hypnotics are usually prescribed to control anxiety, induce sleep, relax muscles, and act as a mild tranquilizer.

14. The three main types of sedative-hypnotics are barbiturates, non-barbiturates, and benzodiazepines.

15. Barbiturates include Seconal (reds), Nembutal (yellows), Tuinal (rainbows), Amytal (blue heavens), and phenobarbital.

16. Non-barbiturate sedative-hypnotics include Doriden, Quaaludes, Miltown, Placidyl, and dozens more.

17. Benzodiazepines include Valium, Librium, Dalmane, Xanax, Halcion and a dozen more.

18. Sedative-hypnotics work on specific sections of the brain; i.e., the brainstem and midbrain to induce sleep.

19. Tolerance to sedative-hypnotics develops rather quickly.

20. Withdrawal from a sedative-hypnotic dependence can be extremely dangerous and life threatening: convulsions, nausea, breathing difficulty and major health problems are common.

21. Valium, the most widely prescribed tranquilizer, stays in the body for days, even weeks. Withdrawal from prolonged benzodiazepine use can be life threatening.

22. Quaaludes are only available from illicit sources. The drug causes an overall sedation, mild euphoria, and suppression of inhibitions.

23. Alcohol is the oldest psychoactive drug known to man. It is legal and found in beer, wine, and hard liquors.

24. Initially, alcohol suppresses inhibitions so it seems to act like a stimulant, but as the depressant effect takes over it slows reflexes; depresses respiration and heart rate; disrupts reasoning and judgement.

25. As a person grows older, the liver and body are less able to handle the same amount of alcohol, so the person gets drunk sooner.

26. Withdrawal from prolonged use of alcohol can be life threatening. Hallucinations, convulsions, and irregular heart rates are common.

27. Alcohol and sedative-hypnotics used together can be especially life threatening. They cause a synergistic (exaggerated) effect which can suppress respiration and heart functions to dangerous levels.

28. Four to eight thousand people in the United States die each year from the synergistic effect of alcohol and another depressant. An additional 50,000 people are treated in emergency rooms because of polydrug abuse.

QUESTIONS

1. What are the three major categories of downers?

2. Name the four minor categories of downers.

3. What are the overall effects of downers?

4. What is the difference between opiates and opioids?

5. Name three opiates and three opioids.

6. What are the body's own, natural painkillers called?

7. What are the most common effects of opiates and opioids?

8. Name three ways heroin can be put into the body.

9. Which is more dangerous, opiate/opioid withdrawal or overdose?

10. What is China White and why is it dangerous?

11. What are the three categories of sedative-hypnotics?

12. What are reds and yellows?

13. Name three reasons why sedative-hypnotics are prescribed by physicians.

14. What is the most widely prescribed opiate/opioid?

16. Why is withdrawal from prolonged use of sedative-hypnotics dangerous?

17. Why do many people think alcohol is a stimulant?

18. What is reverse tolerance in regards to alcohol?

19. What is a synergistic effect, and why is it dangerous?

20. Why is withdrawal from prolonged use of alcohol dangerous?

21. Give two examples of synergism.

1924

The Juice of the Jungle Vine That Cures FEAR

In the Heart of South American Jungle Growing the "Courage Flower" Vine, Caapi, Growing About the Tree in the Center, and One of the Searchers for the Precious Growth Holding His Rifle Ready to Repel Savage Attack.

At Last Medical Science Feels That It Has Found in the "Courage Flower," Caapi, a Non-Habit Forming Draught to Overcome Mankind's Greatest Enemy.

Science Resorts to All Sorts of Means to Overcome Fear. Below is a Photograph of a Patient in a Washington Emergency Hospital Having His Mind Diverted by a Radio Concert as Surgeons Operate on Him.

FEAR—A Notable Interpretation of Mankind's Curse by Sybil Thorndike, Famous English Actress.

1988

Navajo Woman Sues State Over Use of Peyote

Associated Press

Sacramento

A Navajo woman from Fresno is suing the state for rejecting her application to become a prison guard because she had eaten the hallucinogenic plant peyote as a sacrament in the Native American Church.

In a lawsuit filed in U.S. District Court in Sacramento, Sherry Mitchell said her right to exercise religious freedom under the First and 14th Amendments and the state Constitution have been violated.

She and her attorney, Jay B. Petersen of the California Indian Legal Services, asked the court to order the state Personnel Board and the Corrections Department to

Brooklyn's Narcotic Farm
Marajuana Field

AMAZING DISCOVERY NEAR BRIDGE

1934

POLICE RAID

CRAFTY DETECTIVE WORK; 2 ARRESTS

Hidden by buildings Brooklyn's "Jungle," almost a stone's throw from Brooklyn Bridge, a whole flourishing field of Cannabis Indica was found from which is made marajuana, Mexican narcotic, was discovered by detectives yesterday.

The discovery followed a raid on an apartment at Concord st. where two men were arrested. The raid, directed by the police narcotic squad, came as a result of fine work of clever detective work by police with the coöperation of the U. S. Army.

Two members of the 16th Infantry were taken into custody by military authorities at the same time.

The Cannabis Indica field, by 100 feet, is in the center of a group of ramshackle buildings in the block bounded by Washington, Nassau, Adams and Concord sts.

Largest Area

Police said it is the largest cultivated area of the weed found in the East in recent years. They believe it has been one of the local sources of the narcotic from which marajuana cigarettes are made.

1983

Psychedelic drugs making a comeback

By Nicole Yorkin
Herald staff writer

Hallucinogenic drugs, thought of until recently as a defunct symbol of the psychedelic '60s when their use on the West Coast was considered "epidemic," are making a comeback among young people who never heard the horror stories that helped push hallucinogenics out of the mainstream of drug use.

Helpless drug—termed lysergic acid (LSD) the "phantom" on the nation's campuses — of students in the schools were reported experimenting with it — was bombarded with young people, drug's influence, public behavior, by jumping out of bridges and toward others.

THE SAN FRANCISCO SUNDAY CHRONICLE

PCP Users Present a Special Problem for Police

By RON HARRIS, *Times Staff Writer*

At 5:30 a.m. on Aug. 4, 1977, Los Angeles police Sgt. Kurt Barz responded to a call at 557 N. Hoover St. He found Ronald Burkholder, 35, a biochemist, running naked down the street, beating on cars and climbing a street sign.

Barz, a solid six feet and 190 pounds, approached Burkholder, 5 feet, 9 inches and 138 pounds, and the two struggled. Twice Burkholder was able to take away his night stick, Barz reported.

Barz said he kicked Burkholder in the groin. "There was no reaction at all," he told the court during a lawsuit that arose from the incident, "no change of expression, no utterance, no indication he felt anything."

The struggle grew more intense. Barz shot and killed Burkholder.

A coroner's report concluded that Burkholder had been under the influence of PHP, an analog of PCP, producing the same effects. Last month, a jury ruled that Barz had acted improperly and awarded Burkholder's mother and daughter $425,750.

Thousands of Incidents

The Burkholder incident was one of the Los Angeles Police Department's earliest encounters

Drug Blocks Out Pain, Imparts Super Strength

charge of physical training at the police academy.

"It's a tough situation," said Steven E. Lerner of the California PCP Training and Prevention Project at UCLA. "Police control techniques are usually based on inflicting pain. Here you have guys that don't feel any pain and possess great strength. You beat on them and they don't feel it."

The problem of subduing PCP suspects frustrates law enforcement agencies and angers some community groups, who say police are brutalizing suspects.

Sound Waves and Bean Bags

Desperate for solutions, the Los Angeles police have looked at everything from new martial arts techniques to exotic guns that shoot sound waves, bean bags and water projectiles. Two officers are expected to return this week from a three-week, eight-city tour of police departments in search of methods to control PCP suspects.

At present, police policy on PCP suspects calls for using a TASER gun, a device that fires electrodes into the body, emitting a debilitating electrical charge. The stun gun and nets, used mostly by the Sheriff's Department, have proven 70% effective.

Those two methods have drawbacks: There are not enough TASERS. The net cannot be used in enclosed areas and it requires what police call "a rather cooperative suspect."

'A Touchy Situation'

"If a guy is running down the street, it's pretty hard to throw a net on him," Dionne explained.

"It's a touchy situation. If those methods fail you just try to muster enough troops and use body weight to subdue the suspect. But if an officer is in fear of his life, that's justification for use of deadly force."

Most officers feel that any encounter with a suspect on PCP is life-threatening.

"What do you do with a guy on dust?" one officer asked rhetorically. "You run like hell."

"I don't like to think about it," said another. "You hear that an officer (is) involved in a shooting, you drop everything and go," Dionne said. "If an officer says it's PCP, it's the same

1987

Although illegal throughout most of the world, the desire to advertise is still strong among some growers of marijuanja, particularly in Hawaii.

CLASSIFICATON

Uppers stimulate us and downers depress us. All Arounders (psychedelics can act as stimulants or depressants, but mostly they distort our perceptions of the world, a world in which logic takes a back seat to intensified sensations. From alphabet soup psychedelics to naturally occurring plants used in religious ceremonies, all arounders represent a diverse group of substances.

The four main classes of psychedelics are the Indole psychedelics which mimic certain brain hormones; the phenylethylamines that closely resemble molecules of adrenaline and amphetamines; the cannabinols found in marijuana (hemp) plants; the anticholinergics such as belladona; and those in a class by themselves such as PCP.

Common name	Active ingredients	Street names
INDOLE PSYCHEDELICS		
LSD	Lysergic acid diethyl-amide	Acid, sugar, window pane, blotter, barrel
Mushrooms	**Psilocybin**	Shrooms, magic mushrooms
Iboga plant	Ibogaine	African LSD
Morning glory seeds or Hawaiian wood-rose	Lysergic acid amide	Heavenly blue, pearly gates, wedding bells
DMT	Dimethyltryptamine	Businessman's special
Yage	Harmaline & DMT	Ayahuasca, caapi, cohaba, snuff
PHENYLETHYLAMINE PSYCHEDELICS		
Peyote cactus	**Mescalines**	Mesc, peyote, buttons
STP, (DOM) (synthetic)	4 methyl 2,5 dimethoxy-amphetamine	Serenity, tranquility, peace pill
STP-LSD Combo	dimethoxy-amphetamine with LSD	Wedge series, orange and pink wedges, Harvey Wallbanger
MDA, MMDA, MDM, MDE, etc.	Variations of methylene-dioxy amphetamine	Love drug, XTC, ecstasy, Adam, Eve
2CB	4 bromo 2,5 dimethoxy phenethylamine	
U4Euh	4 methyl aminorex	Euphoria

CANNABINOLS (MARIJUANA, ETC)

Marijuana	THC-tetrahydro-cannabinol	Grass, pot, weed, herb Acapulco gold, joint, reefer, dubie, etc.
Sinsemilla	High potency, seedless flowering tops of female marijuana plants	Sens, skunk weed, ganja
Hashish, hash oil	THC (refined from marijuana) Bhang	

ANTICHOLINERGICS

Belladonna, jimsonweed, datura, wolfbane, thornapple	Atropine, scopolamine	Deadly nightshade

OTHER PSYCHEDELICS

PCP	Phencyclidine	Angel dust, hog, peace pill, krystal, krystal joint, ozone, Sherm
Nutmeg and mace	Myristicin	
Amanita mushrooms (fly agaric)	Ibotenic acid, muscimol	Soma
Kava root	Alpha pyrones	Kava-kava

LSD

PCP

MDA

DMT

Unlike uppers and downers, all arounders represent a diverse group of chemical compounds, all of which are capable of producing a psychedelic state..

THE EFFECTS

Though psychedelics are found throughout the world, the majority of these drugs, except for marijuana, are found and used in the Americas and Africa. Hundreds of primitive tribes such as the Aztecs, Toltecs, Navajos, and Huicholes have used peyote, psilocybin, yage, morning glory seeds, and dozens of other substances for religious, social, magical, and medical reasons.

Psychedelics interfere with the normal balance of the brain. They mimic some naturally occurring neurotransmitters and disrupt others. More than uppers and downers, the effects of all arounders are very dependent on the size of the dose, the basic emotional makeup of the user, the mood at the time of use, and the surroundings when taking the drug. For instance, first- or second-time users may become nauseous, extremely anxious, and depressed, while experienced users may induce in themselves a feeling of euphoria. A user with a tendency towards schizophrenia could get a really bad reaction from LSD or PCP because it would exaggerate those unstable tendencies. Someone who is basically agressive might become more so while an immature user might become more childlike. Many psychedelics, particularly marijuana, have been called, "The mirror that magnifies."

Physical Effects

LSD and most other hallucinogens stimulate the sympathetic nervous system. This results in a rise in pulse rate and blood pressure. It can produce sweating and palpitations. The stimulation of the brainstem can overload the sensory pathways, making the user very conscious of all sensation.

Mental Effects

Psychedelics have a strong effect on our emotional center (the limbic system) influencing mood and emotion. They even affect the visual centers, producing visions ranging from flashes of light to complete scenes. They impact the reticular formation making the user extremely conscious of sensory input. They suppress the memory centers and other higher cerebral functions such as judgment and reason. Since the effects do vary so much with psychedelics, we will expand on the effects of each individual drug.

Metabolized by liver in 10 - 12 hrs

LSD

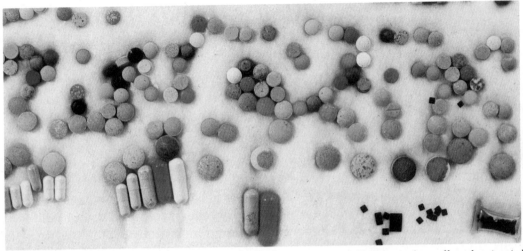

The effective dose of LSD is so small that it can be delivered in many guises. Tablets can be swallowed, saturated bits of gelatin or impregnated paper can be absorbed under the tongue, and impregnated sugar cubes can be eaten.

"Acid," "blotter," "barrels," "sunshine," and "window panes" are just some of the street names for LSD. Developed in the late 40's as a possible cure for schizophrenia, it was popularized by Dr. Timothy Leary and others in the 60's as a way to "Tune in, turn on, and drop out."

LSD is remarkable for its potency. Doses as low as 25 micrograms (mics), 25 one millionths of a gram, can cause mental changes and psychedelic effects. Effects appear 15 minutes to one hour after ingestion. The usual dose of LSD is 100 to 200 micrograms. The current low dose (30 to 50 mics) acid gives more stimulatory than psychedelic effects.

LSD can cause physical effects of a rise in heart rate and blood pressure, a higher body temperature and some sweating, much like amphetamines.

LSD user: We had some acid which we called the 'Victor Mature LSD' because it made you grind your teeth like he did in the movies. That was because it had so much speed in it."

LSD creates mental effects of sensory distortions and illusions by its overloading effect on the brainstem, the sensory switchboard for the mind.

LSD user: "In a real strong acid, the old ones, you'll see the walls melting like candles, and running water down the wall. That kind of hallucination, never anything real solid like a bottle...'Is it there or not?' The thing that got me really crazy was hearing a dog or airplane or passenger car miles away and you didn't know whether that was real or an hallucination." You remember the psychedelic hum...hummmmmm?"

LSD user: "I stuck my hand in this flame and then I went, 'Uh-oh, my hand is in the flame,' and I pulled it out and it didn't burn, but later that night, you know, my hand started blistering and I'm going, 'Oh no, I got burned.'"

The amount of acid, the surroundings, the user's mental state, and physical condition all determine the reaction to a drug. Because of its effect on the emotional center in the brain, a user is open to the extremes of euphoria and panic. Inexperienced users, or even experienced users who take too high a dose, can feel acute anxiety, fear over loss of control, paranoia, and delusions of persecution or of grandeur.

LSD user: "You would all of a sudden look at a clock and say, 'All right, I'll come down now.' And then, the writing would

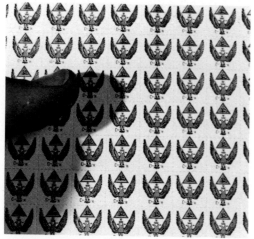

A sheet of blotter acid (LSD); each perforated square contains a drop of dried LSD, sufficient for one dose.

still be on the wall and you'd still be hearing the sounds and you'd go, 'No, I'm not going to come down. I'm never, never going to come down. I'm never going to be sane again. They're going to lock me up.'"

The best treatment for someone on a bad trip is to talk him or her down in a calm manner, without raising one's voice or appearing threatening. Also, one needs to provide a quiet, peaceful environment, reduced stimuli, and continued reassurance that the drug is being metabolized from the body and the user will recover from the bad trip.

The drug is metabolized by the liver in about 8 to 12 hours and as it's neutralized, the psychedelic effects disappear. However, certain chronic after effects are recognized. First, those with a preexisting mental instability can be nudged into more severe mental disturbances. Next, some otherwise normal users can be thrown into a prolonged psychotic reaction or severe depression. Finally, some people have mental flashbacks to sensations experienced under the influence of LSD, and the flashbacks might happen at dangerous times.

All Arounders
PSILOCYBIN
(Magic Mushrooms)

Psilocybin is the active ingredient in a number of psychedelic mushrooms. Psychic effects are obtained from doses of 20 to 60 mg and generally last for 5 to 6 hours. Both wild and cultivated mushrooms vary greatly in strength so one strong plant might have as much psilocybin as 10 weak ones.

Most mushrooms containing psilocybin are bitter and may cause nausea, vomiting, and other physical symptoms before the mental effects take over. The mental effects include visions perceived with the eyes closed and altered states of consciousness. However, the mental effects are not consistent and depend on the setting in which the drug is taken. In certain North American Indian cultures, ceremonies using the mushrooms are performed by shamans, usually women, to help treat illness, solve problems, foresee the future, and contact the spirit world.

Recently, users have found new supplies of the mushrooms such as a mail order market for growing your

Psilocybin mushrooms ready for harvesting. Most mushrooms sold in the U.S. are dried and old.

own. Some users tramp the countryside looking for a certain species. Unfortunately, the major danger in "shroom" harvesting is mistaking poisonous mushrooms for those containing psilocybin. Some of these (i.e., Amanita Phalloides) can cause death or permanent liver damage within hours of ingestion.

visual hallucinations

One of the many ads encouraging the home cultivation of psychedelic mushrooms to avoid the potentially lethal problem of harvesting poisonous mushrooms by mistake.

MESCALINE (PEYOTE) & OTHERS

Mescaline is the active component of the peyote cactus which is still eaten for religious practices by the Southwestern Plains Indian tribes such as the Huichol, Tarahumara, and Cora. In fact, the Native American Church with 250,000 members uses the peyote cactus as a sacrament. As early as 300 B.C., the ancient Aztecs, Toltecs, and Chichimecas were using peyote for religious purposes.

A mature peyote cactus (Lophophora williamsii) bud is ripe for harvesting. Each bud contains about 45 mg. of mescaline. It can take from 2 to 10 buttons to get high.

The tops of the cactus are cut at ground level and dried into peyote "buttons." They are either eaten (7 to 8 buttons is an average dose) or boiled and drunk as a tea. The effects of mescaline, which last approximately 12 hours, are very similar to LSD with an emphasis on colorful "visions." Users term it the "mellow LSD," but real hallucinations are more common with mescaline than with LSD. Unfortunate-

ly, each use of the drug is usually accompanied by a severe episode of nausea and vomiting.

wavy flexability

IBOGAINE

Made from the African Iboga plant, ibogaine is a long-acting psychedelic and stimulant. It produces a profound catatonic reaction, more intense than that experienced with PCP. It is rarely found here. Its use is generally restricted to native cultures in Africa.

MORNING GLORY SEEDS

These seeds contain an LSD-like substance in low concentration. Used by Indians in Mexico before the Spanish arrived, several hundred seeds have to be taken to get high so the nauseating properties of the drug are exaggerated. Many commercially sold morning glory seeds are dipped in poison to prevent their use as a psychedelic.

DMT

Dimethyltryptamine is a naturally occurring, easily synthesized psychedelic substance. It is usually snorted or smoked. South American, tribes prepare it from several different plants as a snuff called yopo, cohoba, vilca, cebil or epena. In the U.S. it is usually synthesized. It causes intense hallucinations lasting about 30 minutes or less. The short duration of action gave rise to its nickname, "businessman's special."

YAGE

Yage, a psychedelic drink made from an Amazonian vine (ayahuasca, or vine of the soul), causes intense vomiting, diarrhea, and then a dreamlike condition. It lasts up to 10 hours. The drink contains both harmaline and DMT as its active ingredients.

STP (DOM) (4 methyl 2,5 dimethoxy amphetamine)

STP, also called the "serenity, tranquility, and peace pill," is similar to mescaline but synthetic. It causes a 12-hour intoxication characterized by intense stimulation and several mild psychedelic reactions. There are, however, reports that it is a "thicker," "duller" trip than those experienced while on mescaline or LSD.

STP/LSD COMBO

The two drugs are combined to increase the stimulation and the psychedelic effects of the individual drugs. This combo, popular in the late 60's, was sold under the street names of "pinks" and "purple or orange wedges."

MDA, MMDA, MDM, MDE, (Designer psychedelics)

This set of synthetic drugs uses laboratory variations of the amphetamine molecule. First discovered over 70 years ago, the drugs can cause feelings of well being and euphoria along with stimulatory effects, side effects and toxicity similar to amphetamines. The differences among the drugs has to do with duration of action, stimulation of visual perception, and degree of euphoria.

BELLADONNA, JIMSONWEED (THORNAPPLE), DATURA, HENBANE

Also called nightshade, these plants are believed to have been used in witches' brews. The main active ingredients, scopolamine and atropine, can cause a form of delirium, making it hard to focus, speeding up the heart, and dilating the eyes. They also create intense thirst, some hallucinations, and a separation from reality for up to 48 hours.

AMANITA MUSHROOMS

Most members of this family, except the fly agaric and the panther mushroom, are deadly. The effects of the nonpoisonous ones are dreamy intoxication and delirious excitement, though there is some toxicity. The effects start a half hour after ingestion and can last for four to eight hours.

NUTMEG, MACE

At the low end of the "desirable" psychedelic drug spectrum, nutmeg and mace, both from the nutmeg tree, cause varied effects as mild as a floating sensation to a full blown delirium. So much has to be consumed, that the user is left with a bad hangover and a severely upset stomach.

PCP

Phencyclidine or PCP, also called "angel dust," "ice," "peep," "KJ," "Shermans," or "ozone," is the most misrepresented drug around. It was originally created as a general anesthetic for humans. However, the frequency and severity of toxic effects soon limited its use to veterinary medicine which was later discontinued. Now, the only supplies are illegal. PCP can be smoked in a joint, snorted, swallowed, or injected. Its psychic effects have been described as mind-body disassociation or sensory deprivation. It appears to distort sensory messages sent to the central nervous system. It stifles inhibitions and deadens pain.

This cat is being prepared for surgery using the anesthetic, PCP. A large dose causes catatonia.

PCP User: "If you smoke it, depending on how strong the joint is, you just kind of get a floating sensation about one minute after you take your first few tokes. And you just get a really numbed sensation. I mean, there are actual rooms I go in that don't exist. Some people would call it a psychotic state."

Since PCP is so strong, particularly for first time users, the range between a dose that produces a pleasant sensory deprivation effect and one that induces catatonia, coma, or convulsions is very small. Low dosages (2 to 5 mg) produce first mild depression, then stimulation. Moderate doses (10 to 15 mg) can produce a desirable sensory-deprived state. They can also produce extremely high blood pressure and very combative behavior. Other adverse reactions to moderate doses include an inability to talk, a rigid robotic attitude, confusion, agitation, and paranoid thinking. Dosages just a little higher, above 20 mg can cause catatonia, coma, and convulsions. Large PCP doses have also produced seizures, respiratory depression, and cardiovascular instability. PCP also induces amnesia while under its influence.

PCP User: "I've had seizures before on it and banged my head really hard, continually on hard objects and got lots of bumps and everything and felt them the next few days but never realized I was doing it or never felt hurt from it."

The effects of a small dose of PCP will last one to two hours but the effects of a large dose can last much longer (up to 48 hours), longer than those produced by a similar dose of LSD. Further, current evidence shows that PCP is retained by the body for several months in fatty cells. The PCP stored in fat can be released during exercise or fasting resulting in a true chemical PCP flashback. This also results from the drug's recirculation from the brain, to the blood, to the stomach, to the intestines, then back to the blood and brain. This is called enterogastric recirculation.

PCP is not widely used by the general street population because of the frequency of bad trips associated with it. PCP is often sold as THC or mescaline to unsuspecting drug users. When the psychic effects kick in, the surprised user can really have a bad trip.

However, PCP can cause an emotional addiction resulting in high levels of abuse in certain populations.

KETAMINE (Ketalar, Ketaject, Super-K)

This close relative of PCP, Ketamine, is still available by prescription. It is used to control severe pain such as pain from burns and is not as closely watched as other restricted drugs. It's usually injected but can be evaporated to solid crystals, powdered and smoked, snorted, or swallowed.

1936

DOPE FOUND GROWING
IN BROOKLYN GARDEN

1986

Increases in Potency of Marijuana
Prompt New Warnings for Youths

By PETER KERR

State Widens
This Year's
Marijuana War

By Birney Jarvis

The state's Campaign
Against Marijuana Planting
will expand its eradication program to two...

1985

Illinois Valley pot raids net 600 plants; 5 jailed

GRANTS PASS — Five people were arrested on drug charges Monday and over 600 growing marijuana plants were seized in simultaneous raids at four Illinois Valley locations.

Marijuana Spray
Spoils Dope Ring's
$5,000,000 Dream

WEEDS GO

1988

Pot Plants
From India Are
Big in Thailand

Reuters

Prachinburi, Thailand
A hardy, tall, quick-growing strain of Indian marijuana is proving a hit with Thai traffickers, said police who have destroyed two tons of it.

MITCHUM IN
MARIJUANA
ARREST

1949

By RUTH BRIGHAM

HOLLYWOOD, Sept. 2 (INS).
Movie Hero Robert Mitchum, a marijuana smoking party.

1937

1984

U.S. judge halts paraquat use

Court agrees government must consider the environmental impact

WASHINGTON (UPI) — A federal judge today temporarily blocked the Drug Enforcement Administration from spraying the herbicide paraquat to eradicate illegal marijuana fields growing on federal lands.

Grifa is one of the Spanish words for marijuana (along with "mota"). It was a patented name for a brand of marjuana cigarettes that was going to be marketed if marijuana ever became legal. Other names like "Acapulco Gold" and "Panama Red" were also patented for this projected eventuality.

The marijuana plant produces a useful fiber (hemp), an edible seed, an oil, a medicine, and several psychoactive substances. Parts of the plant, including the flowers and leaves, can be smoked or eaten to alter the physical and mental states of the user.

Marijuana is also written about endlessly in every newspaper and magazine, researched in dozens of laboratories, smoked in hundreds of countries, and forbidden by thousands

Marijuana propaganda, popular in the late 30's and 40's, depicted the drug as the devil (Moloch) incarnate and its peddlers as devil servants. Note, learned men and judges are shown with their backs turned to the problem, ignoring or denying its existence.

of laws. Add to this the fact that the marijuana of the late 80's is a different drug than the marijuana of the 60's and you can see why confusion reigns in medical, political, law enforcement, and user circles.

The major difference with the new marijuana is the potency of its main psychoactive ingredient, THC. Potency has shot up from a 1% to 3% concentration in the 60's and 70's to an 8% to 14% concentration in the 80's. So, all the studies done in the 60's and 70's with a more dilute form of the drug or with refined THC are inaccurate. In addition 200 to 300 other substances in the cannabis plant have been identified, and while their psychoactive qualities remain under study, there's no doubt that their existence vastly complicates any research. And finally, while a drug like alcohol or cocaine is converted into just a few other metabolites (chemicals) by the body, marijuana is converted by the liver into 45 or more different, potentially psychoactive substances.

In contrast to marijuana users in the early 70's, users in the 80's begin smoking at a much earlier age and are more likely to become habitual users than experimenters. The most significant increase has been among 12 to 17-year-olds. Regular use by high school seniors surveyed in 1980 was over 10%.

There are three species of marijuana (Cannabis); the most common, and most psychoactive, is Cannabis sativa.

Female flowering top of Cannabis sativa with relatively long slender leaf projections.

Another species, Cannabis indica, used to have a lower concentration of THC. New modifications have resulted in a much stronger variety of this plant called "skunk weed."

Immature Cannabis indica with shorter, stout leafs.

Cannabis ruderalis, a short species of the cannabis bush, has virtually no psychoactive ingredients.

Cannabis sativa and indica come in many varieties and can be grown almost anywhere in the world. The biggest change in growing methods has been the **sinsemilla** growing technique. Contrary to popular belief, sinsemilla is not a separate plant.

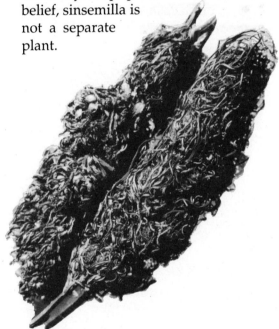

Harvested and dried flowering "bud" of Cannabis indica. Premium "ganja" marijuana, ready for packaging and sale at $200 to $300 an ounce.

The sinsemilla technique, which involves separating female plants from male plants before pollination, can be used to increase the THC concentration of any kind of cultivated cannabis.

Marijuana leaves and flowers can be crushed and rolled into cigarettes. They can also be used in food or in drinks. The leaves can also be chewed. In India, marijuana is divided into three different strengths, each one of which comes from a different part of the plant. Bhang is the stem and leaves with the lowest potency. Ganja is made from the stronger leaves and flowering tops, and charas, or hashish, is the concentrated resin from the plant.

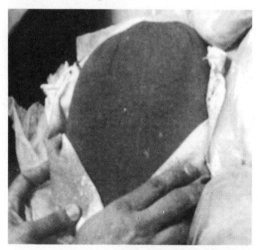

A brick of hashish, usually containing 10% to 20% THC. In India, one of its other names is "charas."

The sticky resin, which contains most of the THC, can be collected and pressed into cakes. This concentrated form is called **hashish**. It is usually smoked in pipes but can be added to a "joint" to enhance the concentration of THC. Since hashish is more concentrated, it is easier to smuggle.

Hash oil can be extracted from the plant (using solvents) and added to foods or used to enhance the psychoactive content of marijuana joints. It can contain up to 40% THC.

THC has also been extracted and purified for use in medicines. Synthetic THC was approved for use in the U.S. in 1985. In fact, the medicinal use of marijuana was referred to more than 4,000 years ago in ancient Chinese medical texts. At the turn of the century, drug companies such as Parke Davis, Squibb, Lilly, and Burroughs Wellcome manufactured extracts of the marijuana plant for use in various medicines.

Worldwide, according to the United Nations, marijuana in its many forms is used by more than 200 million people.

A-4   Sunday, October 9, 1988 ★ ★

Glaucoma patients fighting hazy laws on marijuana use

By Kevin Davis
FORT LAUDERDALE NEWS & SUN-SENTINEL

HOLLYWOOD, Fla. — Elvy Musikka can't see why she should go blind when there's a simple way to save her sight.

Musikka is a glaucoma patient whose use of marijuana was declared a medical necessity Aug. 15 by a Broward County judge. She's still waiting for the federal govern-

ment to give her the drug she says she is legally entitled to.

"My loss of sight is definitely a result of this ridiculous law," said Musikka, already blind in her right eye. "I am going blind."

Since her acquittal by Browar Circuit Judge Mark Polen on charge of growing pot in her ba yard, Musikka has been get marijuana from her friends w she can.

"Anyone who's helping n

The Effects

Within 20 minutes of smoking, marijuana can induce (depending on the strength) a dreamlike effect in which the user is a bit confused and separated from the environment. It produces a feeling of deja vu where everything seems familiar but really isn't. There is also a detached, aloof feeling and difficulty concentrating.

Smoker #1: "The highs are different depending on what kind it is and what kind of mood you're in. I've smoked it at times and not got high at all."

Like most psychedelics, the mental effects of marijuana are very dependent on the mood of the smoker and the surroundings. Marijuana acts almost as a mild hypnotic, exaggerating mood and personality, and making the smoker more suggestible to other's feelings.

Smoker #2: "Sometimes you can't just let out feelings when you're straight. But if you're with your girlfriend or someone close, you can let out your feelings a lot and the way you feel about things."

Marijuana can act as a stimulant or depressant depending on the variety and amount of chemical that is absorbed in the brain, but most often, it acts as a relaxant, making users sleepy, drowsy, and more inner-focused so they are less socially interactive.

Smoker #3: "It makes time go by fast, sometimes slow, depending on if you're watching the clock or if you're bored."

The loss of a sense of time is responsible for several of the perceived effects of grass. Dull, repetitive jobs seem to go by faster. In Jamaica, cane field workers used to smoke ganja to make their hard and repetitive jobs pass by more quickly.

Smoker #2: "You get real hungry; you get the munchies. The other thing is I don't do it when I play sports, especially serious sports, or when you're going out with the kids at P.E. It slows you down."

Marijuana impairs tracking ability (the ability to follow a moving object, such as a baseball, with one's eyes).

A major concern of health professionals is the damaging effect that marijuana smoking has on the lungs and breathing passages. A single joint contains the same amount of tar and other noxious substances as approximately 14 to 16 filtered cigarettes. These toxins irritate the throat and lungs. Frequent "pot" smoking has been associated with an increased risk of lung cancer, bronchitis, and emphysema. Some evidence also suggests that heavy use can depress the immune system, making users susceptible to a cold, the flu, and other viral infections.

Other physical effects include an increased heart rate, decreased blood pressure, decreased pressure behind the eyes (pills or joints are used as a treatment for glaucoma), and decreased nausea (pills, joints, or even injection are used for cancer patients undergoing chemotherapy).

An assortment of marijuana rolling papers. Note the fancy designs compared to standard tobacco papers.

User #3: "If you go home and have homework to do that night and you say, 'O.K. I'm going to get stoned before I do my homework,' you're never going to get your homework done."

Marijuana has been shown to slow learning and disrupt concentration. It has a specific effect on short term memory. Short term memory, very different from long term memory, is a processing of information to be retained for only a short period of time such as a grocery list, a proper assortment of tools for a certain job, or facts crammed into the head for an upcoming exam.

Marijuana impairs this process. However, it has very little effect on long term memory, which is the processing of information for a long period of time such as a theory in physics that has been worked on for several weeks.

User #2: "If I didn't smoke none of it when I went to school, I would have done a lot better, but if someone has some stuff you haven't had for a while and says 'What about a dubie?', you just light up some and go to class real stupid."

Although the research is controversial, many chronic users show a certain apathy and lack of motivation. They have a strong tendency to neglect their life's problems and delay their emotional maturation and growth. A number of long term users report the sensation of coming out of a fog when they finally give up daily use of grass.

A collection of hand rolled marijuana joints, ready for a light. A joint, in the schoolyard will go for anywhere from $3 to $10.

Closeup of cured sinsemilla (unpollinated female flowering top of marijuana plant). Notice the abundance of small hairlike projections along all parts of the vegetative material. These are actual THC crystals.

Smoker #4: "It feels good if you quit for a while. You just don't use it for a long time. It does feel better if you don't smoke it every day."

We do know that marijuana causes a temporary disruption of the secretion of the male hormone testosterone. That might be critical to a user with hormonal imbalance or somebody in the throes of puberty and sexual maturation. It also slightly decreases organ size in males, temporarily.

More concentrated forms of marijuana result in a true psychedelic effect, where actual physical stimuli are perceived in a unique way; e.g., flowers taking on different shapes and scenery taking on different forms. Most often, colors become more intense and music sounds louder and more distinct when smoking strong marijuana.

Such extreme reactions can lead to acute anxiety or temporary psychotic reactions when individuals believe that they have lost control of their mental state and have become psychotic. There's often paranoia or a belief that they have damaged themselves severely or that their underlying insecurities are insurmountable.

Of great concern about marijuana is the discovery that it persists in the body for up to six months after a single joint is smoked though the major effects are over within 4 to 6 hours after smoking. These residual amounts in the body may disrupt some physiological functions for a much longer period though research is skimpy on this point.

Smoker #1: "If you smoke it and smoke it, you can't get no higher after a while; it's just a waste of smoking."

Tolerance to marijuana occurs in a rapid and dramatic fashion. Although high dose chronic users can recognize the effects of low levels of THC in their

A poster distributed by CAMP (Campaign Against Maijuana Planting) has aggressively attacked the illegal growing of marijuana since the early 1970's. Despite their best efforts, every state has its own marijuana crop. Many growers now cultivate their crop indoors, in greenhouses and large warehouses, to avoid CAMP detection from the air or by informants.

systems, they are able to tolerate much higher levels without some of the more severe emotional and psychic effects experienced by a first time user.

Smoker #3: "Burns you out to the point that you can't get up for work the next morning. It's what I call, 'the marijuana hangover.'"

Chronic use of marijuana has now been demonstrated to cause a mild physical withdrawal syndrome. Symptoms include headaches; anxiety, depression, restlessness, sleep disturbances, change in brain waves, craving for the drug, and irritability. These problems may persist for several weeks after quitting the drug.

The 1980's has made us take a different view of the addiction potential of this substance. Today, many people smoke the drug in a chronic, compulsive way and have difficulty discontinuing their use. Like cocaine, heroin, alcohol, nicotine, and other addictive drugs, marijuana does have the ability to induce compulsive use in spite of negative consequences in a user's life. Finally, all available research on marijuana was based on a THC calculation of 20 mg per marijuana cigarette. Current street "joints" are routinely analyzed to contain 40 mg or more of THC. Thus, researchers really aren't sure what they're dealing with in the marijuana of the 80's or 90's.

1. The most commonly used psychedelics are marijuana, LSD, PCP, peyote, psilocybin (magic mushrooms), and MDMA (or other variations of the amphetamine molecule).

2. A major physical effect of psychedelics, other than marijuana, PCP, or anticholinergics, is stimulation.

3. The most frequent mental effects of psychedelics are intensified sensations, particularly visual ones, suppressed memory centers, and disrupted judgment and reasoning.

4. The effects of all arounders are particularly dependent on the size of the dose, the emotional makeup of the user, the mood at the time of use, and the user's surroundings.

5. LSD is extremely potent. Doses as low as 25 micrograms (25 millionths of a gram) can cause intoxication.

6. Like many other psychedelics, LSD overloads the brainstem, the sensory switchboard for the mind, and creates distortions and illusions.

7. Psilocybin is the active ingredient in "magic mushrooms."

8. After initial nausea or vomiting, visual delusions and a certain altered state of consciousness are the most common effects of mushrooms.

9. Mushrooms and peyote buttons have been used in religious ceremonies by many Indian tribes.

10. Mescaline is the active ingredient of the peyote cactus.

11. Eating peyote buttons, or drinking them in a prepared tea, causes color-filled visions and vivid hallucinations after an initial nausea and physical stimulation.

12. Belladonna and other nightshade plants contain scopolamine and atropine. In low doses, these substances cause a mild stupor, but as the dose increases, delirium, hallucinations, and a separation from reality are common.

13. PCP (angel dust) is an anesthetic, now illegal, which, besides deadening sensation, disassociates users from their surroundings and senses.

14. Effects of the drug PCP include amnesia, extremely high blood pressure, and combativeness. Higher doses can produce tremors, seizures, catatonia, coma, and even kidney failure.

15. Marijuana, which is usually smoked, can also be eaten.

16. Current street marijuana is 3 to 7 times more potent than the marijuana of the 60's and early 70's.

17. The sinsemilla technique of growing Cannabis sativa or Cannabis indica is a major reason for the increase in potency of marijuana.

18. Smoking marijuana can cause a dreamlike effect, a certain sedation, and a mild self-hypnosis making users more likely to exaggerate their mood and react to the surroundings.

19. Some of the negative effects of marijuana are lowered testosterone levels, a decrease in the ability to do complicated tasks, a temporary disruption of short term memory, decreased tracking ability (an impairment of eye-hand coordination), and a loss of the sense of time.

20. Large amounts of marijuana can cause anxiety reactions, paranoia, and some hallucinations.

21. Chronic marijuana users show a certain apathy, a tendency to neglect life's problems.

22. When stopping chronic marijuana use, one can suffer a withdrawal syndrome which includes headache, anxiety, depression, restlessness, and sleep disturbances.

QUESTIONS

1. Name five psychedelics.

2. What factors are most important in determining the effect of a psychedelic on the user?

3. What is the most common physical effect of most psychedelics?

4. What sense is most affected by psychedelics?

5. What part of the brain is overloaded by LSD?

6. What is the best way to treat someone on a bad LSD trip?

7. Where, in nature, is psilocybin found?

8. What is the most uncomfortable physical effect of psilocybin (magic mushrooms) and peyote?

9. From which plant is mescaline extracted?

10. What are the major effects of scopolamine and atropine?

11. What are the major effects of a low dose of PCP? What about a moderate to high dose?

12. What is the biggest difference between a marijuana cigarette from 1970 and one from 1989?

13. What are hashish and hash oil?

14. What is the deja vu effect of marijuana?

15. What are the known negative effects of marijuana?

16. Does tolerance develop to marijuana?

17. What are the withdrawal effects when stopping chronic use of marijuana?

INHALANTS, OTHER DRUGS
& POLYDRUG ABUSE

INHALANTS

The three main types of inhalants are organic solvents (hydrocarbons), volatile nitrites (amyl, butyl, isobutyl), and nitrous oxide. The substances are inhaled from bottles, soaked rags, bags, balloons, or gas tanks.

ORGANIC SOLVENTS

The use of industrial solvents and aerosol sprays to induce a state of intoxication is most widespread among 10 to 20 year-olds. These volatile liquids include gasoline, kerosene, chloroform, alcohol, airplane glue, lacquer thinner, acetone, benzene (nail polish remover, model cement), naphtha (lighter fluid), carbon tetra-chloride, fluoride based sprays, metallic paints and most recently, typewriter correction fluids.

Inhaling these substancess produces a temporary stimulation and reduced inhibitions before the CNS depressive effects begin; dizziness, slurred speech, unsteady gait, and drowsiness are seen early on. Impulsiveness, excitement, and irritability may also occur. As the CNS becomes more deeply affected, illusions, hallucinations, and delusions develop. The user experiences a dreamy euphoria culminating in a short period of sleep. Delirium with confusion, psychomotor clumsiness, emotional instability, and impaired thinking are seen. The intoxicated state may last from minutes to an hour or more.

Complications may result from the effect of the solvent or other toxic ingredients such as lead in gasoline. Injuries to the brain, liver, kidney, bone marrow, and particularly the lungs can occur and may be from either heavy exposure or individual hypersensitivity. Death occurs from respiratory arrest, cardiac arrhythmias, or asphyxia due to occlusion of the airway.

Huffing: soaking a rag in turpentine, paint, or another solvent and then inhaling it. Huffers use a wide variety of substances but usually have a liquid of choice.

VOLATILE NITRITES

Inhalation of amyl nitrite "poppers" to alter consciousness and enhance sexual pleasure has emerged in recent years. This use has been particularly prominent in urban male homosexual society. When amyl nitrite was returned to the pre-scription drug category, entrepreneurs began to market other nitrites (butyl, isobutyl) under a variety of names; i.e., Locker Room, Rush, Bolt, Quick Silver, Zoom, etc.

Emphasism

last up to 1 hr

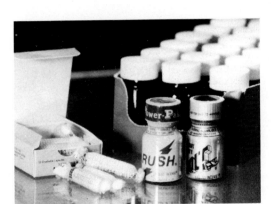

Isobutyl, butyl, or amyl nitrite, sold under various trade names fom the 1970's, were some of the first successful designer drug trends. For example, a prescription drug, amyl nitrite, was chemically rearranged to create a legal derivative, and sold as a room odorizer, to circumvent drug laws.

The major effect of nitrites is the relaxation of all smooth muscles in the body including those around the blood vessels. More blood flows to the heart and brain, and less to other parts of the body. Effects start in 7 or 10 seconds and last about 30 seconds.

There is a rush of blood to the brain that may be followed by severe headaches, dizziness, and giddiness. A tolerance develops rapidly to the gas, though prolonged use may cause nitrite poisoning, vomiting, shock, unconsciousness; or blood problems.

NITROUS OXIDE

This is one of the earliest documented abused inhalants. Now known as "laughing gas," it was first developed and abused by Joseph Priestly in 1776. Currently available in large blue painted gas tanks for dental offices and bakeries, whipping cream aerosol cans and small metal cylinders, nitrous oxide is abused for its mood-altering effects. Within 8 to 10 seconds of constant inhalation, the gas produces a giddiness and stimulation often accompanied by profound laughter. There is a buzzing or ringing in the ears along with a sense that one is about to collapse or pass out. These feelings quickly stop when nitrous oxide leaves the body.

Dangers with the abuse of this gas include exploded or frozen lung tissue and frostbite of the tips of the nose and vocal cords from direct inhalation out of a large pressurized tank. This risk is minimized when inhaled from a balloon inflated with the gas. Long term exposure also causes nerve and brain cell damage due to lack of sufficient oxygen in the blood (nitrous oxide replaces oxygen). Further, nitrous oxide use can lead to dependence. Also, there is the danger of passing out and getting hurt from the fall.

Gas cartridges (capsules) of nitrous oxide sold for whipping cream but often diverted to the inhalant abuser.

The Drugs
OTHERS

A toad indigenous to Santa Cruz county in California, Australia, and South America is a living and hopping psychoactive drug. Bufotenine, a powerful psychedelic compound, is secreted from its skin and has been abused for decades. It's illegal to own the toad.

It's amazing what substances and methods people will use to get high: inhaling typewriter correction fluid, drinking hair tonic, snorting nutmeg, ingesting C4, a plastic explosive, smoking herbal medicines, and swallowing antihistamines. Steroids, cough suppressants, over-the-counter diet pills, and even ginseng root are also abused. It's not only the inherent qualities of the drug but also society's attitude toward the substance that determines which drugs are available for abuse. For example:

Heroin was prescribed as a cure for alcoholism and even morphine addiction. Cocaine was available in soda pops (e.g. Coca-Cola) to "perk us up" until it was restricted in 1914. Marijuana growing and its medicinal use was legal until 1938.

And finally, there is no limit to the imagination of street chemists in either synthesizing now illegal drugs such as Quaaludes, PCP, Fentanyl, and the like or in creating new drugs such as the amphetamine alphabet-soup psychedelics: MDA, MDMA, and MDE.

The danger, of course, is that street drugs have not been tested and are not made under any kind of control so contaminants can have disastrous results. For example, recently, a group of China White heroin users (really a synthetic Demerol derivative-MPPP) were found to have an 80% incidence of Parkinson's disease symptoms (rigid muscles, loss of voluntary body control) caused by contamination of the drug with MPTP, a byproduct of sloppy synthesis in the laboratory. As more and more untested synthetic drugs hit the street, produced by illicit chemists, we can expect to experience more tragedies like the MPTP nightmare.

Medicine

Surprising Clue to Parkinson's
A California street drug is linked to the disease

When George Carillo arrived at the Santa Clara Valley Medical Center in San Jose one steamy July day in 1982, he seemed more a mannequin than a man. The 42-year-old heroin addict was bent over and twisted, drooling and unable to speak, almost every muscle was immobilized. No one knew what to make of his condition, so a call went out for Dr. J. William Langston, the hospital's chief neurologist. Langston took one look and was amazed. Carillo's symptoms suggested that he had been suffering for at least a decade from Parkinson's disease, a nervous system disorder that causes tremors and a gradual loss of mobility. But that hardly seemed plausible. Parkinson's rarely strikes anyone under the age of 50.

Using stiffened fingers to scrawl answers to doctors' questions, Carillo managed to provide a few clues. The symptoms had come on suddenly after he and his girlfriend, Juanita Lopez, 31, had tried a new synthetic heroin. Though the drug had caused an odd burning sensation when injected and hallucinations, they continued to use it for three days, two days later both had frozen into living statues.

With help from colleagues at Stanford University, where he teaches, Langston located Lopez and had her hospitalized. A tip from a neurologist in Watsonville, 30 miles away, led him to two more cases a pair of brothers, both addicts in their 20s, with advanced Parkinson's symptoms. By now Langston was alarmed. He called a

Langston with a model of the MPTP molecule

press conference to announce that bad heroin was on the streets; he urged that anyone suffering from stiffness and tremors come forward. The appeal uncovered three more cases.

The seven cases in Santa Clara County attracted the attention of local drug-enforcement officials and Parkinson's researchers at the National Institute of Mental Health (NIMH), who joined the hunt to identify the deadly ingredient in samples of the drug obtained by police. Their task was made easier by an alert toxicologist at the

county crime laboratory, who recalled the 1977 case of a Maryland graduate student who had developed Parkinson's symptoms after injecting himself with a home-brewed opiate. The student had been trying to produce a substance similar to the pain-killer Demerol, but had accidentally created a related chemical called MPTP. Langston asked Stanford University Chemist Ian Irwin to test the samples for the drug. Sure enough, MPTP was there.

While public health authorities worried about additional cases of drug-induced Parkinson's and police pondered how to stop the sale of a drug that was not illegal (see box), medical researchers could hardly contain their excitement. The tragic outbreak in California could hold the key to understanding and treating Parkinson's disease, which afflicts some 350,000 Americans.

The scientists quickly turned to the task. For years research on Parkinson's disease has been limited by the lack of an animal model on which to test new drugs and treatments. Would MPTP induce Parkinson's in animals? The answer: NIMH Researchers Sanford Markey and R. Stanley Burns soon discovered, was no in rats but yes in monkeys. Says Markey: "That was probably the biggest breakthrough in this story."

The next step was to find out how MPTP did its damage. Doctors have known since the 1930s that Parkinson's occurs as a result of the deterioration of a small, darkly pigmented region of the brain called the *substantia nigra*. This region produces most of the brain's supply of dopamine, a vital chemical in the transmission of nerve signals. Normally, people lose 5% to 8% of the cells in this region each decade of their

Death by Design

They look like heroin, they act like heroin, and they satisfy an addict's urge just like the real thing. But when subjected to a chemist's scrutiny, the narcotics that have been flooding California turn out to be something else. They are "designer drugs"—designed, that is, to get around the law.

The drugs are created by underground chemists who tinker with the molecular structure of illegal narcotics to produce variants that are not explicitly banned by federal law. Thus it is legal to make and use designer drugs. But it is by no means safe, as those who toyed with MPTP have learned.

Police in Orange County, Calif., first encountered designer drugs in 1979, when they found two young addicts lying dead near samples of a heroin-like powder. Thirteen more users had died before Forensic Chemist Donald Cooper of the U.S. Drug Enforcement Administration managed to identify the substance. It was a designer version of the anesthetic fentanyl, which

Heroin look-alikes

is widely used during prolonged surgery. The variant was many times as powerful as heroin; just a little could be an overdose.

The drug was outlawed in 1981, but another modified fentanyl instantly appeared on the streets; when the second drug was banned, a third popped up. So far, eight designer-like drugs have appeared, one of them a thousand times the strength of heroin. All told, they have killed at least 90 people.

California authorities believe that 20% of the addicts in the state have used designer dope. And, says Pharmacologist Gary Henderson, an expert on designer drugs at the University of California at Davis, the drugs are now favored by affluent cocaine users as a way of taking the "edge" off coke.

Experts suspect that the designer fentanyls are the work of a single evil genius (who must now be very wealthy; some $2 million worth of drugs can be produced from $200 worth of chemicals). Cooper says that the lab work is so sophisticated that "I just don't think more than one person could be doing it."

TIME, APRIL 8, 1985

61

Some of the more unusual drugs that are abused are:

ANTIHISTAMINES

Antihistamines are taken to control allergic reactions, suppress the symptoms of respiratory infections such as the flu or colds, or control asthma. The drug is prescribed in dozens of compounds and found in numerous over-the- counter preparations. Unfortunately, antihistamines can also affect our mood and reasoning; depression, drowsiness and fuzzy thinking are common side effects. One of the combinations used by some drug abusers are an antihistamine and Talwin (an opioid) known as "T's and Blues." Some people become compulsive about their use of antihistamines, mostly for the depressive (sedating) effect of the drug. Overuse can cause respiratory and circulatory problems, addiction, and even hallucinations from high doses..

DESIGNER DRUGS (UNCONTROLLED ANALOGUES)

Two recent "designer" psychedelic drugs are 2-CB (4 bromo 2,5 dimethoxy phene-thylamine) and U4Euh (Euphoria or 4 methyl aminorex). Both substances are synthetic amphetamine-like derivatives which produce major psychedelic effects and are just now becoming more available to street drug users.

CAMEL DUNG

Some arab countries produce hashish by force feeding ripe marijuana plants to camels. Their four chambered stomachs compact the marijuana into hashish camel dung.

C4 EXPLOSIVES

Modern veterans have been known to ingest C4 or cyclonite plastic explosives for their psychedelic effects. Tremors and seizure activity can result but usually not an explosion as it takes a blasting cap to set off the chemical.

EMBALMING FLUID (formaldehyde)

Mortuaries have been broken into and robbed of their embalming fluid. It can either be directly abused (inhaled for its depressant and psychedelic effects) or it can be used in the manufacture of other illicit drugs. Some users soak marijuana in the fluid and smoke it. Called "clickers" or "clickems," the mixture gives a PCP like effect. Formaldehyde is a known carcinogen.

GASOLINE

In spite of the toxicity of leaded or unleaded gasoline, a few kids and adults have been known to mix it with orange juice and drink it. The life expectancy of these abusers is particularly short. Most often it is inhaled for depressant and psychedelic effects.

STEROIDS: *See "Drugs in the Environment-Sports," page 186.*

POLYDRUG ABUSE

Cocaine/alcohol user: "Alcohol was the great buffer for coke. Pills were also good, but booze...because coke is such a social thing and so is alcohol, the two just mix so beautifully together. For me, my drinking just came alive at that time, and it was usually never one without the other."

Polydrug use and abuse can be intentional or accidental. The user might want to exaggerate or temper the effect of a drug, or the doctor, treating a patient for a variety of illnesses with different medications, might forget such factors as drug synergism, cross dependence and cross tolerance. People can overdose or become addicted to doses of a drug that are usually too small in and of themselves to cause addiction. For example, a person who drinks alcohol finds that he's having trouble with sleep and takes a sedative. He would have an increased liability of addiction or overdose to both drugs. And though each drug works on different parts of the brain, the physical addiction comes from the combination of the drugs' effects. In fact, most studies of drug abusers in this country show that addicts abuse a multitude of different drugs that are available to them. They may have a preference to cocaine but will take alcohol, Valium, heroin, marijuana, or any sedative to help them deal with the hyperactivity caused by cocaine.

Popular polydrug combinations are

The mixture of **Doriden** and **codeine** which is known as **"loads,"** **"sets"** or **"setups," "four by fours,"** or **"fours and doors."** Both are downers.

The combination of **cocaine** and **marijuana** is known as "c**hampagne," "caviar,"** or **"gremmies."** The marijuana is used to take the edge off the stimulation of cocaine.

The combination of **cocaine** and **alcohol** is called a **"crack cooler"** when mixed in a wine cooler. This combination also dulls the stimulation of cocaine.

The combination of **heroin** and **cocaine, heroin** and an **amphetamine,** or **heroin** and **Ritalin** are all known as **"speedballs."** The combination of an upper and a downer, called speedballing, makes it easier to overdose because when the upper kicks in, you think you need more and more downers and then all of a sudden, the downers kick in and you've taken too many. It's a roller coaster ride since each drug is metabolized at a different rate and each drug affects different sites of the brain. When smokable cocaine is smoked with tar heroin, the combination is called **"hot rocks."**

Cocaine mixed and smoked with **PCP,** known as **"spacebase"** or **"whack,"** provides the user with an intense rush followed by the long-lasting psychedelic effects of the PCP.

Cocaine has also been mixed with **crank** or amphetamines to produce a euphoric, long-lasting stimulation. This combination has been called **"super crank."**

Crank (methamphetamine) mixed with **Cogentin** or **Artane** produces a stimulation psychedelic effect that is sought after by a number of speed freaks. Cogentin and Artane are medications used to counteract the side effects of antipsychotic drugs (i.e. Thorazine).

Other combinations are

Alcohol and **Valium** or **Valium** and **methadone.** When users of the last combination become tolerant to the methadone, the Valium kicks in, making the depressant effect that much stronger. Even antidepressant drugs like Sinequan and Elavil have been used with methadone for this purpose.

Recently, a benzodiazepine called **Clonopin,** very similar to Valium, is taken with **methadone** or **heroin** to bolster the effects of both drugs. This has become quite widespread, creating a new illicit market for this diverted prescription drug.

Quaalude and **Benedryl,** a sedative and an antihistamine, when used together are called a **"Mandrake."**

Opiates/opioids (heroin, codeine, Dilaudid) are mixed with **antihistamines** like Phenergan or Benadryl to counter the nausea and itchiness of the opiates.

Usually, when there is a drug problem, there is a primary drug of choice, but if it's in short supply, the user will likely use whatever drug is available. Oftentimes, this results in multiple chemical dependencies.

REVIEW

1. The three main types of inhalants are volative solvents, volatile nitrites, and nitrous oxide.

2. Volatile solvents consist of fluids such as gasoline, kerosene, airplane glue, nail polish remover, lighter fluid, carbon tetrachloride, and even embalming fluid.

3. The effects of volatile solvents, mostly depressant, include dizziness, and slurred speech. Impulsiveness and irritability give way to hallucinations and delusions. Eventually, delerium, clumsiness, and impaired thinking occur.

4. Prolonged use of volatile solvents, especially leaded gasoline, can lead to brain, liver, kidney, bone marrow and especially lung damage. Death can occur from respiratory arrest or cardiac irregularities.

5. Volatile nitrites, "poppers" such as butyl or isobutyl nitrite are sold as Bolt, Rush, and Locker Room. The major effects are muscle relaxation and blood vessel dilation causing a blood rush to the head. Dizziness and giddiness also occur. Too much can lead to vomiting, shock, unconsciousness, and blood vessel problems.

6. Other drugs used for their psychoactive effects include antihistamines, designer drugs, even typewriter correction fluid

7. Antihistamines, used to control allergic reactions, comes in hundred of compounds, i.e., cold and asthmatic medicines. They can cause drowsiness, fuzzy thinking and eventually, respiratory and circulatory problems.

8. Designer psychedelic drugs which are mostly variations of amphetamines, create many of the effects and side effects associated with speed.

9. Almost all drug users who come in for treatment have problems with more than one drug.

10. Using more than one drug creates a synergistic effect, that is, more effects than just adding up the separate effects.

11. The more widely used polydrug combinations are Doriden and codeine "loads" or "fours and doors;" cocaine and alcohol; heroin and cocaine or heroin and speed "speedballs;" Talwin and antihistamines "T's and blues".

12. Designer heroins, fentanyl and Demerol derivatives are often misrepresented as "China White" heroin.

13. Designer Demerols (MPPP and others) are often adulterated with MPTP which causes irreversible Parkinson's disease.

QUESTIONS

1. What are the three main types of inhalants?

2. Name 3 different types of volatile solvents.

3. Name 3 different volatile nitrites.

4. What are the major effects of volatile solvents?

5. What are the major effects of volatile nitrites?

6. What is the main use of antihistamines?

7. What are the main side effects of antihistamines?

8. What are the main effects of designer psychedelic drugs?

9. What are synergistic effects?

10. What is a "speedball"?

11. What are "loads" or "sets"?

12. What are "T's and blues"?

13. Why is alcohol or Valium taken with cocaine?

14. Give three examples of "speedball" combinations.

15. What street names are used to indicate the combination of smokable cocaine with PCP?

16. List two designer heroins sold as "China White."

17. What is the major cause of Parkinson's disease among heroin abusers?

18. Why are drugs like Cogentin and Artane taken with crank (methamphetamine)?

19. What are "hot rocks" and "crack coolers"?

20. Describe the effect of taking antihistamines with opiates/opioids.

21. List two reasons for the development of polydrug patterns.

Kids Who Sell Crack

The drug trade has become the nation's newest—and most frightening—job program

The homeboys call him Frog. But as he swaggers through the Rancho San Pedro Housing Project in East Los Angeles, Frog is a cocky prince of the barrio. His mane of lustrous jeri curls, his freckled nose and innocent brown eyes belie his prodigious street smarts. Frog is happy to tell you that he rakes in $200 a week selling crack, known as rock in Los Angeles. He proudly advertises his fledgling membership in an ultra-violent street gang, the Crips. And he brags that he has used his drug money to rent a Nissan Z on weekends. He has not yet learned how to use a stick shift, however, and at 4 ft. 10 in., he sometimes has trouble seeing over the dashboard. Frog is 13 years old.

NFL Gives Teams More Leeway for Spot Drug Testing

By CHRIS COBBS, *Times Staff Writer*

SAN DIEGO—Team doctors have new authority to order random tests for suspected drug abusers under conditions spelled out in a recent memo from the National Football League Management Council.

Team physicians, acting on input from position coaches, trainers and strength coaches, now can direct a player to submit to a urinalysis based on a cumulative pattern of danger signals outlined in the memo, a copy

Steroid Use Rampant Among Olympians

By Michael Janofsky with Peter Alfano
New York Times

At least half of the 9,000 athletes who competed at the Olympics in Seoul may have used anabolic steroids in training to enhance their perfor-

es banned by the IOC, as many as 20 other athletes tested positive and were not disqualified, said Dr. Park Jong Sei, the director of the Olympic drug-testing lab in Seoul.

"Maybe this is true," Juan Antonio Samaranch, the IOC president, said this week of the drug-test re-

which are believed to enhance muscle growth, has revealed several other facets of the issue:

■ Estimates of how many Olympic athletes used steroids in training range from 10 percent by Park — a figure he called conservative — to 99.9 percent by David Jen-

"It's an affront to anyone who thinks about the problem," Halpern said.

And with the testing procedures so complex and the ramifications potentially as damaging to the sport as to the athlete, not even people with firsthand knowledge of always certain enough to make accurate judg-

tt, a sports therapist years, worked closely from several countries Olympics, including and the American Lewis.

ed recently at his of-y, Scott said that ath-ny of the smaller na-Olympics "definitely ig people were being Johnson was only added, because of the "foul-up."

nated that 20 percent el athletes use drugs d absolute disregard being." He added that he athletes who com-ul had used some amount of performance-enhancing substances in training.

Ultimately, deterring drug use

How Babies Suffer When Mothers Use Cocaine

Babies born to mothers who used cocaine while pregnant show three major symptoms — tremors, extreme irritability and severe respiratory problems, according to a recent study.

Dr. Rick Fulroth, a pediatrician at Highland Hospital and a member of Stanford University's neonatology staff, said the study he co-wrote also found "some pretty scary stuff" about these babies' growth patterns.

Thirty percent of the infants whose mothers used only cocaine had significantly smaller than normal heads and 20 percent of them had significantly lower than normal birth weights, he said. Tests show children born with these physical characteristics can have low IQs and do poorly in school later in life.

Along with problems evident at birth, doctors also worry about the effects on the baby's brain cells, Fulroth said.

Some doctors fear the pregnant mother's use of crack may lead to long-term or permanent brain damage.

Fetuses become exposed to crack when it passes from the mother's bloodstream through the umbilical cord and into the baby's bloodstream. The cocaine then triggers spasms in the infant's blood vessels, and the spasms can cut the vital flow of oxygen and nutrients from mother to baby. That oxygen and food are critically needed for the baby's proper mental and physical development.

Most drug-exposed babies are short on resources, socially isolate ous, chaotic, violent and perverse Durfee, coordinator of child abus the Los Angeles County Departm

"Why are these people fools' than others because they have m

housing project and are surrounded by drugs and violence, when the welfare check comes, if there are people in your neighborhood hustling drugs, you have a different life than a woman in the suburbs with more resources to fall back on."

Sadly, some mothers hooked on crack may be purposely using the drug to induce premature births when they tire of pregnancy, unaware of the serious damage they may be causing to their unborn babies, said Dr. Jim Green, head of

Workers' Substance Abuse Is Increasing, Survey Says

By MILT FREUDENHEIM

Executives and Federal officials say the use of cocaine and crack is growing rapidly in the workplace, significantly compounding the effects of drug and alcohol abuse, which cost business more than $100 billion a year.

In a recent survey to be released today, a majority of the employers who responded said that 6 percent to 15 percent of their employees have an alcohol or drug problem. Absenteeism, medical expenses and lost pro-

caine is unsafe," Dr. Wienck said. "He uses very poor judgment." Because of distorted thinking, "the quality of his work is frequently diminished," he said.

Substance abuse among G.M.'s 472,000 workers and their dependents cost the automotive company $600 million last year.

The growing concern is evident in recent surveys, other studies and interviews with executives and Government officials.

The survey that will be released today found that the situation has worsened in the last five years. It was con-

a notion on nt and want

f women have caine doesn't

How medicines can turn the elderly into drug abusers

By Susan Paynter

So many people over 60 have become unintentional drug abusers, even 'addicts', that physicians and pharmacists are starting to sound an alarm.

Doctors say abuse of prescription and over-the-counter drugs is more common among the elderly because it is masked in the responsibility of doctors or-ders. Multiple drugs for chronic complaints, this eyesight memory loss and age's effects on the body are just a few things ganging up on the elderly to make drug-induced confusion.

Marti Jones, professor of pharmacology at Washing-ton State University, heads a new program sending senior pharmacy students out to talk to older people about drugs. He says the big problem is duplication of medicines which causes a variety of side-effects from over sedation to blurred vision.

stimulat' by becoming paranoid, disoriented and even belligerent.

To help them manage, nursing homes use a range of 'psychoactive' drugs According to the Journal of American Geriatrics about 75 percent of nursing home patients get at least one such drug.

Still, Dr Jerry Pleur of the University of Washington's School of Pharmacy says they work with such homes shows they keep closer track of patients' medical schedules and dosage than most people get living with their families.

Dr. Weinecke also gave He the pro process as well.

N.Y. swaps needles for lives

Officials hope to reduce AIDS rate among addicts

By George Raine
OF THE EXAMINER STAFF

NEW YORK — A foam rubber mattress is serving nicely as a door for the home and shooting gallery that Doc maintains in a hollowed out above in an abandoned build-ing on Avenue C. Not a hint of light seeps through. It's a rather cozy setting for Doc, Mike, Lloyd and Sal to get high and happy, huddled around a couple of stubby candles.

No one here really wants to talk about AIDS and how the virus that causes it can be picked up from needles heroin users often share. The topic has the same chilling affect on Doc's get-together that the rats did when they started fighting over peanut butter behind the divan.

Just as surely as denial is here on the Lower East Side, one flight up the fire escape just behind the mattress.

There are more than 200,000 intravenous drug users in New York. It is believed that 60 percent of them are infected with the human immunodeficiency virus. That fact

There are more than

D R U G S I N T H E
EVIRONMENT

DRUGS IN THE ENVIRONMENT

Despite the greatly increased awareness of drug abuse in our society, there persists a social denial about its impact on our immediate environment. All too often, drug addicts are thought to fit a certain stereotype. As mentioned in our introduction, that stereotype is of a male from a lower socioeconomic background, poorly educated, ghetto-barrio-chinatown bred, and socially disenfranchised.

If the staff of the Haight-Ashbury Drug Detox Clinic has learned anything during the past two decades and 30,000 plus clients, it's the fact that this stereotype is completely inaccurate. Addicts come from both sexes, wide backgrounds, all cultures, and diverse socioeconomic spheres. There is no immunity to the compulsive properties of certain drugs and addiction is a non-biased condition. Drugs don't care who you are or where you come from. As users continue to abuse drugs to alter their perceptions, they continue to gradually progress into toxic and problematic drug use.

Recent studies on select populations and their propensity to develop drug or alcohol problems support our clinic's observation. They indicate an increased or overrepresentation of drug and alcohol abuse among the most intelligent, skilled, and talented individuals of our society. Physicians, nurses, and Mensa (a society for those with high IQs) members are 6 to 8 times more likely to be addicts than are members of the general population. Priests seem more prone to alcoholism than the rest of us. Gifted and highly motivated youth go on to higher rates of suicide and drug abuse.

Recognition of this wide distribution of drug abuse in our society illuminates the broad impact that drugs have on our environment. As we look more closely at this, we begin to appreciate the unique and special needs of some communities--the youth, the elderly, working men and women, pregnant women, students--all of whom must be considered to effectively address their problems with drugs.

Drugs in our Environment
PREGNANCY

By ANTHONY J. PUENTES, MD
Medical Director, Santa Clara County
Health Department, Bureau of Drug
Abuse Services

Overview

Drug and alcohol use during pregnancy is a growing national problem. The number of infants with drug and alcohol-related birth defects has increased dramatically over the past several years. For example, in the San Francisco Bay Area, there has been a five to tenfold increase in the number of babies born addicted to drugs such as heroin, cocaine, and PCP.

Drug abuse during pregnancy occurs in women of all ethnic and socio-economic backgrounds. Studies now indicate that at least 10 to 15 percent of all pregnant women in this country are using drugs like alcohol, cocaine, crack, marijuana, sedatives, heroin, amphetamines, and PCP. Fetal Alcohol Syndrome (FAS) is the third most common birth defect and the leading cause of mental retardation in the United States.

Medical research has established that most psychoactive substances, when ingested during pregnancy, may be harmful to the developing fetus. The exposure of a fetus to harmful drugs is an issue of critical concern and the problems associated with substance abuse during pregnancy are now beginning to be understood.

Maternal Complications

Drugs and alcohol abuse during pregnancy puts women at high risk for a long list of medical and obstetrical complications during pregnancy. Anemia, sexually transmitted diseases, hepatitis, and poor nutrition are among the most common medical problems of drug and alcohol dependent women. The use of intravenous drugs, such as heroin or amphetamines, puts women at risk for other complications such as endocarditis (a heart infection), or even fetal death. The use of contaminated needles further increases the risk of a woman's becoming infected with the AIDS virus and passing the disease to her unborn child. Eighty percent of children with AIDS in the United States were born to mothers who were or are I.V. drug abusers, or sexual partners of I.V. drug abusers. The life expectancy of an infant born with AIDS is less than two years.

Multiple drug use is now commonplace and can further complicate a pregnancy. A typical pregnant drug addict is in poor health and presents herself for treatment late in pregnancy. She is without any prenatal care or medical interventions and often lives a chaotic lifestyle.

Fetal & Neonatal Complications

Since psychoactive drugs are those substances which are able to cross one of the most rigid and impervious barriers of the body, the blood-brain barrier, they can easily cross the placental barrier, the membrane separating the baby's and the mother's blood *(page 173)*. So, when a pregnant woman uses drugs, her fetus will also be exposed to the same chemicals. In addition, many drugs can pass into a nursing mother's breast milk and expose a developing fetus to dangerous chemicals.

Because of the infant's or fetus's metabolic immaturity, each surge of effects that the mother receives gives the baby multiple surges. Thus, psychoactive drugs can be expected to cause greater problems for the fetus than for the mother.

Medical research on the effect of drugs on the fetus is extremely difficult to perform and has only been seriously undertaken in the last 10 to 15 years. Knowledge is being accumulated through inference from animal research and observations of women who have admitted to drug use or have been in treatment for drug abuse during pregnancy.

The health of the fetus can be affected by a variety of maternal, fetal, and environmental factors. Factors such as maternal age, health, genetics, or stress certainly play a role in influencing the development of the newborn. Fetal physiology and genetics, as well as environmental exposure to elements such as radiation, drugs, or other dangerous chemicals, can all cause an abnormal fetus.

It is very difficult to isolate a single drug's effect from a variety of other factors when explaining a complication in fetal development. Certainly, polydrug exposure can further complicate the picture.

The period of maximum fetal vulnerability is the first twelve weeks. During this first trimester, development and differentiation of cells into fetal limbs and organs takes place. This is when drugs pose the greatest risk.

The brain and nervous system develop throughout the entire pregnancy and beyond . Thus, the fetal nervous system is vulnerable to damage no matter when a woman uses drugs.

The second trimester involves further maturation of the already developed body parts. Drug exposure at this stage in pregnancy creates a risk of abnormal bleeding or spontaneous abortion.

The third trimester involves maturation of the fetus and preparation for birth. Dangerous drugs such as heroin or cocaine can cause severe · withdrawal in the fetus and perhaps premature birth.

Since drugs can have an effect on the fetus throughout pregnancy, it is crucial that a pregnant woman abstain from all unnecessary drug exposure.

An additional complication is that the fetal metabolism is very immature compared to that of the mother. As a result, drugs can persist in the fetus for a longer period of time and in higher concentrations then in the adult. Drugs like Valium or cocaine and their metabolites may remain in the fetal or newborn's system for days or even weeks longer than in the mother. Withdrawal or intoxication in a baby born exposed to PCP may last for days, weeks, or even months after birth.

The problems of fetal drug exposure extend beyond the period of pregnancy. Definite syndromes of neonatal withdrawal, intoxication, and developmental or learning delays have been attributed to a variety of drugs, including alcohol.

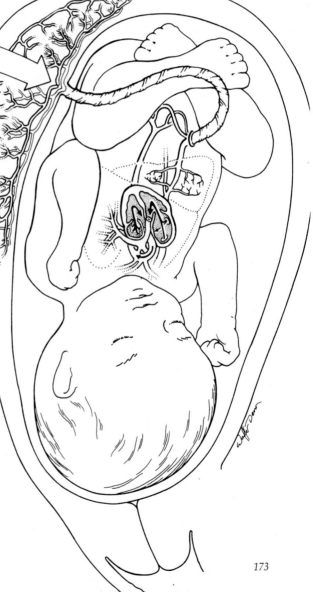

Maternal blood supply is delivered to the fetus via placenta

The developing baby (and its circulation) is protected by the placental barrier which screens out agents that would affect the fetus. All psychoactive drugs breech this protective barrier and affect the baby, usually more than the mother, particularly when the drug is sequestered in the amniotic fluid.

SPECIFIC DRUG EFFECTS

Despite the difficulties with scientific research on the fetal effects of drug use during pregnancy, medical scientists have identified a variety of specific prenatal and postnatal symptoms and conditions due to alcohol and other psychoactive drugs.

Alcohol

Fetal Alcohol Syndrome (FAS) and Fetal Alcohol Effects (FAE) are well documented in the literature. As we said, Fetal Alcohol Syndrome is the third most common cause of mental retardation in the United States.

The Fetal Alcohol Syndrome has a number of well-defined abnormalities and occurs in the babies of chronic alcoholic women who drink heavily during pregnancy. FAS abnormalities occur in three categories:

• Growth retardation in almost 50% of all FAS cases.

• Central nervous system abnormalities, including developmental and mental retardation in all cases.

• Structural abnormalities consisting of characteristic facial, skeletal, and organ defects.

Growth defects have been seen in infants of mothers who drank even moderately during pregnancy. Sig-nificantly decreased birth weights have been observed among infants born to women who averaged only one ounce of alcohol per day during pregnancy.

Neurological damage and mental retardation are permanent and average IQ's are in the low 60's. Structural abnormalities consist of smaller head size, short eyelids, defective midfacial tissue, abnormal creases in the palms of the hand, and defects in the walls separating the heart chambers.

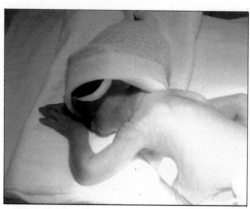

When babies are born prematurely, whether due to drugs or natural forces, the cost of intensive neonatal care, usually to the community, is thousands of dollars a day.

Five to forty-one percent of FAS infants also have minor abnormalities of the joints, benign tumors of blood vessels, ear defects, drooping eyelids, cleft palates, and smaller eyes and fingernails.

FAS children have a growth rate about two-thirds of the norm, though this may even out as they approach adolescence.

Fetal Alcohol Effects (FAE) refers to the occurrence of negative effects on the fetus but not necessarily all the characteristics described in FAS.

To answer the question of **how much alcohol intake is required to produce FAE or FAS,** several studies have attempted to define a safe level of alcohol intake during pregnancy. Some recent studies indicate that alcohol use greater than nine shots per day of 100 proof whiskey, or about one and a half bottles of wine per day, increases the frequency of all abnormalities associated with fetal alcohol syndrome. Alcohol consumption of as little as one ounce twice a week has been associated with a significant increase in spontaneous abortions.

Alcohol withdrawal in the mother may cause premature labor while alcohol consumption up to and even during labor has resulted in increased nausea and vomiting, low blood pressure and blood sugar, and depression in both mother and newborn.

Alcohol withdrawal can also occur in the addicted newborn resulting in irritability, restlessness, agitation, and increased chance of neonatal mortality. Nursing mothers also pass alcohol to their babies in their breast milk which can result in sedation and lethargy in the infant.

Despite an array of research studies, the exact relationship between alcohol dose and fetal outcome is unknown. However, most physicians now agree that there is no known safe amount of alcohol use during pregnancy. Abstinence is considered the only safe approach.

In 1988, Federal legislation mandated the posting of alcohol warning labels, cautioning pregnant women of the dangers of drinking during pregnancy.

Cocaine and Amphetamines

With the increasing, widespread use of cocaine, particularly smokable cocaine (crack, free base), there has been a dramatic increase in cocaine-affected newborns. In the United States, there are 5 to 7 million heavy cocaine users (compared to one half million heroin addicts). One third are women (and increasing yearly) with an average age in their late twenties, the very fertile childbearing years. One can only assume that a large number of these women use cocaine during pregnancy.

Currently, in some parts of the country, up to 60% of drug-impaired babies are born to cocaine or amphetamine-abusing mothers. Even more alarming is the recent disclosure that as many as 20% to 25% of babies born in county hospitals of large metropolitan areas are born cocaine affected. Research on the effects of cocaine and amphetamines during pregnancy is very limited. Nevertheless, some definite conclusions can already be drawn.

Cocaine and amphetamines are both strong stimulants. They result in markedly increased heart rates and constriction of blood vessels. These effects, in turn, cause dramatic elevations in blood pressure in both mother and fetus. Rapid fluctuations in both maternal and fetal blood pressure can have serious consequences.

Constriction of blood vessels will result in a decreased blood and oxygen supply to the placenta and fetus. An impaired blood and oxygen supply can result in retarded fetal development. Increased maternal and placental blood pressure can result in a premature separation of the placenta from the wall of the uterus. This abnormal separa-

Cocaine Use Linked To Infant Defects

New York

Animal experiments suggest that cocaine use during pregnancy can produce infants with long-term abnormalities in the brain systems that control sensation, movement and emotions, a researcher said yesterday.

This occurs despite the frequent absence of physical defects in the offspring, said Diana Dow-Edwards, a researcher at the State University of New York Health Science Center in Brooklyn.

In a separate report, a researcher said he has found that cocaine use by pregnant women may retard the brain growth of their

ing in the infants of cocaine-using mothers.

For example, Chasnoff said, "it appears that these infants are probably having an increased rate of seizures in the neonatal (newborn) period." That could be due to a hypersensitivity in the brain similar to what Dow-Edwards has observed in rats, he said.

Chasnoff also reported that infants of cocaine-using mothers have a significantly smaller head size than normal infants, suggesting a retardation in brain growth.

Chasnoff said cocaine-affected infants are excessi...rience...

tion, or abruptio placenta, has been reported several times, presumably as a result of the acute hypertension associated with cocaine use. An abruptio placenta will result in an acutely critical situation, usually resulting in spontaneous abortion or premature delivery. Abruptio placenta can be a life-threatening situation for both mother and fetus.

Acutely elevated blood pressure in the fetus can cause a stroke in the brain of the fetus even before it is born. Fetal blood vessels in the brain are very fragile and may be easily damaged as a result of exposure to cocaine while in utero. In fact, cases of in-utero stroke and postnatal seizures have been reported with cocaine use during pregnancy.

Third trimester use of cocaine can induce sudden fetal activity and uterine contractions within minutes after ingestion. Women have been rushed to the hospital in premature labor shortly after using cocaine.

Infants who have been exposed to cocaine during pregnancy, often go through a withdrawal syndrome characterized by extreme agitation, increased respiratory rates, hyperactivity, and occasional seizures. These babies are tremulous and deficient in their ability to interact with their environment. They are highly irritable and difficult to console. These effects may be due to drug withdrawal, intoxication, or both.

Cocaine is metabolized much slower in the fetus, and its metabolites remain in the fetus and newborn for several days after ingestion. This slower excretion can prolong neonatal withdrawal and intoxication.

Cocaine- and amphetamine-exposed babies are often growth retarded and may have smaller heads. This growth deficiency may be a result of the decreased fetal blood and oxygen supply resulting from the vasoconstricting properties of the drugs.

There are reports of cocaine babies born with abnormalities of the genito-urinary tract and with severe intestinal disease.

Cocaine-exposed infants are known to have a 10 to 20 times greater chance of dying from Sudden Infant Death Syndrome (SIDS) than the general population. Studies are currently under way to investigate abnormal sleep and breathing patterns in these high risk newborns.

Investigation of long term developmental and psychological effects of cocaine and amphetamines is only just beginning.

Opiates & Opioids

Opiate drugs such as heroin, morphine, codeine, demerol, dilaudid, percodan, etc., have been shown to have negative impacts on pregnant women and their babies. For example, pregnant heroin addicts have greater risk for miscarriages, abruptio placenta, stillbirths, and severe infections from I.V. use such as endocarditis, septicemia, hepatitis, and, of course, AIDS.

Babies born to heroin addicted mothers are often born prematurely and are smaller and weaker than normal. Heroin addicted newborns often go through a period of withdrawal sickness referred to as the Neonatal Narcotic Withdrawal Syndrome. Prenatal exposure to heroin has also been associated with abnormal neurobehavioral development. These infants have abnormal sleep patterns and are also at greater risk for Sudden Infant Death Syndrome (SIDS).

Pregnant women addicted to opiates will go through several periods of drug withdrawal each day. These withdrawal periods alternate with "rushes" following drug injection. These dramatic fluctuations are believed to be harmful to the fetus and contribute to the variety of maternal/fetal complications.

If a mother becomes truly addicted to opiates, so does the fetus. After birth,

and depending on a variety of factors such as the mother's daily dose of drugs, other drug use, and other narcotic use, opiate exposed infants may exhibit the Neonatal Withdrawal Syndrome. Narcotic withdrawal in a newborn may appear shortly after birth or take 7 to 10 days to develop.

A brochure (in English and Spanish), produced by the Santa Clara County Health Department in California, warns pregnant women of the dangers of drugs.

Manifestations of the Neonatal Narcotic Withdrawal Syndrome include hyperactivity, irritability, incessant high pitched crying, increased muscle tone, hyperactive reflexes, sweating, tremors, irregular sleep patterns, increased respiration, uncoordinated and ineffectual sucking and swallowing, sneezing, vomiting, diarrhea, and other symptoms. In severe cases, failure to thrive, seizures or even death may occur. These withdrawal effects may be mild or severe and may last from days in mild cases to months in severe instances.

Most cases of neonatal narcotic withdrawal can be treated with good nursing care and normal maternal/infant bonding behaviors. Only in severe cases is medication for the infant required. Opiates have been found in breast milk in sufficient concentration to expose newborns. Breast feeding by addicted mothers may continue to expose their infants to these drugs as long as they continue to use. The risks and benefits of breast feeding for a drug using woman should always be discussed with a physician. As with other types of drugs, the long term effects on opiate addicted babies is not clearly understood.

PCP

As with other psychoactive drugs, PCP (phencyclidine) readily crosses the placental barrier and exposes the developing fetus to its effects. Worse, PCP seems to concentrate in amniotic fluid (the fluid that surrounds the fetus in the womb) and may actually expose the fetus to greater concentrations of the drug than those in the rest of the mother's body.

Some people store PCP in fat tissue which can release the drug days, months, and even years later, causing an actual chemical "flashback" and toxic effects. Thus, a mother who may have given up the drug before getting pregnant, still bears a small risk of passing the drug on to her baby during pregnancy.

Very little is known at this time of the effects of PCP on a developing or newborn infant. This is partially because PCP is a relatively new drug (significant abuse dates only to the 1970's). Additionally, PCP is often misrepresented as other drugs. The mother may not even be aware of her PCP use. It has been sold as THC, mescaline, psilocybin, Quaalude, and cocaine as well as many other substances with exotic nicknames, making it difficult to recognize.

Finally, PCP using mothers are often polydrug users, making it difficult to isolate the effects of PCP alone.

The research to date shows that PCP use during pregnancy has led to some serious neurological and behavioral defects in infants. The characteristics of PCP-exposed babies include intense irritability, emotional liability with inconsolability, abnormal muscle tone, tremors, inability to coordinate simple motor tasks, and abnormal response to stimuli. Follow-up studies of these children show continued irritability, difficulty with motor coordination, and occasionally, slow development. Long term studies of older PCP exposed children suggest abnormalities in attention span, organizational abilities, and learning abilities. Most studies, however, are only preliminary.

Some infants have been born with extremely toxic levels of PCP in their blood and have had major developmental and behavioral disorders through early childhood.

PCP has also been detected in the breast milk of nursing, PCP-using mothers. Because of fat storage and drug redistribution, former PCP-abusing mothers can also have tainted breast milk. The extent and potential hazard of this phenomenon are not currently known.

Marijuana

Research into the effects of marijuana on pregnancy is severely lacking, and it is assumed that the incidence of marijuana use by pregnant women is grossly underestimated. In fact, most marijuana-exposed newborns go undetected.

The main psychoactive chemical in marijuana, THC, has been shown to cross the placental barrier and have significant effects on the fetus. Studies have reported reduced fetal weight gain, shorter gestations, and some congenital anomalies. In fact, women who use marijuana were found to be five times more likely than non-users to deliver babies with features similar to those identified as part of the Fetal Alcohol Syndrome.

Marijuana use can cause a more difficult labor and delivery compared to the labor and delivery of non-using mothers. Studies of marijuana use by pregnant women have demonstrated increased incidences of premature labor, prolonged or arrested deliveries, abnormal bleeding, increased operative deliveries, abnormal fetal tests, meconium staining (fecal release by the fetus in the womb), and the need for manual removal of the placenta.

Researchers have also found neurological abnormalities, indicating nervous system immaturity in the newborns of regular marijuana users. These babies had abnormal responses to light and visual stimuli, increased tremulousness, "startles," and a high-pitched cry typically associated with drug withdrawal. However, unlike infants undergoing narcotic withdrawal, marijuana babies were not excessively irritable.

Although there is a lack of conclusive research on long-term development and growth problems from fetal marijuana exposure, some defects can be related to the effects of this substance on the reproductive system of the father and the mother as well as fetal development. Further, one must remember that marijuana today is five to eight times more potent, by THC concentration, than marijuana of the early 1970's. The research data available at this time has been based upon a high daily marijuana THC dosage of 20 mgs per joint. The usual street joint of high grade marijuana today contains 40 mg of THC, twice the concentration of the test dose. New research using higher concentrations is needed to reevaluate the risk of marijuana on pregnancy and the fetus.

Prescription Drugs

Over-the-counter and prescribed medications are clearly the most common drugs used by pregnant women. It has been estimated that at least two thirds of all pregnant women take at least one drug during pregnancy, usually vitamins or simple analgesics such as aspirin.

Physicians must be especially careful when prescribing medications to treat conditions such as maternal discomfort, anxiety, pain, or infection. Studies have shown a variety of prescription drugs to be harmful to the human fetus. Sedatives-hypnotics are among the most studied of these drugs.

Drugs such as Valium or Xanax (benzodiazepines) freely cross the placental barrier and because of the immature fetal metabolism, accumulate in the fetal blood at levels much greater than in maternal blood. This phenomenon will occur at dosages that are normally safe for the mother alone. Besides high fetal concentrations of the drug, excretion is also slower. The drugs and their metabolites will remain in the fetal and newborn systems days or even weeks longer than in the mother resulting in dangerously high concentrations of the drug leading to fetal depression, abnormal heart patterns, or even death.

Studies have indicated an increased risk of cleft lip and/or palate when Valium was used in the first 6 months of pregnancy. Other, less common anomalies have also been noted. Of special interest is the fact that some researchers have found that women who combined cigarette smoking with sedative use had a 3- to 7- fold increased risk of deliverying a malformed infant compared to those who smoked but did not use sedatives.

A newborn addicted to benzodiazepines may exhibit a variety of neonatal complications. Infants may be "floppy" and have poor muscle tone, they can be lethargic, and have sucking difficulties. A withdrawal syndrome, similar to narcotic withdrawal, may also result. These manifestations of withdrawal may persist for weeks.

Since Valium and its active metabolites are excreted into breast milk, it has been implicated as a cause of lethargy, mental sedation/depression, and weight loss in nursing infants. Since Valium can accumulate in breastfed babies, its use in lactating women is ill-advised.

Anticonvulsants such as phenobarbital and Dilantin are now believed to markedly increase a pregnant woman's chance of delivering a child with congenital defects. Antibiotics such as the tetracyclines can cause a variety of adverse effects on fetal teeth and bones and can result in other congenital anomalies.

Maternal metabolic and biochemical changes associated with pregnancy may dramatically alter the way a woman's body will handle a drug. For example, altered absorption, metabolism, or excretion of a given drug may require dosage modifications. All these changes will also influence how a fetus is affected.

For a more comprehensive discussion of prescription drugs' effects on pregnancy, the reader is referred to *Drugs In Pregnancy and Lactation* by Briggs, et. al. Williams and Wilkins, Baltimore, 1986.

Nicotine

Smoking during pregnancy is particularly dangerous because tobacco smoke contains more than 2,000 different compounds including nicotine and carbon monoxide. Both have been shown to cross the placental barrier and reduce the fetal supply of oxygen.

The percentage of female smokers in the overall population has steadily increased from 5% in the 1920's to about 35% in the 1980's. By comparison, smoking by males has decreased from 50% to about 35% during the same period of time.

Since the 1930's, it has been known that nicotine and its major metabolite, cotinine, can cross the placental barrier and show up in the amniotic fluid. Further, cotinine has also been detected in the amniotic fluid of non-smoking women (although in much smaller amounts) as a result of their passive exposure to smoking by others.

Smoking has been shown to decrease male sperm motility and sperm count. There is some indication that heavy smoking hastens menopause by some one to two years.

Recent studies now indicate that women smokers with a heavy habit are about twice as likely to miscarry and have spontaneous abortions as non-smokers. Nicotine damages the placenta and has adverse effects on the developing fetus as well. Stillbirth rates are also higher among smoking mothers.

As with many other psychoactive substances, smoking decreases newborn birthweights. Babies born to mothers who smoke heavily weigh on the average 200 grams (7 oz) less, are 1.4

Study of Smoking's Effect on Fetuses

A 2½-year study of pregnant women has provided new evidence that cigaret smoking is harmful to the fetus, researchers said yesterday.

The study, conducted on 935 pregnant women in the Baltimore area, showed women who stopped or reduced smoking while pregnant gave birth to infants significantly heavier and longer than newborns of mothers who continued smoking at their usual level, researchers said.

"I think this is very strong evidence that the fetal growth is retarded by maternal smoking," said Mary Sexton, an associate professor at the University of Maryland School of Medicine and co-author of the study ... and by the National ...

nant women — a treatment group that was counseled to stop or cut down on smoking and a control group that was only observed.

Women were selected who smoked at least 10 cigarets a day before their pregnancy. They represented a broad range of race, education, income and age.

Sometime during their pregnancies, 20 percent of the control group and 43 percent of the treatment group quit smoking. Nineteen percent of the treatment group and 13 percent of the control group cut down on smoking.

The results showed that the infants born to mothers in the treatment group had a mean birth weight of 3278 grams — 92 grams heavier than the infants born to mothers in the control group. The treatment group babies were 0.6 centimeters greater in length.

... ences be-

centimeters shorter, and have a smaller head circumference compared to babies from non-smoking or non-drug-abusing mothers.

Although the incidence of physical birth defects is very low in babies born to smoking mothers, there is still a significant increase in some birth defects. Specifically, cleft palate and congenital heart defects occur more frequently with smoking mothers. Smoking results in increased carbon monoxide and carboxyhemoglobin in the mother's blood. This decreases the oxygen capacity of blood and can potentially result in some minor brain and nerve defects which may be hard to detect. Several studies have shown that nicotine is toxic and creates lesions in that part of animal brains which controls breathing. This has been suggested as a possible reason for the increase in "Sudden Infant Death Syndrome" (crib death) seen in babies born to mothers who smoke heavily.

Babies born to heavy smokers have been shown to have increased nervous nursing (weaker sucking reflex) and possibly a depressed immune system at birth resulting in more pneumonia and bronchitis, sleep problems, and less alertness than other infants.

Long lasting effects of smoking exposure before birth can be retarded development and slowed maturation. Reading, math comprehension, language skills, psychomotor tasks, and IQ test scores of these children lag behind those skills in other children even up to the age of one. There has also been some research that links mothers who smoke excessively to an increased incidence of hyperactive offspring.

Nicotine is also excreted into breast milk and there have been rare but actual reports of nicotine poisoning in breastfed infants of mothers who smoke heavily. Further, smoking may decrease breast milk production causing smoking mothers to wean their children earlier than non-smokers.

Severe nicotine poisoning and even death have resulted from the ingestion of cigarette "butts" or their left over filters by infants and even young adolescents. As with other poisons, parents should exercise care in keeping such substances out of the reach of young children.

Treatment Issues

Clearly, the potential problems of drug use during pregnancy suggest that women with a drug problem should ask advice and seek professional help as soon as possible. Appropriate help and treatment for the chemically dependent pregnant woman is an issue that has traditionally created controversy and debate. What is now clear is that the numerous problems facing these women must all be dealt with to insure a healthy outcome for both mother and infant. The proper treatment of substance abuse in pregnant women requires a comprehensive approach from a variety of health care and social service providers as well as a desire on the woman's part to become drug free and to protect her baby.

It is critical for health professionals to recognize pregnant women with drug or alcohol problems, and to help them begin appropriate substance abuse treatment as early as possible. Intervention is necessary to reduce alcohol and drug related birth defects. Providing specific services (e.g., methadone treatment for pregnant heroin addicts) attracts the pregnant woman to treatment early in pregnancy, thus providing access to essential medical care, parenting training, drug abuse counseling, and referral to other services. Abstinence from all mood-altering chemicals is viewed as an integral part of recovery.

As a result of a heightened awareness of the problem of drug abuse in pregnant women, a variety of programs are now emerging in the United States that specifically treat the pregnant drug user/addict. Unfortunately there are still inadequate resources to help treat all women in need. It is hoped that in the years to come, more private and public funding will be made available to help this population of mothers and infants.

Tuesday, February 21, 1989   San Francisco Chronicle

SPECIAL REPORT/THE COST OF CRACK

Living Hell Of Infant's Drug Battle

By Elaine Herscher
Chronicle Staff Writer

The tiny baby girl is shrieking nonstop like a trapped bird, her face red and contorted, her body in constant motion.

In her second day of life, she is not snuggling in her mother's arms like other newborns. The four-pound infant is in a plastic chamber, withdrawing from heroin and crack cocaine.

The two drugs cause different symptoms, but it is the crack withdrawal that is making her inconsolable. She is too jittery to eat. She is so irritable and hyperactive that it will take four doses of sedative to calm her down.

She is expected to spend two weeks in the intensive-care nursery withdrawing from the drugs and putting on enough weight to leave.

But that is not the worst. It will be years before it is known how deeply she has been affected by constant exposure to crack in the womb.

"It's very disturbing to see the effects of drug use on both the family and the infant," said Colin Partridge, attending neonatologist at San Francisco General Hospital, where the black-haired newborn lies in an incubator.

Sicker Babies

These babies are in the hospital longer, they are sicker babies, they may have birth defects or brain damage related to the drugs," Partridge said. "It's difficult to be an infant these days as it is, let alone when you have strikes against you."

The toll is not only on the infant and her family. By the time she has lived for a year, this one crack baby will have cost San Francisco taxpayers nearly $40,000.

She will run up a hospital bill of $25,000, with half paid by Medi-Cal and the other half by the city. Because the mother's addiction has already lost her one child to Children's Protective Services, the baby probably will be placed in foster care, which, along with court costs, will come to $24,000 for the first year.

But this is by no means the sickest baby that doctors will see.

The heart-wrenching ones are born as much as 14 weeks premature and weigh 1½ to 2 pounds. A frequent side effect of crack use is that the placenta separates from the womb early, causing the birth to come too soon.

"What you're talking about is a tiny baby who can't eat, can't breathe, has skin that is extremely fragile, may get infections easily and could possibly hemorrhage in the brain," said Roberta Ballard, Mount Zion Hospital's chief of pediatrics.

Without being hooked to a respirator, kept in an incubator and fed through tubes, a baby like this will die. Its lungs and chest wall are too thin for the infant to breathe, and although being on a respirator can cause chronic lung problems later in life, there is no other choice.

The baby's blood vessels are so tiny they do not carry enough blood to maintain body temperature. Its intestines do not function at all, and the baby must be fed intravenously. Often the blood vessels are too small to accept an IV line, and a feeding tube has to be run through the fragile infant's umbilical cord.

In effect, doctors and nurses have to recreate the womb that rejected this baby after filling him full of potentially lethal drugs.

"A baby like this will cost $1,500 a day, with the total bill ranging from $100,000 to $200,000 for a baby that when it's all over wasn't wanted in this world and may have lasting health problems," Ballard said.

Hundreds to Be Born

Hundreds of these babies will be born in San Francisco this year.

At San Francisco General, 80 percent of mothers who test positive for drugs are crack cocaine users. About 12 percent of the babies delivered there are crack addicts. Last year, the hospital cared for an estimated 250 crack babies.

Other hospitals are also besieged by crack babies.

St. Luke's Hospital in the Mission District, for example, treats at least 10 crack babies a month, and in a recent two-week period, treated eight newborns for cocaine addiction, hospital social worker Gretchen Phelps said.

"This is very unfulfilling. You stay up nights with these babies trying to keep them alive, and you realize there's an unacceptable home situation they're going to, without a caring set of parents," said Robert Piecuch, attending neonatologist at Mount Zion, which has an ultra-sophisticated nursery that regularly treats the city's sickest crack babies.

Medical practitioners and social workers say they are amazed at how easily pregnant crack addicts forget they are having babies.

"Crack users' can't relate to the fact that they are pregnant. They can only relate to their drug-seeking behavior," said Karen Huntley, co-ordinator of San Francisco General's high-risk obstetrics clinic.

The absence of maternal feeling among some crack users is chilling.

Recently, in the middle of the night Partridge was called into the hospital nursery to resuscitate a one-pound, three-ounce baby, 14 weeks premature, the offspring of a habitual crack user in her late teens.

"When I told the mother, (the baby) was critically ill, she said, 'I was going to get an abortion, but I was too busy,'" said Partridge.

"I said, 'Do you want to touch your baby.' Your baby is dying.' The only thing she said is, 'What time's breakfast?'" The young woman vanished right after her meal.

A doctor examined a four-pound infant afflicted with cocaine and heroin addiction

YOUTH AND SCHOOL

I n the late 1980's, all the headlines shouted about the crack cocaine epidemic. They talked about the gangs in the inner cities who ran the drug trade and about 16-year-olds buying BMW's. In fact, in some cities, the youth guidance centers, or juvenile halls, were clogged because of the cocaine trade (as many as 85% of the juveniles in the San Francisco Youth Guidance Center are there because of drug use). Most of the involvement was thought to be confined to inner city youth, so called "high risk" teenagers (and even younger children).

The well known study by Lloyd Johnston, Ph.D., of high school seniors (generally thought to be low risk) from 1975 through 1984 entitled "Monitoring the Future," reflects the problems. In the study, high school seniors from all over the country admitted that

• 29% currently used (within the past 30 days) an illicit drug;

• 47% had used an illicit drug within the past year;

• 25% currently used marijuana, 40%

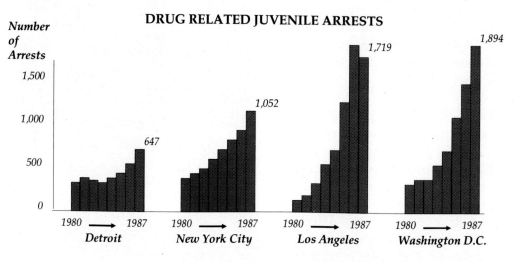

DRUG RELATED JUVENILE ARRESTS

Number of Arrests

Detroit: 647 (1980 → 1987)
New York City: 1,052 (1980 → 1987)
Los Angeles: 1,719 (1980 → 1987)
Washington D.C.: 1,894 (1980 → 1987)

But, drug use is widespread and has not been confined to the "high risk" groups. And despite our increased awareness and a small decline in substance abuse from 1980 through 1985, drug use and abuse among so-called "low risk" American youth is not so low.

within the past year, and 5% smoked it on a daily basis;

• Amphetamines were second to marijuana as the most frequently used illicit drug with 17.7% of the sample having used these within the past year;

• 12% used cocaine within the past year with regional variations. This figure has most probably climbed recently but not as much as the headlines would imply.

As to legal drugs:

• 93% of high school seniors had tried alcohol; about one in twenty were drinking daily; and 39% had ingested 5 or more drinks in a row at least once in the past two weeks;

• 29% used cigarettes; 19% were daily smokers.

Reports of other drug use are scattered about in the study;

• Inhalant use had increased to some 7.9% over the past year (1984);

• Over the counter "diet pills" showed a 10% current use with higher levels of use in women;

• Over the counter "stay awake" or stimulant pills had 6% current use and their use had been increasing since 1982;

• There was 4% Quaalude, 5% barbiturates, and 6% tranquilizer use;

• 5.2% had used an opiate/opioid other than heroin over the last year; 0.5% had used heroin in that period;

• 4.7% LSD and 2% PCP use were found though regional variations seem to indicate much higher use of PCP in Washington DC and Los Angeles.

Although not part of this study, another item of great concern is the increased use of smokeless tobacco by youth. Chewing tobacco and snuff, or "dip," still contain enough nicotine to bring about habitual patterns of use and increase the risk of mouth cancers.

Clove cigarettes, sold as Krakatoa, containing nicotine plus another chemical, eugenol, have also become increasingly popular among youth in recent years.

The United States' levels of substance abuse are estimated to be the highest found in any developed country in the world. This is particularly alarming from two perspectives: first, drug use among our youth gives us a preview of future levels of drug abuse in our society; and drugs are generally more potent and toxic in youth due to physiologic and emotional immaturity.

Chemical differences, different hormonal levels, reduced body fluids and cells, decreased blood elements, immature kidney and liver function, as well as incomplete development of the blood brain barrier, all contribute to greater effects and toxicity in young users from a typical adult dose of psychoactive drugs. It is for this reason that pediatric doses of drugs are based upon body weight or surface area measurements. Thus, youth are more susceptible to the toxic and adverse side effects of drugs and can more readily progress to substance abuse problems.

Further, adolescents have immature levels of sex hormones which are also quite susceptible to drug disruption.

fect of increasing short term memory, motivation, and learning. Continued or high dose use, however, greatly impairs learning.

These are just some of the considerations which raise great concern over the

Can you identify at-risk teen behavior?

Parents get pep talk from Ashland counselor

continued high level of drug abuse by American youth.

Many current drugs of abuse like marijuana, the opiates/opioids, and the new rage, anabolic steroids (rhoids) can potentially alter sexual development or function.

The psychological and emotional growth of youth can also be affected by psychoactive drugs during the critical years of maturation. All psychoactive substances alter or distort moods, feelings, emotions, and thought patterns.

The adolescent years are critical to the development of learning and the acquisition of academic skills. Depressant drugs, marijuana, and psychedelics all impair learning to some degree. Stimulants have the transient ef-

Nowhere does prevention play a more important role than in addressing drug abuse problems in our youth. Primary prevention should start even in kindergarten with parent-educator programs and the incorporation of established drug prevention lesson plans within the school's overall curriculum.

Secondary prevention efforts with peer educator programs, prevention curriculum, Students Against Drunk Driving, positive role models, health fairs, etc., can be effective in minimizing experimentation with drugs.

Tertiary prevention efforts with student assistance programs, teenage Narcotics/Cocaine/Alcohol Addictions Anonymous Meetings, peer intervention teams, and other activities geared at getting drug abusers into early treatment have effectively decreased the negative impact of drugs on youth.

Important work in preventing substance abuse in youth continues to be developed by researchers like Steven Glenn, Ph.D., in South Carolina and Richard Jessor, Ph.D., in Colorado. They present four antecedents or "predictors" of future drug use in children. These four antecedents do offer many stimulating considerations for the development of a comprehensive youth drug abuse prevention program. The four antecedent factors which, by age 12, seem to differentiate future drug abusers from future non drug abusers are

1. **Strong sense of family participation and involvement.** By age 12, those children who feel that they are significant contributing members of their family unit, that their participation is important to and valued by their families, seem to be less prone towards substance abuse in the future.

2. **Established personal position about drugs, alcohol, and sex by age 12.** Children who had a position on these is-sues, whatever that position may be, and who could articulate how they arrived at their position, how they would act on that position, and what effect their position would have on their lives seem less likely to develop drug or alcohol problems.

3. **Strong "spiritual" sense of community involvement by age 12.** Youth who feel that they are significant to and contribute to their community and the greater society around them, that they are individuals with a role and purpose in society, also seemed less likely to develop significant drug or alcohol problems.

(4) **Attachment to a clean and sober adult role model other than one's parents by age 12.** Children who can list one or more non drug-using adults for whom they have esteem, and to whom they can turn for information or advice seem less prone to develop drug abuse problems. These positive role models play a critical role in the formative years of a child's development and are often persons like a coach, a teacher, activities leader, minister, relative, neighbor, or family friend.

These factors underscore the need to develop a drug abuse prevention program early and continue such programs through the school years and even into adulthood.

SPORTS

Athletes, like others, abuse "social" or illicit psychoactive drugs. These drugs, presented in greater detail in other chapters, are used by athletes to enhance their training or performance. Principally, the uppers like

Cocaine Caused Bias' Death, Autopsy Reveals

"crank," "whites," or "black beauties," (all amphetamines) are used for the purpose of enhancing performance whereas cocaine is most often used as a motivating or reward substance. Because competition, in itself, creates adrenalin in the body, depressant drugs like alcohol, Valium, barbiturates, Quaalude, and even marijuana are used to help calm an athlete after a good game or ease the agony of defeat. Opioids like codeine, Darvon, Vicodin, etc., originally used for post performance pain and pain of major injuries also can lead to drug problems for the athlete.

Drug use by athletes has also expanded to include a vast array of often-times bizarre and exotic substances. Although the majority of these "ergogenic" (strength, endurance, or performance enhancing) substances are not psychoactive, they are still abused by athletes.

STEROIDS called "rhoids," are a major drug of abuse by athletes. There are two major types: anabolic and adreno cortical.

ANABOLIC STEROIDS

Testosterone, Dianabol, and Stanozolal are basically male hormones which accelerate training by increasing muscle mass. They also have psychoactive effects such as increasing confidence and aggressiveness with an elevation of mood. Major toxic and adverse effects include increased risk of injury (tendon strength remains the same while muscle mass increases), masculinization of women (body hair and baldness), rebound feminization of males (gonado atrophy), and liver cancer.

Boys using steroids estimated at 500,000

By Celia Hooper
CHICAGO (UPI) — As many as 500,000 U.S. high school boys have taken anabolic steroids, most trying boost football and wrestling performance, others seeking to improve with the

ADRENO CORTICAL STEROIDS

Cortisone, Prednisone, Decadron, etc., are used appropriately to decrease inflammation and swelling in injured tissue and promote faster healing. Unfortunately, they are also abused to permit injured athletes to continue their performance. These chemicals can also affect mood and even induce psychotic thoughts when used in high doses.

HCG

Human chorionic gonadotropin or HCG (isolated from placenta) as well as clomiphene or tamoxifen are occasionally used after anabolic steroid treatment in an attempt to restart the body's own testosterone production. These also have serious toxic effects on the liver and reproductive system.

HGH

Human growth hormone has also been used by athletes to accelerate their training. HGH increases tendon strength in addition to increasing muscle mass. Severe side effects of acromegalia (hand, feet and skull abnormalities) and bone overgrowth may result from the use of this substance.

GINSENG ROOT

This plant extract is also used to help develop muscles rapidly. The root does contain small amounts of anabolic steroids but can cause blood problems in massive doses.

PERIACTIN

An antihistamine used for colds and allergic reactions, Periactin is believed to also increase strength and cause weight gain. Its side effects include decreased sweating, sedation, and decreased performance.

Substances and methods used to increase performance by affecting stamina or endurance include

BLOOD DOPING

The injection of extra blood, either one's own or that of someone else, is used to increase endurance by increasing the number of blood cells available to carry oxygen. Blood from another person also carries the potential danger of exposure to hepatitis, AIDS, serum sickness, transfusion reactions, and other problems. In lieu of increasing the

Blood-Doping Dilemma

Olympic Cyclist Rogers Says It Raises Other Questions

By KENNETH REICH,
Times Staff Writer

To Olympic cyclist Thurlow Rogers, blood doping is only part of a much larger problem faced these days by athletes in all sports.

That problem, according to Rogers, who was sixth in the men's Olympic road race at Mission Viejo last summer, revolves around which artificial stimuli to athletic performance are going to be accepted, which are going to be banned, and which it is actually feasible to ban.

Rogers—one of 16 members of the 24-member U.S. cycling team who declined to take a blood doping transfusion—mentioned a number of such artificial aids and said athletes and coaches are often confused about what is acceptable, or what public opinion, not to mention Olympic authorities, may shortly rule unacceptable.

He said that during recent European competition it became common knowledge that the East German cyclists were taking injections of glucose and mineral solutions at night.

"But we don't do these things, like glucose or minerals," he said. "One of the big reasons is that we don't have team doctors. We're ... tours. We say, 'We'll ride ... them, they

'And what about ... nology?'

in, saying that was an error.

"Of the 10 road racers, male and female, only one was blood doped," he said. "Our group was experienced from European trips, than most of the others ... team. We knew that there ... questions about the effective ... the procedure, and we had ... the altitude training. So w ... really think it would do ... much good."

Rogers said that he ... tempted to have a blood ... sion, but had been stoppe ... that something might go ... he also wanted to ... say to himself later, if h ... he had done so without ... such tactics.

"I like knowing ... Olympic team on my ... skill, and that I didn ... other guys who gav ... five years like I did a ... it," he said. "You'v ... your friends, and I' ... honestly. Hopefull ... pete the same way ... He added that ... pleased when th ... Committee instit ... drug tests for Ame ... "It's good not ... about what is po ... "On drugs, we ... going to be a re ... great, because ... do anything to ... they don't ca ... their bodies af ... thing. It sc

191

number of blood cells, athletes have taken baking soda, magnesium, or potassium citrate, all of which raise the PH of blood, allowing it to carry more oxygen. There has been no proof that this will improve performance and several deaths have resulted from this dangerous practice. Penpoxi- fyline is another drug used to improve the blood doping technique.

CAFFEINE

It can increase performance slightly at blood levels of 10mg/ml. Unfortunately, it begins to have serious toxic effects on the heart and blood vessels in levels just 50% higher than that. About 10 cups of coffee drunk over a short period of time would be needed to achieve the 10mg/ml level.

BEE POLLEN

Bee pollen is felt to increase endurance by decreasing the recovery time of the body. It can also cause a severe allergic reaction and even a fatal shock in people allergic to these pollens.

B-15

Pengamic Acid or Calcium Pangamate (also inaccurately called Vitamin B-15) has been used to keep muscle tissue better oxidated and at peak efficiency longer. The downside of this is an extremely high rate of liver cancer within 7 years of its use.

PRIMAGEN

This drug increases the body's production of testosterone and is currently used by European athletes for that purpose (with all the attendant excess testosterone risks).

VITAMIN B-12

This drug is believed to increase health and ward off illness. It is injected into the body.

ADRENALIN & AMYL OR ISOBUTYL NITRITE

This combination is taken by weight lifters just prior to their performance to increase strength.

EPHEDRINE

This drug is available in hundreds of legal, over-the-counter cold and asthma medicines, is used to increase strength and endurance.

ORNITHINE & ARGININE

Both of these amino acids, and other nutritional aids like Octacocenol (from wheat germ oil) and Verona (a Brazilian herb containing 3% to 5% caffeine) are also used to increase growth or improve performance. Use of high doses of these amino acids used can lead to kidney damage.

DMSO

DMSO (dimethylsulfoxide) is used like adrenocortical steroids to decrease inflammation and promote healing. It is also abused by letting injured athletes perform before an injury has healed. DMSO at 80% to 100% concentraton is effective in decreasing inflammation. This concentration will also burn the skin unless sufficient tolerance has been induced. In high concentrations, DMSO is toxic to the liver and has been associated with cataract formation in the eye.

NSAID's:

These nonsteroidal anti-inflammatory drugs, used to promote healing and decrease inflammation, include Butazoliden, Clinoril, Motrin, Advil, Indocin, and others. These all potentially have toxic effects on the gastrointestinal tract and blood.

ANESTHETIC (like lidocaine) and ANALGESIC (like codeine) and DARVON

These combinations are also used by athletes to perform while still injured. This can result in more damage and even addiction to the opiate/opioid pain killers.

INDERAL

Even drugs like Inderal (a heart and blood pressure medicine) and LASIX (a diuretic or water pill) have been used by athletes to increase performance in a quest for that competitive edge.

This abundance of diverse and exotic drugs used by athletes fully exposes our society's myth about the institution of sports. We often believe that drug abuse in sports means abuse of illicit drugs such as cocaine. We have not dealt with the larger questions in athletics: the widespread use of legal drugs and the institutional denial of the responsibility of organized sports to protect the health of the athlete.

There probably exists the same level of illicit drug abuse in athletes as in our overall society. But in our exploitation of athletes, pushing them on and rewarding them only for greater achievements and performances, we have all participated in exposing them to a more diverse array of pharmacologic substances which are almost always misused, abused, and very dangerous to their overall health.

We must be willing to wrestle with this and provide first an institutional environment that is not conducive to drug abuse and that rewards not only athletic performance but also the dedication and training that goes into being an athlete. Only then can we institute the prevention and educational programs which can effectively reduce the abuse of drugs by the athlete.

WORK

Studies on the impact of drug abuse in the American workplace have resulted in the estimates that substance abuse cost our industries about $43 billion in 1979, increased to $60 billion in 1983, and is projected to cost us over $120 billion by the late 1980's.

Detailed analysis of these substance abuse related costs reveals not only an impact on industry but also an impact on the substance abusers themselves.

1. Loss of productivity: A substance abuser compared to a non drug-abusing employee is

• Late 3 to 14 times more often;

• Absent 5 to 7 times more often and 3 to 4 times more likely to be absent for longer than 8 consecutive days;

• Involved in many more job mistakes;

• Likely to have lower output, make a weaker salesperson, experience "work shrinkage" that is, less productivity despite more hours put forth;

• Likely to appear in a greater number of grievance hearings.

2. Medical Cost Increases: Substance abusers as compared to non-drug abusing employees

• Experience 3 to 4 times more on-the-job accidents;

• Use 3 times more sick leave;

• Overutilize health insurance for themselves and for their families;

• File 5 times more workman's compensation claims;

• Increase premiums for the entire company for medical and psychological insurance;

• Endanger the health and well being of co-workers.

3. Legal cost increases: As tolerance and addiction develop, a drug-abusing employee often enters into some form of criminal activity. Crime at the workplace brought about by drug abuse results in

• Direct and massive losses from pilferage, embezzlement, sales of corporate secrets, and property damaged during commitment of a crime;

• Increased cost of improved company security: more personnel; urine testing costs; product monitoring; quality assurance; intensified employee testing and screening;

• More lawsuits, both internal and external;

- Expanded legal fees, court costs, and attorney expenses;

- Loss of "good will" and negative publicity from drug use and trafficking at the workplace, employee arrests, the perception that there are more substance abusers than just those arrested, and manipulation of client contracts or goods.

In response to the increased problem of drugs in the workplace and its resultant drain on profits and productivity, many employers have instituted the mutually beneficial and extremely effective Employee Assistance Programs, or EAP. Those EAP programs which enjoy the greatest success are ones that strike a balance between the legitimate and immediate needs of management to minimize the negative impact that drug abuse has on their business with a genuine and sincere concern for the better health of the company's employees.

The EAP is designed to be an additional resource for employees. It is a benefit to them which, if effectively organized and utilized, can assist with a wide range of life and health issues and not just substance abuse problems. Many models for these programs exist which can be both a self-referral resource for the employee or an alternative to more stringent discipline by a supervisor for poor work performance.

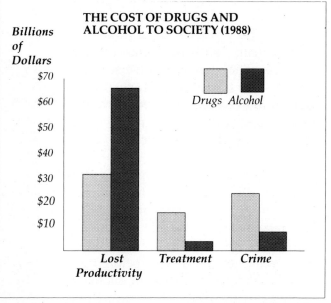

THE COST OF DRUGS AND ALCOHOL TO SOCIETY (1988)

Placed into the concept of a full prevention program, the successful EAP can effectively bring to the American workplace a broad based strategy to address the full spectrum of substance abuse prevention needs.

Many different EAP models have been created and those with the greatest success share two overall design features:

1. They "frame" the EAP drug abuse services in a full spectrum prevention program with efforts focused at minimizing employee attraction to drugs as well as helping those with problems to get into treatment.

2. They utilize an approach in which drug abuse problems are addressed in the context of a diverse range of ser-vices provided for a wide spectrum of employee problems (emotional, rela-tionship, financial, wage garnishment, "burnout," etc.).

These two design features have the distinct advantage of lessening the apprehension of employees about taking advantage of the available services for fear of being labeled as a drug abuser; preventing drug problems before they start; and identifying drug problems in employees who are in "denial" (they don't accept the fact that they have a problem) and who at first utilize the EAP for another problem.

The EAP is comprised of six basic components:

(1) Prevention/education/training;

(2) Identification and confidential outreach;

(3) Diagnosis and referral;

(4) Treatment, counseling and a good monitoring system;

(5) Follow-up and focus towards aftercare (relapse prevention);

(6) Confidential record system and effectiveness evaluation.

Placing these components in a full spectrum prevention program, the EAP could provide the following services:

Primary Prevention: Both corporate and individual denial should be addressed with a systems oriented approach to prevention.

Education and training about the impact of substance abuse should be provided at all levels in the corporation: the administration, unions, and line staff. These segments should all agree on a single corporate policy on drugs and alcohol abuse. An EAP program should be established as an employee benefit designed to assist in a broad range of employee problems. Informational materials should be available and readily accessible to employees about drug and alcohol abuse, the EAP itself, and referral resources. Routine health fairs or union meeting presentations should be organized with curricula and lesson plans developed to help prevent drug abuse.

Secondary Prevention: Both education and training need to be focused on identification and early intervention. Drug identification, and information about the major effects of drugs on behavior should be incorporated into the prevention curriculum. The corporation's legal, grievance, and escalating discipline policies need to be scrutinized and possibly reworked in regards to the EAP. Security measures (urinalysis, staff review, monitoring, etc.) need to be established which are both appropriate and humane. These measures could operate both as deterrents to use as well as methods of identifying the abusers.

Tertiary Prevention: The EAP will need to formalize its intervention approach allowing for confidential self referral, peer referral, and supervisor initiated referral to the EAP. A diagnostic process should be established along with a number of appropriate treatment referrals. Treatment should be confidential, but the EAP should have access to and an ability to monitor the treatment to insure for proper follow-up aftercare and continued recovery efforts. It is important, however, that the employment status of workers be evaluated on work performance and not on their participatory effort in the EAP.

Employee Assistance Programs which are well conceived and which strike a balance between the corporation's security needs and a genuine concern for the better health and welfare of each individual employee have demonstrated not only great effectiveness but also tremendous cost savings to the corporation. Several studies in major corporations such as Southern Pacific, General Motors, Alcoa Aluminum, Eastman-Kodak, and others, have documented a 60% to 85% decrease in absenteeism; 40% to 65% decrease in sick time utilization and personal/family health insurance usage; 45% to 75% decrease in on-the-job accidents; as well as other cost savings once the EAP system was put into operation.

Drugs in the Environment
AGING

Overuse (as opposed to occasional use) of psychoactive drugs by the elderly is often overlooked, ignored, or passed off as a minimal health concern of old age. All too often, the attitude is one of "They've lived a full life and made their contribution to society so why disturb their lives now? If they want to abuse drugs at this age whom will it harm? They deserve to be able to abuse drugs now." These attitudes highlight one of the greatest myths in substance abuse, that the continued abuse of drugs is enjoyable, fun, and full of contentment.

Our experience with all chemically dependent people, the elderly included, is just the opposite of this. Addiction is a progressive illness with an initial "honeymoon" phase where psychoactive drugs are exciting and pleasurable. They enable one to cope with negative feelings and produce euphoric and pleasant feelings. But, continued use leads to progressive physiologic, emotional, social, relationship, family, and spiritual consequences that users find intolerable. Oftentimes the elderly abuse psychoactive drugs to deal with their feelings of loneliness, being unwanted, not respected, and rejected by their families and the workplace. The effect of drugs to suppress these feelings and alter states of consciousness is only transitory and ultimately increases problems of low self-esteem and self-worth.

No systematic measure of drug abuse within the elderly has been made as it has within other age groups. Our experience has been that elderly substance abusers are exposed to a wide range of drugs and, as a group, present diverse drug abuse problems, which include the abuse of alcohol, illicit drugs, prescription drugs (which they sometimes share with one another) and even over-the-counter drugs.

The human body's physiologic functioning and chemistry are very different in the elderly compared to young people and midlife adults. This results in an abnormal response to drugs in the aged as compared to younger adults. Generally, the elderly's enzyme and other bodily functions become less active, conditions which impair their ability to inactivate or excrete drugs. This makes drugs stronger and more toxic in the elderly. For example, Valium is deactivated by liver enzymes but after the age of 30, the liver, little by little, loses its ability to make these deactivation enzymes. Thus, a 10 mg dose of Valium taken by someone age 70 will result in an effect equal to a dose of up to 30 mg taken by someone age 21.

The aged are also more likely to have other concurrent illnesses which may greatly alter the effects of drugs in their bodies or make them more sensitive to the toxic and adverse side effects. Conditions like diabetes, liver, heart, and kidney disease all affect or are affected by drug abuse. Further, drugs used to treat these concurrent illnesses along with a greater use of over-the-counter drugs by the aged give rise to a greater potential for drug interactions. Such interactions frequently have synergistic effects on psychoactive drugs (actions which exaggerate their effects). These interactions, combined with a physiologic state that also exaggerates the toxic effects, are a prescription for disaster.

Age does not endow a person with an immunity to the negative effects of drugs or chemical dependence. In fact, the opposite is closer to reality. Impaired body systems that usually accompany the aging process make the elderly more sensitive to negative drug consequences. Thus prevention, education, and treatment services targeted for the aged are important, unmet needs.

The most commonly abused drugs in the elderly are alcohol; prescription sedatives like Valium; codeine; Darvon and other opioid analgesics; narcotic cough syrups; and over-the-counter sedatives or sleep aids. Note however, that all abused drugs are candidates for abuse by the elderly. Even cocaine and marijuana addiction have been treated in patients 70 years or older.

NEEDLE USE, INFECTIONS AND AIDS

In New York City, in 1988, through tests at various treatment centers, it was found that over half of the intravenous (I.V.) drug users tested positive for the HIV (AIDS) virus. (HIV means Human Immuno Deficiency Virus, the infection which causes AIDS). This means that in 10 years, most of them will probably be dead. Some have estimated the infection rate to be even higher, approaching 80%. Whatever the numbers, the figures are staggering. And these figures don't include all the other diseases that needle use can promote. In New York, by the beginning of 1988, there were close to 5,000 AIDS cases among heterosexual I.V. drug users. In San Francisco, there were 62 cases among heterosexual I.V. drug users.

Education as prevention remains our most effective weapon against the spread of AIDS. Comic books, flyers, posters, ads, and TV commercials all help spread the word and by mid-1988 began stemming the spread of the HIV contagion.

The problems with needle use come from several sources.

Needle kits are called "outfits," "fits," "rigs," "works," "points," and many other names. Besides putting a large amount of the drug in the bloodstream in a short period of time, needles also inject other substances like powdered milk, procaine, or even Ajax, often used to cut or dilute drugs. They can also inject dangerous bacteria and viruses. I.V. injection is called "mainlining," "geezing," "slamming," or "hitting up."

NUMBER OF AIDS CASES REPORTED TO THE WORLD HEALTH ORGANIZATION
(IN THOUSANDS OF CASES)

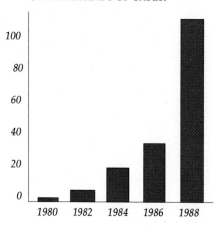

Usually, the veins of the arms, wrists, and hands are used first. As these veins become hardened due to the constant sticking, the user will inject into the veins of the neck and the legs. As it becomes difficult to locate usable veins, addicts will also shoot under the skin ("skin popping"). They will also shoot into a muscle in the buttocks, shoulder, or legs ("muscling"). If they become desperate as they run out of places to shoot themselves, they will inject into the neck, foot, and even the dorsal vein in the penis.

Household bleach, repacked into convenient pocket size bottles with instruction labels, provides some disinfectant protection to fight the transmission of AIDS and other infections.

Because of the contamination of street drugs, unsafe or non-sterile needle practices, and particularly the sharing of needles, users can contract viral hepatitis, an infection of the liver. Besides AIDS, this is the most common disease in needle users.

Another common problem is endocarditis, a sometimes fatal condition caused by certain bacteria that lodge and grow in the valves of the heart.

Needle use can cause abscesses at a contaminated injection site or they can put bits of foreign matter in the bloodstream which can lodge in the spine, brain, lungs, or eyes and cause an embolism or other problems. Needle users can also contract cotton fever, a very common disease. The symptoms are similar to those of a very bad case of the flu. It is thought to be caused by bits of cotton lodging in various tissues or by infections carried into the body by cotton fibers injected into the blood.

And then there's **AIDS.** AIDS is a disease that is most often fatal. AIDS means "Acquired Immune Deficiency Syndrome." The way it causes its damage is by destroying the immune system that normally fights infection so the affected person becomes susceptible to many infections and diseases such as pneumonia, Karposi's Sarcoma (cancer), or dozens of others which can prove fatal. Usually, it's a combination of many infections. Many needle users test positive for the HIV (AIDS) virus because they shared a needle used by someone already infected. What happens is that bits of infected blood from an AIDS carrier lodge in the needle. If the needle is dirty and not disinfected, the AIDS virus is passed when the other user sticks the needle into the body.

It is impossible to overemphasize the danger of using infected needles because I.V. use of a drug bypasses all the body's natural defenses such as body hairs, mucous membranes, body acids, and enzymes. And AIDS itself destroys the body's last line of defense, the immune system.

In fact, recent research shows that in and of themselves, opiates and other drugs of abuse weaken the immune system. This means that a user's body can't fight off an illness as well as a drug-free person.

Needle user: "I told this guy that was sharing some speed with me that I had AIDS and that he should clean the needle but he was so strung out and anxious to shoot up that he pulled a knife on me and made me give him the needle."

The increased risk of AIDS is multiplied because
• drugs impair judgment,
• drugs lower inhibitions.
Both effects will lead users into high-risk drug and sex practices.

Another important point is that multiple exposures increase the risk of infection. Of course, if the immune system is already weakened, then even one exposure can infect the user.

There are several strategies to stopping the spread of AIDS in the I.V. drug-using community. You can try to stop the flow of drugs into the country. You can identify and quarantine those with AIDS. You can hand out free needles to all I.V. drug users. You can get all drug abusers to give up I.V. drug use. You can teach drug users how to clean needles. It's the last strategy that seems to be the most practical and the most effective at this time.

In San Francisco, the Mid-City Consortium and the Urban Health Studies of the Haight-Ashbury Free Medical Clinics started an outreach program, meant to reach the I.V. drug users who are not in treatment and therefore not normally aware of how

Bleach kills the AIDS virus that gets into used needles. By cleaning them with bleach you will help protect yourself from getting AIDS, and it will not damage the needle.

1. BLEACH

FILL SYRINGE   EMPTY SYRINGE

FILL   EMPTY

2. WATER

FILL SYRINGE   EMPTY SYRINGE

FILL   EMPTY

Make sure you don't shoot or drink the bleach.

For more facts about AIDS and cleaning needles:  **Call 863-AIDS**

© 1987 San Francisco AIDS Foundation

AIDS is spread. Outreach workers from the Consortium, armed with AIDS educational materials, free bottles of bleach, and free condoms, go out to the shooting galleries, crack/rock houses, dope pads, and other areas to distribute these materials. It's an intervention into behavior without intervening into drug use. The drug use intervention part of the total policy is handled by the other sections of the clinic.

The problem with education about the risks of sharing needles that is too closely tied to treatment is that it misses the larger segment of I.V. drug users who are not ready for treatment and therefore at the highest risk for AIDS.

In San Francisco, with a more tolerant policy toward relapses and toward users who can't clean up during their first few tries in the treatment centers, the user is at least in contact on occasion with a treatment facility that can intervene or present important information. Users alienated by the treatment community or in denial will also be hard to educate.

In just a short period of time, drug users' awareness about the dangers of AIDS and the need to clean needles jumped from a few percent to 85 percent. By 1988, the HIV positive segment of the I.V. drug-using population in San Francisco was 15 to 17 percent compared to 60 to 80 percent in New York. Part of this HIV infection rate difference between the two coasts is certainly due to the educational effort. Other differences seem to be the greater presence of shooting galleries in New York, the limited number of treatment facilities, the difficulty in obtaining new needles, and language barriers.

Outreach worker: "At one shooting gallery in New York that I visited, users came in, shoved their money through one hole in the wall, then shoved their arms through another hole in the wall and received an injection. Russian roulette with real bullets seemed safe compared to this practice."

Drugs in the Environment
DRUG TESTING

© 1988, Marlette-The Atlanta Constitution-Permission of Creators Syndicate, Inc.
'So this is how he knows if we've been bad or good!...'

Along with the national concern about drug abuse, there has been an increasing call for the use of drug testing in all walks of life. The Federal Government has even issued a mandate for a **"drug free workplace."** Drug testing has been used for years to determine the blood or breath alcohol level of drivers suspected of drunk driving, of ex-convicts or felons on probation, and of others suspected of a crime. Recently though, some laws have been proposed and even enacted, calling for random testing of special groups, testing of job applicants, testing of all federal employees, and even random testing of teachers and students. The legal, moral, and ethical debate will continue for years. We will discuss

- the different tests used to determine the presence of drugs in the body,

- the length of time it takes for certain drugs to leave the body,

- the accuracy of the various methods of testing,

- the consequences of false positives and false negatives in drug testing.

THE TESTS

First, it is important for everyone to know that there are many different laboratory procedures used to test for drugs. One can test for drugs in the urine, blood, hair, saliva, and even different tissues of the body. Each test possesses inherent differences in sensitivity, specificity, and accuracy as well as other potential problems. The more common methods are

Chromatography, especially Thin Layer Chromotography or TLC:

This method is practical, able to search for a wide variety of drugs at the same time, and fairly sensitive to the presence of even minute amounts of chemicals. The major drawback is its inability to accurately differentiate drugs that may have similar chemical properties. For example, ephedrine, a drug used legally in over-the-counter cold medicines, may be misidentified as an illegal amphetamine.

Enzyme Multiplied Immuno-Assay Techniques or EMIT

These tests are extremely sensitive, very rapidly performed, and fairly easy to operate. However, they cannot usually distinguish the concentration of the drug present and may show positive tests results to environmental traces of a drug; e.g., the presence of marijuana caused by breathing in the air at a rock concert. Also, a separate test must usually be run for each specific suspected drug. Thus, an EMIT test run for only heroin and cocaine, would miss the presence of marijuana, PCP, or any other non-tested drug. EMIT tests can also mistake non-abused chemicals for abused drugs. For example, the presence of opiate alkyloids in the poppy seeds of cakes and pastries can cause a false positive test for opiates. The chemical in Advil or Motrin may be mistaken for marijuana.

Gas Chromatography/Mass Spectrometry combined or GC/MS

This method is currently the most accurate, sensitive, and reliable method of testing for drugs in the body. However, it is very expensive, requires highly trained operators, and is a very lengthy and tedious process in comparison to other methods. Being very sensitive, it can detect even trace amounts of drugs in the urine and therefore requires skilled interpretation to differentiate environmental exposure from actual use.

Hair analysis

Researched by Dr. Werner Baumgartner at the Janus Institute in Los Angeles, analysis of hair samples for drugs of abuse may prove to be more practical and even more accurate than other methods. The chemical properties of most psychoactive drugs are such that they are absorbed and stored in human hair cells, so the drugs can be detected almost as long as the hair stays intact, even many decades after the drug is been taken. Further, hair grows at a fairly constant rate for most people so hair cut close to the scalp may be able to give an accurate 6 months history of drug use. This could give a better picture of the degree of drug use (to differentiate recreational use from addictive use) and decrease the frequency of testing. About 40 strands of hair are needed for accurate testing since each individual strand can be tested for the presence of only one drug. Shampoo, excessive sun, bleach, etc., do not seem to affect the results. Recently, a second technique of hair analysis has been developed. Since good detection procedures call for a second test unrelated to the first test to confirm a positive reaction, there will probably be an increase in drug testing by hair analysis in the future.

Currently, some two dozen methods are used to analyze body samples for the presence of drugs. None of these methods is totally foolproof.

DETECTION PERIOD

A great number of factors influence the length of time that a drug can be detected in someone's blood, urine, saliva, or other body tissues. These include an individual's drug absorption, metabolism, distribution, excretion, and the specific testing method employed. With a wide variation of these and other factors, a predictable drug detection period would be, at best, an educated guess. Despite this, the public interest requires that some specific estimates be adopted. For urine testing, these estimates can be divided into three broad periods: latency, detection period range, and redis-tribution.

Latency

Drugs must be absorbed, circulated by the blood, and finally concentrated in the urine in sufficient quantity before they can be detected. This process generally takes about 2 to 3 hours for most drugs except alcohol which takes about 30 minutes. Thus, someone tested just 30 minutes after using a drug, would probably (but not always) test negative for that drug. A chronic user or addict, however, should have enough chemicals already present to test positive within that time frame.

Detection period range

Once sufficient amounts of a drug enter the urine, the drug can be detected for a certain length of time to be detected by urinalysis. The rough estimates for the more common drugs of abuse are

DETECTION PERIOD RANGE

Alcohol	1/2 to 1 day
Amphetamines (crank, speed, ice)	2-4 days
Barbiturates	
Amobarbital, Pentobarbital	2-4 days
Phenobarbital	up to 30 days
Secobarbital (reds)	2-4 days
Valium, Xanax, etc.	up to 30 days
Cocaine (coke, crack)	12-72 hours
Doriden (loads)	2-4 days
Marijuana	
Casual use to 4 joints per week	5-7 days
Daily use	10-15 days
Chronic, heavy use	1-2 months
Opiates/Opioids	
Dilaudid	2-4 days
Darvon	6-48 hours
Heroin (morphine measured)	2-4 days
Methadone	2-3 days
PCP	
Casual use	2-7 days
Chronic, heavy use	several months
Quaalude	2-4 days

Again, these are merely rough estimates with wide individual variations. Thus, an individual delaying a urine test 5 days because of cocaine abuse will probably, but not definitely, test negative for cocaine.

Redistribution, recirculation, sequestration, and other variables

Long acting drugs like PCP, marijuana, and the benzodiazepines can be distributed to certain body tissues or fluids, concentrated and sequestered there, then be recirculated and concentrated back into the urine. This can result in a positive test following negative tests and several months of abstinence. PCP, the most studied drug in this situation, has been found concentrated back into stomach acids or body fat, then rereleased, resulting in a positive urine test. Additionally, there are a few reports of infants and youth testing positive for PCP many years after their intra-uterine exposure to the drug.

ACCURACY OF DRUG TESTING

Despite many claims of confidence in the reliability of drug testing, independent, blind testing of laboratory results continue to document high error rates for many testing programs.

Technological problems

The discussion of different tests and detection periods has already addressed some problems with false positive results. Other false positive tests result from: some herbal teas containing coca leaf, and therefore testing positive for cocaine; phenylpropanolamine and dextromethorphan in many cold products are often misidentified as amphetamines and opiates respectively;

Benadryl is mistaken for methadone; Midol, Primatine-M, Elavil, and Tofranil, for opiates; Tegopen (an antibiotic), for benzodiazepines; Novrad (a cough medicine), for Darvon; poppy seed cake, for opiates; Advil and Motrin, for marijuana; and many others, just because of the limitations of the testing technology.

Handling Problems:

Errors also result from the mishandling of urine and other specimen samples taken. Tagging the specimen with the wrong label; mixing and preparing the testing solutions incorrectly; calculation errors; coding the samples and solutions; logging and reporting of results; exposure of samples to destructive conditions or to drugs in the laboratory have all resulted in inaccurate tests.

Specimen manipulations

Though there is much concern over the possibility of false positive tests, in actuality, false negative results constitute the bulk of urine testing errors. These result from laboratories being overly cautious in reporting positive results and from specimen manipulation by the testee.

Many manipulations, some effective and some just folklore, have been used by drug abusers to prevent the detection of drugs in their urine. These include diluting the urine with water;

putting cleanser, vinegar, salt, or baking soda in the urine bottle; drinking vinegar or Golden Seal Tea before testing; taking a dye like Pyridium before testing; taking water pills like Lasix to dilute urine in the bladder; substituting someone else's urine or even synthetic urine for their own; and even catheterizing and substituting urine in their own bladder before testing.

These attempts to manipulate urine testing have grown to such proportions that "clean pee" (drug free urine), has become a profitable black market item. Further, recent designer drugs create a major problem in drug testing. Many have no standard to test against and some are so potent (the effective dose so small), that they will be impossible to identify in the body.

Inaccurate tests also result from disease states, pregnancy, medical conditions, interference of prescribed drugs, and individual metabolic conditions. We even have a case where a diabetic women's urine fermented its sugar into alcohol with the yeast present along her genital tract, after the sample was taken and before it was tested. She was inappropriately accused of falling off the wagon.

CONSEQUENCES OF FALSE POSITIVES AND NEGATIVES

Concerns about false positive test results are well publicized, debated,

and feared. The prospect that people could lose their jobs, be denied employment, or even lose their freedom over an erronious positive, certainly underscores such concerns. Even the most accurate testing program cannot, at this time, insure that false positive tests won't occur.

Less publicized or feared but just as critical are the false negative results. These prevent the discovery of drug abuse and feed the already strong denial process in the user. They permit the addict to progressively become more impaired and dysfunctional until a major life crisis occurs. False negatives represent a considerable threat to public safety with a conductor, pilot, or even driver who is allowed to function in a diminished capacity. False negatives also present an obsticle to effective treatment and intervention plans.

Random Drug Tests For Truckers Barred By Judge in S.F.

By Harriet Chiang
Chronicle Staff Writer

The Transportation Department suffered a first-round loss in court yesterday when a U.S. district judge in San Francisco temporarily barred any random testing for the nation's 3 million truck drivers.

Judge Marilyn Hall Patel issued a temporary restraining order preventing the federal government ...nting ...ly testing ...ant carri-

include airline pilots, railroad workers, mass transit employees and maritime workers. Last week, the Teamsters Union and the union representing railroad workers filed separate lawsuits in U.S. District Court in San Francisco to try to block the new rules.

The truckers, who make up the bulk of those affected, filed their lawsuit in San Francisco the same day that Transportation Secretary James Burnley announced ...gulations. The truckers ...iolate their

Extremely potent drugs and designer drugs also present a major problem of false negatives. LSD and fentanyl derivatives cause reactions at the microgram level which make them difficult to locate in any body sample. New designer drugs which have never been developed before meant that drug tests have no standards for their identification. These drugs, therefore, go undetected in almost all tests.

Despite the many problems with drug testing, it is still an effecive intervention, treatment, and monitoring tool. Addicts who have become totally disabled because of their addiciton often state that they wished they had been tested and identified before their lives had been destroyed. Drug abusers in treatment often request increased urine testing to help them focus on their need for confirmed abstinence. It also helps them resist peer pressure; "Hey, I can't use. I have to be tested." Treatment programs have no better tool to deal with the strong denial and dishonesty in addicts during early treatment than the confrontation of continued positive tests. Continued employment of recovering addicts in jobs that expose the public to high risk would not be acceptable without a reliable drug testing program.

With the technology available at this time, the best chance for a reliable drug testing program would include

1. Direct observation of the body specimen being obtained for testing to minimize sample manipulations.

2. Established, rigid chain of custody over the sample to minimize recording and mix-up problems.

3. Utilization of the most accurate testing methods available (i.e. GC/MS), with mandatory second, confirmatory test via a different method.

4. Testing for a wide range of abused drugs and not just the primary drug of addiction. This is to both identify the now prevalent pattern of poly-drug abuse and to monitor for drug switching or substitution.

5. Incorporation of a detailed medical and social history in the interpretation of lab results, i.e., "Is the testee being treated for a medical condition with prescription or over-the-counter drugs which interfere with testing?

A major controversy in drug testing is the question of mandatory random testing versus probable cause testing. The need for public protection is weighed against civil and individual rights. Given our founding fathers' philosophy and the repulsive element of an observed test, necessary for a reliability, testing only when there is probable cause to suspect drug abuse seems the best alternative at this time. But, how many of us would be willing, or would not feel demeaned, to urinate in front of a stranger?

REVIEW

1. Ten to fifteen percent of all pregnant women in this country are using psychoactive drugs: alcohol, cocaine, cigarettes, and marijuana.

2. The principal danger from drugs comes from the drug itself which crosses the placental barrier between mother and fetus. Associated dangers of drug abuse include poor nutrition, sexually transmitted diseases, and diseases from dirty or shared needles.

3. Drugs are particularly dangerous to the fetus because its defense mechanisms such as a drug neutralizing metabolic system, an immune system to fight infections, and well developed organs to handle the effects are not yet developed. For example, each surge of effects from a drug the mother takes gives multiple surges to the defenseless fetus.

4. Major problems from drug use during pregnancy include a higher rate of miscarriage, blood vessel damage, severe withdrawal symptoms, and a much higher risk of SIDS, or "sudden infant death syndrome."

5. The problems of drug abuse during pregnancy last well beyond the birth of the baby. Withdrawal, intoxication, and developmental delays are commonplace.

6. Fetal alcohol syndrome (FAS) is the third most common cause of mental retardation in the United States.

7. In some parts of the U.S., about half the drug-affected infants are born to cocaine or amphetamine-abusing mothers.

8. Cocaine and amphetamines are particularly traumatic to the circulatory system of the infant, causing increased blood pressure and heart rate, stroke, and premature placental separation.

9. Besides the danger of miscarriages and placental separation caused by opiates or opioids, particularly heroin, the biggest danger comes from contaminated needles. Eighty percent of children with AIDS are born to addicted mothers who use drugs intravenously.

10. Unlike adults, infants in opiate or opioid withdrawal can die.

11. Opiates and most other psychoactive drugs can be found in the breast milk of addicted mothers.

12. Women who smoke marijuana heavily during pregnancy are five times more likely to deliver babies with features similar to those of fetal alcohol syndrome. Sufficient research into this and other problems associated with marijuana use during pregnancy is lacking.

13. At least two thirds of pregnant women take at least one prescription drug during pregnancy, so prescribing physicians should be particularly careful.

14. Women who are heavy smokers are twice as likely to miscarry and have spontaneous abortions; they will have smaller babies; and the babies will have a slower maturation rate and a higher risk of SIDS (Sudden Infant Death Syndrome).

15. The majority of teenagers in juvenile detention centers are there because of involvement with drugs--either using, selling, or buying.

16. A well known study of high school seniors showed that almost a third had used an illegal drug in the past month, mainly marijuana and amphetamines; almost 40% had 5 or more drinks in a row in the past two weeks; 5% were drinking every day; and 20% were smoking cigarettes.

17. The levels of substance abuse among youth in the U. S. is among the highest of any developed country.

18. Youths are more likely to experiment with psychoactive drugs; they are more susceptible to peer pressure; their hormonal systems are in the developmental stage so psychological and emotional maturation can be disrupted or delayed by drug use.

19. Prevention programs (building self esteem, learning about drugs, saying no to peer pressure) throughout a student's years of learning are crucial to developing a lifelong aversion to psychoactive drugs.

20. The main drugs used by athletes are stimulants such as speed, to enhance performance; painkillers such as opiates, to help users play past pain; steroids to increase muscle mass or decrease muscular inflammation; and twenty or more others to affect various aspects of performance and training.

21. Anabolic steroids can create a feeling of increased confidence, agressiveness, and elevation of mood. Toxic effects include masculinization in women; increased injury from disproportionate growth of muscles versus tendons; liver damage.

22. Adreno-cortical steroids such as cortisone decrease inflammation and promote faster healing, but they also increase the chance of injury since the user is playing on damaged tissue. They can also affect mood and even induce psychotic thoughts at high doses.

23. Drug abuse in the workplace costs American business more than 100 billion dollars a year.

24. Drug abuse in the workplace causes loss of productivity; medical cost increases; legal cost increases.

25. The most effective answer to drug abuse in the workplace seems to be EAP's (Employee Assistance Programs).

26. EAP's should have full-spectrum drug prevention programs and should handle other kinds of employee problems besides drug abuse.

27. Good EAP programs have been documented to decrease absenteeism 40% to 65% and to decrease on the job accidents 45% to 75%.

28. As drug users get older, their bodies become less able to neutralize and metabolize psychoactive drugs.

29. The elderly are more likely to have concurrent illnesses which alter and exaggerate the effects of psychoactive drugs. They are also more likely to be taking several drugs which can interact with other drugs such as alcohol.

30. In New York City, from 50% to 80% of I.V. drug users test positive for the HIV virus.

31. AIDS is a disease which destroys the immune system so the user is susceptible to any infection. Drugs also lower the body's defenses indirectly. In addition, drugs impair judgment and lower inhibitions, so users are more likely to engage in dangerous behavior.

32. The best AIDS prevention program is education on the dangers of sharing dirty needles and using drugs.

33. Other diseases caused by dirty needles include hepatitis, cotton fever, endocarditis, abcesses, malaria, tuberculosis, and syphilis.

34. The major types of drug tests are thin layer chromotography (TLC), enzyme multiplied immunoassay technique (EMIT), and gas chromotography/mass spectrometry (GC/MS).

35. The important aspects of testing are the length of time it takes for drugs to leave the body; the accuracy of the various methods; the consequences of false positives and false negatives.

36. It takes 2 or 3 hours for most drugs to enter the urine and be detectable. Alcohol, the exception, takes 30 minutes.

37. False negative tests can be as damaging as false positives. Failure to recognize a serious addiction can be more serious than damage to one's reputation from a false positive.

Drugs in the Environment
QUESTIONS

1. What is the placental barrier?

2. Why are drugs more damaging to the fetus than to the mother?

3. What are two effects to the fetus of alcohol abuse in a pregnant woman?

4. What is FAS?

5. Why do stimulants cause blood vessel and heart problems to the fetus?

6. What is the relationship between drug use during pregnancy and "sudden infant death syndrome?"

7. What is the most widely used psychoactive drug in youth?

8. Name three factors that encourage a teenager to use drugs.

9. Name two factors which would help keep a teenager from abusing psychoactive drugs.

10. Name the two different kinds of steroids used by athletes. Also, describe the main purpose for their use.

11. Why do some athletes use uppers? Why do they use downers?

12. In what three ways do drugs cost U.S. business?

13. What is an EAP and what are its major functions?

14. Why do drugs affect the elderly more than those in their 20's and 30's?

15. What percentage of IV drug users in New York City test positive for the HIV virus?

16. Why is AIDS so deadly?

17. What are two important methods of preventing the spread of AIDS in I.V. drug users?

18. What are two other diseases commonly caused by contaminated needle use in I.V. drug abusers?

19. What are the two fluids that can be used to test for drug use and how long does it take for a drug to be detectable?

20. What three factors in testing would lead to a false negative or a false positive test?

21. List the most common methods used to detect drugs in the urine.

22. Describe four ways to minimize drug testing errors.

1915

AS FIFTEEN DRUG SLAVES ARE TAKEN IN FOR CURE, 20 MORE ARE SHUT OUT.

Drug Fiends Giving Up Fight;
147 of Them in 3 Hospitals

Pitiful Begging by Addicts Who Come Late, but the Metropolitan Hospital Can Take No More Just Now of Those Who Find Federal and State Laws Depriving Them of "Dope."

BELLEVUE GETS PATIENTS FOR A RIGID TREATMENT.

District Attorney Announces His Determination to ... the Utmost.

1919

U.S. CLINIC TO SELL DRUGS TO ADDICTS

AUGUST 7, 1919

Mayor Calls Conference to Perfect Plans for "Clubhouse" Where Cures May Be Made

Collector Wardell Secures Sanction of Government for Novel Experiment in Curbing Habit

1984

Responding to the Demand

Treatment Programs Multiplying

Ten years ago, the heroin addict had few treatment options. But now there are a number of programs to meet the needs of the expanded addict population.

"A lot of these middle-class addicts aren't going to go to some methadone clinic where half the people have tattoos or criminal records," said Richard Rawson, director of the Matrix Center, a drug treatment program in Beverly Hills.

"They're not going to go to some hard-core place where they have to shave their head and wear signs. They've put a lot of pressure on us to come up with new kinds of treatment and new kinds of facilities."

There are about 130 drug treatment programs and hospital clinics in the county—more than double the number in 1975, estimated Robert Roberton, who heads the state Division of Drug Programs. The increase reflects both the growing problem and the growing market for clinics now that an increasing number of companies reimburse employees for drug detoxification.

The traditional treatment for heroin addicts is the substitution of methadone, a synthetic drug that is even more addictive than most street heroin. Methadone detoxification programs provide addicts with a decreasing dosage of the drug, usually over a 21-day period, until the addict is clean. Maintenance—for the hard-core addicts—provides methadone for longer periods, sometimes indefinitely.

Methadone removes an addict's physical need to take heroin, obviates his need to steal for the drug and can be an successful tool for detoxification, some clinic directors say. But its detractors claim that one addictive drug is simply being substituted for another.

About 15 "investigational new drugs" are being tested on heroin addicts in hospitals throughout the country for maintenance and for treatment of withdrawal symptoms, said Dr. Edward Tocus, chief of the Food and Drug Administration's drug abuse staff. When the studies are completed, the FDA will evaluate the data and determine if a drug is "safe and effective," he said.

Beverly Glen Hospital in West Los Angeles is now prescribing an IND—a natural hormone—to treat withdrawal symptoms. A Los Angeles-based group of drug abuse clinics is experimenting with two other INDs—one for maintenance and the other for effectiveness in removing withdrawal symptoms.

Naltrexone, a drug that blocks the effects of opiates and ensures that addicts will not get high if they try heroin, has been approved by the drug agency and, doctors say, has been used successfully at a number of clinics. And doctors have found that withdrawal symptoms can be treated effectively with several medications normally used for treating high blood pressure.

Small, exclusive hospitals like Beverly Glen and Las Encinas Hospital in Pasadena charge several thousand dollars a week for treatment. Most patients have health insurance, but some are wealthy enough to pay cash. Most of the out-patient methadone maintenance centers charge between $100 and $200 a month.

— MILES CORWIN

FROM EXPERIMENTATION TO COMPULSION INTO TREATMENT

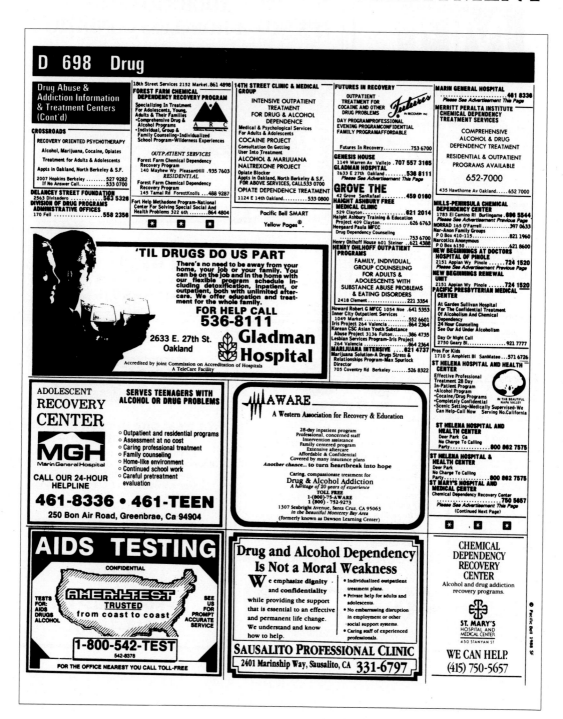

From Experimentation to Compulsion into Treatment

THEORIES OF ADDICTION
(ADDICTIONOLOGY)

In the past two decades, a tremendous amount of research has been generated to help understand the process of drug addiction. This, in turn, has generated volumes of literature and papers on theories of addiction. It becomes difficult to decide which theory to believe. It's important to trust some theory because that belief in turn governs the way we treat addicts. Traditionally, there have been three major schools of thought about addiction.

ACADEMIC MODEL
ADDICTIVE DISEASE MODEL
BEHAVIORAL/ENVIRONMENTAL
  MODEL

ACADEMIC MODEL

In this model, addiction is brought about by the adaptation of the body to the toxic effects of drugs at the biochemical and cellular level. The idea is that "Given sufficient quantities of drugs for an appropriate duration of time, changes in body/brain cells will occur which will lead to addiction." Four changes characterize this process:

• Tolerance: An increased resistance to the drug's euphoric and other effects occurs which necessitates larger and larger doses to maintain a "high." This occurs through several different processes including actual changes in liver cells which help to metabolize drugs more rapidly.

• Tissue dependence: There are actual changes in body cells which occur because of addiction, so the body "needs" the drug to stay in balance. For example, 80 to 120 mg of Valium taken for 42 days causes a buildup of certain chemicals in the brain. The user then has to keep taking Valium to prevent these chemicals from flooding the body, causing possible convulsions and other adverse reactions.

• Withdrawal syndrome: Physical signs and symptoms of tissue dependence appear when the drug is stopped as the body tries to return to "normal." Abrupt cessation from cocaine abuse will result in depression, sleep disturbances, lethargy, muscle aches, and a tremendous craving for the drug.

• Psychic dependence: This results from the direct influence of drugs on brain chemistry. The drug causes an altered state of consciousness and distorted perceptions pleasurable to the user. These reinforce the continued use of the drug. Psychic dependence can therefore result from the misuse of drugs to deal with life's problems or from their use to compensate for inherited deficiencies in brain reward hormones. Further, drugs also have the innate ability to mesmerize or hypnotize the user into continual use (called the positive, reinforcing action of drugs).

ADDICTIVE DISEASE MODEL

This model states that the disease of addiction is a chronic, progressive, relapsing, incurable, and potentially fatal condition that is a consequence of genetic deficiencies in brain hormones and/or neurotransmitters. It also states that it is set into motion by experimentation with the drug by a susceptible host in an environment that is conducive to drug misuse. The susceptible user quickly experiences a compulsion to use, a loss of control, and will continue the use despite negative physical, emotional, or life consequences.

Several studies of twins separated from their genetic parents at birth, along with other human and animal studies, strongly support the addictive disease theory that heredity and not environment govern uncontrolled, compulsive drug use.

For example, the children of alcoholics are at a much greater risk of becoming alcoholics than are the children of non- alcoholics. They seem to metabolize alcohol differently and are born with lower levels of certain brain hormones (met-enkephalin, GABA, seratonin) than those not genetically at risk.

There is reason to hypothesize that similar genetic influences may be found for compulsive use of other psychoactive substances, not just alcohol. It is these alterations in enzyme and other biochemical levels which cause addicts to react differently from nonaddicts to the same drug or life experience.

Addictive disease, under this definition, is characterized by

- Impulsive drug abuse marked by intoxication throughout the day and an overwhelming need to continue use;

- Loss of control over the use of a drug with an inability to reduce intake or stop use;

- Repeated attempts to control use with periods of temporary abstinence interrupted by relapse into compulsive, continual drug use;

- Continuation of abuse despite the progressive development of serious physical, mental, or social disorders aggravated by the use of the substance;

- Episodes or complications which result from intoxication such as an alcoholic blackout, opiate overdose, loss of job, breakup of a relationship, arrest, heart attack, or any other disabling or impairing condition.

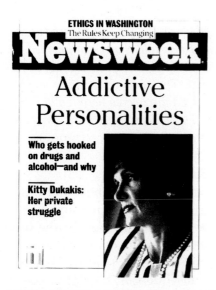

BEHAVIORAL-ENVIRONMENT-ALLY INFLUENCED CHEMICAL DEPENDENCIES

Environmental and developmental influences can also result in changes in brain hormones as seen in animal studies. Chronic stress, for example, can decrease brain levels of met-enkephalin, (a neurotransmitter) in rats, making normal alcohol-avoiding rats more susceptible to alcohol use. Many sociologic studies suggest that peer pressure, media hype, physical/emotional stress, and other environmental factors cause people to seek, use, and sustain their continued dependence on drugs.

In this model, there are multiple levels of drug use from experimentation to addiction. There are five levels.

Experimentation

The person doesn't seek out the drug. He or she is just curious about it or is influenced by friends or society and may take some, only when it becomes available, to satisfy that curiosity. No patterns of use develop and it has no negative consequences in the person's life. Drug use is limited to only a few exposures.

Experimenter: "I remember the first time a friend of mine gave me this little yellow popper and he said, 'Here's a present for you,' and I said, 'Oh, what's this?' And he said, 'Well, it's amyl nitrite you know, and you take it and you snap it, and hold it up to your nose and inhale it.' And so I said, 'Okay'"

Social/recreational

Whether it's a beer at a restaurant, a joint with a friend, or a sniff of cocaine at a party, with recreational/social use, the person does seek out a drug and does want to experience a certain effect, but there is no established pattern. Drug use is infrequent, sporadic, and has little impact on the person's life.

Marijuana smoker: "There's a lot of times you don't get stoned alone. You get stoned with your friends. If you come to school, you say to your friends, 'Hey Johnny, let's get stoned.' Everybody does it."

Habituation

With habituation, there is a **definite pattern of use: the** TGIF high, the five cups of coffee everyday. No matter what happens that day, the person will use that drug. As long as it doesn't affect his or her life in a really negative way, it could be called habituation. This level of use clearly demonstrates that one has lost control of use of the drug. Regardless of how frequently or infrequently a drug is used, a definite pattern of use indicates that **the drug is now controlling the user.**

Drinker: "You would say that I was a habitual user but I don't really think that's the case. So, it is a habit. I like a drink. And the question you know...the question is, 'Could I go a day without having a drink?' I think so but I've never had a reason to try."

Drug Abuse

Our definition of drug abuse is, **"The continued use of a drug despite negative consequences."** It's the use of speed in spite of high blood pressure; the use of LSD though there's a history of mental instability; the alcoholic diabetic; the two-pack-a-day smoker with emphysema. No matter how often you use a drug, if you develop negative consequences in your relationships, social life, finances, legal status, health, or emotional well being and you still use, then you are a drug abuser.

Speed user: "I had an EEG and a CAT scan and I was told that I had lowered my seizure threshold by doing so many stimulants. The reason I actually stopped was because I discovered heroin and I liked it better. I would probably have continued using speed, even with the seizures."

Addiction

The step between abuse and addiction has to do with **compulsion.** That is, if the person spends most of the time either getting, using or thinking about the drug; when, in spite of negative health consequences, mental or physical, the person continues to use it; after withdrawal, the user still has a high tendency to start using again--that's addiction. The user has **lost control of his or her use of the drug** and it has become the most important thing in life.

It is a behavioral pattern of compulsive drug use characterized by an overwhelming use of a drug, the need to secure a supply, and a strong tendency to relapse upon withdrawing from the drug despite the negative consequences that the drug is having on one's life.

Barbiturate user: "I used to walk crooked, my balance was off all the time, my speech got slurred, but I enjoyed it and I liked it, and as many pills as I had, I would take. I didn't really care about overdosing which I did many times. A few times, the police picked me up right off the gutter."

From Experimentation to Compulsion into Treatment
CNS DEFICIENCY SYNDROME

Much of the debate about addiction and its causes hinges on semantics. People reject many theories because of the words used and not because of the facts. We think that a new phrase which embodies the condition known as addiction might overcome many objections people have. The phrase is **CNS Deficiency Syndrome.**

We chose **Syndrome** rather than disease because addiction itself isn't what damages the body. It's the drugs that are used because of addiction that cause the damage: the cirrhosis, the seizures, the psychosis. A disease, on the other hand, in most people's minds, damages the tissues directly: gangrene, influenza, endocarditis. This idea is similar to the thinking that went into the acronym AIDS, Acquired Immune Deficiency Syndrome. AIDS doesn't cause most of its damage directly but rather, sets the stage for other opportunistic infections, the real destroyers.

The words **CNS Deficiency** seemed appropriate because whether it's heredity, overuse of the drug, or environmental factors, it's the brain chemistry that's disrupted, and most often that disruption causes a deficiency of certain neurotransmitters.

For example, in terms of the addictive disease model, many children of alcoholics **inherit a deficiency** of met-enkephalins and certain other neurotransmitters. This makes them more sensitive to alcohol and they react to it more swiftly than others.

Another example, this time of the academic model: people who use stimulants such as cocaine over a period of time become **deficient in norepinephrine** because the drugs squeeze out too much of the neurotransmitter. They also impair the brain's ability to manufacture more. This means that they will need to artificially stimulate their norepinephrine storing brain tissues just to get back to normal, to have enough energy to get up in the morning.

A final example, this time of the behavioral/environmental model: continuous stress will **deplete endorphins in the nerve cells** causing a person to rely on heroin to simulate the action of the missing neurotransmitters in the emotional center of the brain, the area which normally gives the user a feeling of well being.

What we're saying is that no matter how the deficiency or disruption begins, the end result is addiction if the excessive use of drugs is continued. Some arrive at the end point sooner than others. Some never become addicts and remain mildly dysfunctional. To better understand these phenomena, we have devised what we shall call a **COMPULSION CURVE.**

COMPULSION CURVE

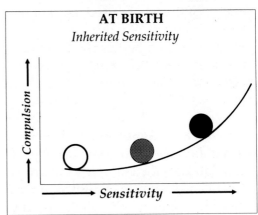

Fig 1

As mentioned previously, there are many models and hypotheses about addiction. Most, however, include factors of genetics, environment, behavior, pharmacology, and psychology. There is a way to unify those major models with a compulsion versus sensitivity curve.

First, it's important to remember that all people are all born with an inherited sensitivity to specific drugs, with a cetain neurochemical balance. Some are more sensitive than others. (*fig 1*)

Then, as we use a drug, we become more sensitive, that is we disrupt our brain chemistry. So we move up on the curve. As one moves up, he or she passess through various use patterns and approaches addiction. Those with a low inherited sensitivity to drugs would have to use a lot of drugs over a longer period of time to push themselves along. It might take them 10 years to become an alcoholic. (*fig 2*)

People in the middle of the scale, with moderate sensitivity, might need 3 or 4 years to slip into addictive behavior. People with a high inherited sensitivity might slip into addiction immediately, after just a couple of weeks of use. Their bodies are primed for addiction. They don't have to induce that deficiency in their brain chemistry. It's already there. (*fig 3*)

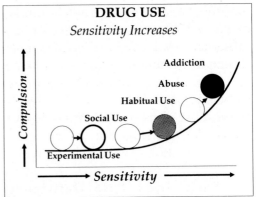

Fig 2

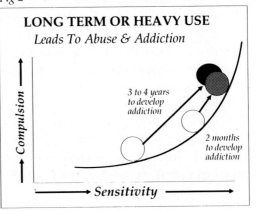

Fig 3

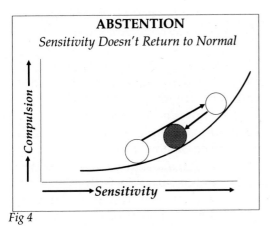

ABSTENTION
Sensitivity Doesn't Return to Normal

Compulsion →

→ *Sensitivity* →

Fig 4

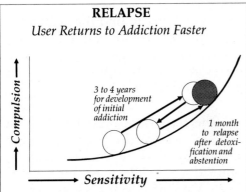

RELAPSE
User Returns to Addiction Faster

Compulsion →

3 to 4 years for development of initial addiction

1 month to relapse after detoxification and abstention

→ *Sensitivity* →

Fig 5

Note that the slope of the compulsion curve is very gradual at the low sensitivity end but dramatically steeper at the high sensitivity end. This is meant to demonstrate the accelerating nature of drug abuse.

So what happens if we stop taking the drug? Do we return to our starting point? The answer is unclear. Current evidence clearly suggests that there will be some rebound in the balance of the disrupted neurotransmitters, but those with inherited high sensitivity will not return to the balance and sensitivity they started with *(fig 4)*.

Other evidence suggests that neurotransmitters may rebound back to normal levels in those with short term, non-inherited disruption but not so with long-term, inherited imbalance. When the sensitivity doesn't return to normal, users are more at risk for addiction the next time they start to use. This is due to a process called "sensitization" or "imprinting." The brain remembers the drug using habits and sensations during abuse of the drug

For example, if it took a person three years to develop barbiturate addiction and then that person abstains from use for a while, it might only take one month to relapse back into abuse or addiction. If it took four weeks to become addicted to cigarettes, it might take just one cigarette now to relapse (fig 5). And regardless of how one gets to the addictive end of the curve, most everyone agrees that once there, it is virtually impossible to return to controlled experimental, social, habitual, or abuse patterns of use. The process leading to addiction can be arrested to minimize the negative impact of drug use, but this cannot be accomplished without abstinence from all psychoactive drugs and utilization of recovery techniques, counseling, 12-step support programs (such as Alcoholics anonymous) or other treatment modalities.

TREATMENT

As in most disease processes, CNS deficiency syndrome is more difficult to recognize or diagnose in its early stages of development. Part of this dilemma is because a person in an early phase of addiction usually has a higher degree of denial and is still functioning. It is in penetration of the defensive use of denial that the concept of CNS deficiency syndrome or addictive disease may have its most potent and beneficial effect.

Substance abusers are often more amenable to admitting their disturbance if they are not held morally, spiritually, or intellectually responsible for their compulsive patterns of destructive, drug-using behavior. According to disease theory, substance abusers are not responsible for the symptoms of their disease. They are, however, responsible for accepting the disease and their program of recovery with the goal of lifelong abstinence.

Along with a credible diagnosis, a rational intervention approach (to convince the user he needs help) must meet the abuser with a sense of optimism and hope. It is important to stress that recovery is not only possible but also a very positive, life-enhancing process. Treatment considerations vary with the specific needs of each addict and drug group of choice. Whereas withdrawal from a combination of alcohol or barbiturate dependence may be life threatening, often requiring hospital detoxification, marijuana with-drawal rarely requires hospital care or adjunctive detoxification medication.

Diagnosis of drug addiction indicates that drug abstinence is the appropriate treatment goal. Individuals who manifest addiction to a particular agent (for example, cocaine) are well advised to abstain from the use of all psychoactive substances. Even a seemingly benign flirtation with marijuana may lead to drug hunger and relapse. It is a common clinical observation that compulsive drug abusers often switch intoxicants only to find the symptoms of addiction resurfacing through another addictive agent. Drug switching is not an acceptable form of recovery-oriented treatment.

The important ingredients of an abstinence-oriented recovery program for any chemical dependence may be summed up in the four components which Vaillant (1983) cites as experimentally validated factors in changing an ingrained habit of alcohol dependence. In our model, the generic term, "drug," is substituted for Vaillant's specific reference to alcohol:

1. Offering the client or patient a nonchemical substitute dependency for the drug such as exercise;
2. Reminding him or her ritually that even one episode of drug use can lead to pain and relapse;
3. Repairing the social, emotional and medical damage done;
4. Restoring self-esteem.

Just as there are many models for addiction so there are many models for recovery but most agree on the following steps for treatment.

The first step is to get the drug out of the system. The user's body chemistry has become so unbalanced that only abstinence will give it time to metabolize the drug and begin to normalize neurotransmitter balance. It takes about a week to detoxify from a drug such as cocaine and perhaps another 4 weeks to 10 months till the body chemistry settles down.

Initial detoxification has included a wide range of approaches ranging from non-medical "cold turkey" treatments to the use of other addictive substances to be used as less harmful substitutes for the addict's drug of choice. These "treatment drugs" range from methadone or phenobarbital to nutritional supplements like tyrosine and d-phenylalanine.

Clonidine dampens the withdrawal symptoms of opiates, and other, newer medications which manipulate body chemistry. It also offers effective detoxification alternatives.

Initial abstinence following detoxification relies on counseling and group interaction to help the addict stay clean long enough for the body chemistry to rebalance. Users need to build a support system that will give continuing advice, help, and information when the user returns to job and home and is subject to all the pressures and temptations that made drug abuse begin. The support groups and 12-step programs like A.A. (Alcoholics Anonymous), N.A. (Narcotics Anonymous), C.A. (Cocaine Anonymous), and others are essential to maintaining a clean, sober, drug-free life style.

In addition, medical approaches like Antabuse for alcoholism, Naltrexone for opiates/opioids, and various amino acids like tyrosine or d-phenylalanine for many of the drug addictions have been used to support the work of the self-help groups by suppressing or reversing the pleasurable effects of drugs or decreasing the drug craving, all of which help encourage the addict to stay clean.

Long term sobriety occurs when an addict finally admits and accepts his or her addiction and surrenders to the long term, one day at a time, treatment process. Continued participation in group, family, and 12 step programs are the key to maintaining long term abstinence from drugs.

Addicts in recovery also need to restructure their lives and find things they enjoy doing that give them satisfaction, that give them the natural highs instead of the artificial highs they came to seek through drugs. Without this, one may have sobriety but will not have recovery.

CODEPENDENCY

Current treatment focuses not only on the addicts themselves, but on their families as well. The use of drugs or alcohol impacts everyone in close contact with the heavy user. Recognized as addictive dysfunctional behaviors in the non-using family members are the conditions of
• codependency,
• enabling, and
• adult children or children of addicts.

Codependency

As an addict is dependent upon a substance, a codependent is dependent on the addict to fulfill some need of their own. For example, a wife may be dependent on her husband maintaining his addiction in order to hold power over the relationship. As long as he's addicted, she has an excuse for her own shortcomings and problems.

Enabling

When a family becomes dependent upon the addiction of a family member, there is a strong tendency to avoid confrontation on the addictive behavior and a subconscious effort to perpetuate the addiction, often led by a person who benefits greatly from that addiction, the "chief enabler."

Children of Addicts (ACoA)

Children of addicts take on predictable behavioral roles within the family which "co" the addiction and which continue on into their adult personalities. In addict families the roles taken on by the children are usually one or more of the following:

1. Model Child-High achievers, overly responsible, chief enablers of addicted parents by taking over their roles and responsibilities.

2. Problem Child-Experiences continual, multiple problems and often manifests early drug or alcohol addiction. They demand and get most of what attention is left from parents and siblings.

3. Lost Child-These are the withdrawn, "spaced out" children, disconnected from the life and emotions around them. Often avoiding any emotionally confronting issues, they are unable to form close friendships or intimate bonds with others.

4. The Mascot Child or Family Clown-Another avoidance strategy is to make everything trivial by minimizing all serious issues. They are well liked and easy to befriend but are usually superficial in all relationships, even those with their own family members.

Effective treatment addresses addiction as a treatable and preventable FAMILY DISEASE. By the end of the 1980's, there was thorough recognition of the impact that addiction has on the entire family system. Increased treatment strategies focus on the addict's family and programs which directly address ACA and codependency have had a dramatic impact on making recovery a more obtainable life process.

From Experimentation to Compulsion into Treatment
DUAL DIAGNOSIS

A steadily growing proportion of chemically dependent individuals under treatment have the condition known as "dual diagnosis." This is defined as a person having both a substance abuse problem along with a diagnosable, significant psychiatric disorder such as schizophrenia, personality disorder, major depressive illness, or bipolar-manic depression disease. Such patients complicate the treatment process because they require special therapeutic skills; but in no way do they warrant the response they receive from both the mental health and the substance abuse treatment systems.

Inability to treat this condition, even an outright refusal to develop treatment strategies for the dual diagnosed client, has resulted in inappropriate and oft times dangerous interactions with these clients who are most often shuffled aimlessly, by a maze of referrals, through the health care system.

Some estimate that there are 30 to 40 million chemically dependent persons in the United States. Of that amount, 10% to 30% may have an additional serious psychiatric problem and another 20% to 35% may have a personality disorder. These estimates are dramatically higher than the estimates made during the 1960's and 1970's. Perhaps an increasing number of people with psychiatric disorders are finding

drug abuse as a way of dealing with their symptoms or maybe it's just an increased awareness of dual diagnosis that accounts for this increase. Whatever the explanation, the conflicts over ways of treating these clients need to be addressed by both mental health and substance abuse treatment personnel.

From the perspective of the mental health treatment community, dual diagnosis represents a threat to drug programs' clinical expertise, assessment skills, and even their underlying concept of recovery or sobriety. It is difficult to differentiate an underlying psychiatric illness from a drug induced toxic psychosis or a post addiction reactive depression. Too often, a diagnosis of mental illness is made early in the treatment or assessment process, resulting in drug programs referring patients who are having drug reactions to the mental health programs, who then reject or send back these individuals because of their drug abuse problem.

Drug treatment programs often lack, or resist developing the expertise needed to diagnose and treat mental health problems. Fiscal and other limited resource problems prevent the expansion of their services to meet the needs of dual diagnosis clients, causing a tendency to establish this condition as an exclusionary criteria for treatment admission in many programs. Even programs with expertise in this area sometimes misevaluate success in prematurely treated drug reaction symptoms as vindication of an underlying psychiatric diagnosis. This also results in an early and inappropriate referral to mental health services.

Another problem inherent in many drug programs is the simplistic view, or even denial, that all problems drug abusers have are a direct result of their substance abuse problem. The tendency is to promote a belief that if one stops taking drugs, then all their life problems will be solved. Thus, dual diagnosis is often ignored and most often, underdiagnosed, by drug and alcohol programs. This underdiagnosing of psychiatric problems by drug programs is further intensified by misinterpretation and misapplication of the 12-step process of recovery.

First, the 12-step process is directed to help sustain a clean and sober life style and is not an appropriate nor effective intervention for the management of a major psychiatric illness. Next, the second step of the 12-step process instills the belief in a higher power to whom one can surrender in order to restore sanity brought about by the addictive disease. This is not meant to address psychiatric problems but the destructive behavior that occurs with drug addiction.

A major problem also results from a general mistrust and lack of understanding about psychiatric illness by the substance abuse treatment community. Often, patients placed on psychotropic medicine receive inappropriate and dangerous advice by the drug treatment community to stop taking their medication because recovery is thought to be total abstinence from all mind affecting drugs. Although the official AA position about this situation is otherwise, various 12-step meetings and drug programs exclude participation by clients who are placed on psychiatric medication.

From the community perspective on chemical dependency treatment, mental health programs are seen to possess an underlying skepticism and ignorance of addiction treatment. Drug addiction is often seen as a symptom of a psychiatric disorder by mental health programs which often focus on addressing subconsious emotional problems to treat a drug problem. This only results in stimulating more anxiety and urges to use in the drug dependent individual, precipitating more, rather than less, drug usage. Alternately, mental health programs exclude substance abusers for lack of understanding and insufficient skills in treating chemical dependency.

All of this is made worse by the lack of 12-step program utilization by mental health programs. AA, CA, NA, etc., remain the most effective and best means of recovery support for substance abusers.

The dual diagnosis patient must be treated for both disorders and is best treated in a single program when appropriate resources are available. At a minimum, both conditions should be addressed without turning the client away.

Substance abuse treatment programs should establish links with mental health service providers and vice versa, such that they can work together in providing the client with their combined treatment expertise. Both need to recognize that mental health and substance abuse treatment are both long term propositions, and therefore they need to establish long range services to address the problem of dual diagnosis.

Triple diagnosis is the added condition of an AIDS affected individual to the dually diagnosed client. Persons with AIDS, an AIDS related condition, an HIV positive bloodtest, or persons who are a partner of someone with AIDS require additional expertise and specific services to effectively address their chemical dependency.

Multiple diagnoses: as the chemical dependencey treatment community becomes more aware of other simultaneous disorders which complicate the treatment of addiction, must willing to accept new challenges such as
- multiple drug addiction (polydrug)
- chronic. pain in the chemically dependent individual
- other medical disorders such as epilepsy, diabetes, sickle cell disease, etc.

These problems require the development of future drug programs which should be holistic, use several modalities, and be multi-disciplinary to meet the challenge of the evolving, complicated, clinical needs of the chemically dependent patient.

REVIEW

1. There are many theories of addiction. They can be divided into three main models: the academic model; the addictive disease model; and the behavioral/environmental model.

2. The academic model states that actual physiological changes of the body due to excessive drug use lead to addiction.

3. The addictive disease model states that addiction is an incurable yet treatable disease that is a consequence of genetic deficiencies in neurotransmitters and brain hormones.

4. The behavioral/environmental model states that environmental and developmental influences, such as stress, can result in changes in brain hormones leading people to seek and use drugs.

5. In the last model, there are multiple levels of drug use: experimental; social/recreational; habitual; abuse; addiction.

6. The CNS deficiency syndrome states that addiction can be any combination of the three theories. It states that genetic deficiencies, excessive use, or environmental influences can disrupt the neurotransmitter balance and lead a user into addiction.

7. The compulsion curve states that we are all born with a certain sensitivity to drugs and that some are more sensitive than others. Users who are sensitive can fall into addiction very quickly, while those with low sensitivity will have to use a lot to fall into addictive patterns.

8. The hardest part of treatment is to get drug abusers or addicts to recognize their problem.

9. The three keys to a treatment program are detoxification, initial abstinence, and long-term abstinence. This means getting the drug out of the system; counseling and group interaction to promote the initial abstinence; long term participation in a group, individual, or family program to foster long-term abstinence.

10. Addicts need to find things that give them the same pleasure they initially sought from drugs. They need a natural high.

11. Dual diagnosis means that many drug users also have an underlying psychiatric problem, so both illnesses must be treated to improve the overall health of the addict.

QUESTIONS

1. What causes addiction according to the academic model of addiction?

2. Describe the body changes which occur with the academic model of addiction.

3. What causes addiction according to the addictive disease model?

4. List 5 characteristics of addictive disease.

5. What causes addiction according to the behavioral/environmental model?

6. What are the five levels of drug use according to the behavioral/environmental model?

7. What is the "CNS deficiency syndrome?"

8. According to the compulsion curve, what is inherited sensitivity?

9. According to the compulsion curve, what moves a person along the compulsion curve from low sensitivity to high sensitivity?

10. How does the compulsion curve slope differ at the low sensitivity end as compared to the high sensitivity end?

11. What is the most difficult thing to overcome when treating addiction?

12. Why are drugs used during drug detoxification treatment?

13. What are the four parts of most drug treatment programs?

14. Once addicted, can the treated addict return to social or recreational use of the drug?

15. Why is habituation considered the dividing line between casual drug using behaviors and intensive drug misuse?

16. What is sensitization or imprinting and what role does it play in addiction relapse?

17. List three types of 12-step peer recovery programs.

18. How does Clonidine help treat the opiate/opioid addict?

19. What does dual diagnosis mean?

20. How is the treatment process complicated by "dual diagnosis?"

21. What percentage of drug addicts now present with dual diagnosis problems?

CONCLUSIONS

The most dangerous psychoactive substance in the United States is nicotine. Anywhere from 300,000 to 400,000 of the country's 56 million smokers die each year from heart disease, emphysema, or cancer, all consequences of smoking. This drug is legal and available over-the-counter.

The next most dangerous substance is alcohol. Over 125,000 people die each year from the direct medical consequences of drinking such as cirrhosis of the liver, from alcohol-related automobile or other accidents, and from alcohol-related murders and suicides. This drug is legal and available over-the-counter.

About 4,000 to 8,000 die each year from sedative-hypnotic/alcohol overdoses. These drugs are legal, available by prescription or over-the-counter.

Only 2,000 people died from cocaine overdoses or abuse in 1988 and perhaps 4,000 from opiates and opioids, particularly heroin. Another 2,000 or so died in drug related murders. None died from marijuana. These drugs are illegal. Of course, who knows how many would die if cocaine and heroin were legal and as readily available as alcohol and cigarettes.

As we said in the introduction, it becomes harder and harder to define what constitutes a drug problem. If we measure it by deaths then surely tobacco and alcohol top the list. If we measure a drug problem by its economic and social impact then you get a different picture.

cocaine, the abusive husband on Quaaludes, the slow student smoking marijuana.

On the other hand, alcohol costs society about 50 billion dollars in lost production, medical benefits, motor vehicle accidents, and administration of

San Francisco Chronicle

The Largest Daily Circulation in Northern California

415-777-1111   25 CENTS

TUESDAY, FEBRUARY 21, 1989

★★★★★

Crack's Incredible Cost to S.F.

City Could Go Broke Over Drug

By Bill Gordon
Chronicle Staff Writer

For example, in cities where identifiable drug addicts were sent to treatment centers and kept off the streets for 60 days to 6 months, burglaries dropped 50% to 75%.

Illegal drugs constitute a 250 billion dollar-a-year business that supports a slew of criminals from marijuana growers in Northern California to organized crime syndicates in Columbia, Mexico, the United States, and almost any country with drugs for sale.

In addition, there's the problem of the day to day impairment of millions of users: the erratic worker shooting

the criminal justice and welfare systems. Tobacco abuse costs are about the same. Those are legal drugs.

Perhaps we need to look at drugs, all drugs, in a broader context. We need to recognize that all psychoactive drugs tamper with the body's natural balance, some to a greater degree than others. We need to judge drugs by the disruption they cause in the body and the amount of damage that disruption can cause. We need to judge drugs by how they interfere with our jobs and with our families. For these reasons, we need to teach and learn about drugs in an objective, absolutely factual manner.

The reason for a "teaching not preaching" approach to drug education is that once we lie about the effects of a drug just to bolster a moral or political point of view, we lose the trust and confidence of those we are trying to teach.

The other reason for a "teaching not preaching" approach is that the other methods of attacking the drug abuse problem have had limited success. For example:

The past 23 years of hard work at the Haight-Ashbury Clinic, with over 30,000 mostly self-referred drug addicts, have definitely shown us that neither the clinic nor the treatment system can ever effectively treat away drug abuse.

For every patient in the program who accepts the recovery process, two more struggle with their inability to totally stop abusing drugs. For each patient in treatment, there are at least ten more who want or need to get into treatment but can't because programs are filled to capacity due to a severe lack of resources and expertise. Then there are an equal number who are either unaware of available services or alienated and distrustful of drug abuse treatment. This doesn't even take into consideration the bulk of substance abusers who are in denial and therefore unable to recognize or admit that their lives are being seriously impaired by the continued use of drugs.

The other approach to the national drug problem has been to police the problem away. Society continues to believe that we can legislate against drugs, enforce those laws, thereby ultimately eliminating drugs by vigorously intercepting supplies and/or limiting distribution.

Everyone, from law enforcement personnel down to the drug pushers and users now agree that this is an impossible task. For every ton of cocaine,

heroin, or marijuana that is confiscated, there are ten or more tons that enter our country undetected. Drug trafficking is very, very profitable and as with every profitable enterprise there are many who will exploit that system for personal gain. Can there be any question that we will never be able to legislate or police drugs into oblivion unless we exact such severe penalties for even minor infractions of drug laws that we change the fabric and meaning of a "free society?"

If we can neither treat nor enforce the problems of drug abuse out of existence, then education offers us the best opportunity to impact the current drug epidemic.

The fundamental economic principle of our society is supply and demand. As long as there exists a major demand for drugs, there will always be an abundant supply. We have continually attacked the supply side of the equation and continue to fail, and worse, lose ground. We can address the demand side of the equation in earnest through education. A concerted, systems oriented, multileveled, flexible, multicultural, longitudinal prevention effort can effectively begin to minimize the negative impact of chemical dependencies in our culture.

MULTI LEVELED: There are various levels of drug awareness:

Primary prevention: education to the drug naive non abusers.

Secondary prevention: education to drug aware experimenters and occasional users.

Tertiary prevention: education to drug users, abusers, and addicts.

We must define which level of education is appropriate for the target audience and develop separate approaches and strategies.

FLEXIBLE: The various educational strategies developed must remain flexible and responsive to specific needs. For example, national statistics show that kids of 10 and 11 are beginning a flirtation with drugs, so a secondary effort here might be more to the point than a primary effort. On the other hand, the target audience might be people who grew up in the 60's and 70's smoking grass who now need more information about the stronger effects of the higher potency strains available in the 80's, in order to convince them to stop. If the drug sophistication level of a target audience is different from that expected, then the educational strategy should be changed to meet the audience's need.

MULTICULTURAL: Cultural characteristics and semantics vary tremendously in our country. When we compare languages, manners and mores in a rural, midwestern community versus a coastal, urban ghetto, we can see the need for translating and molding the information to the community language so it can be truly understood.

LONGITUDINAL: The most important aspect about drug abuse prevention education is the need to recognize that these efforts must start at a very early age, and then continue through the school years and beyond. A curriculum with multiple lesson plans needs to be developed at each age or drug sophistication level.

SYSTEMS ORIENTATION: This effort requires universal participation. No matter where we live or what we do, we must all devote some time to helping ourselves and others better understand the effects of substance abuse and its impact on our lives.

It is too much to expect youth or even adults to resist the temptations and peer pressure to abuse drugs alone. The combined efforts of the community, parents, teachers, churches, law enforcement agencies, etc., in a concerted prevention effort has been shown to be extremely effective in minimizing drug problems.

Drugs are their own worst enemy. The more knowledge, honest and balanced knowledge, one has of drugs and their actions, the less attractive they become. It is our sincere hope that this book and other materials including films and tapes that we have produced, will be of benefit in that educational process.

SUGGESTED EXERCISES

1. Collect all the ads for legal psychoactive drugs (alcohol and tobacco included), that are found in magazines around the home. Then discuss "What are these ads trying to sell?" (i.e. fame, fortune, sex).

2. For one week, collect all the newspaper stories related to drugs (legal and illegal). Discuss if the articles are hype, or if they seem to reflect what is going on in your neighborhood, state, or country?

3. Ask some friends or a parent to describe exactly how their bodies feel (physically and mentally) after a cup of coffee, after a cigarette, or after drinking alcohol. Note measurements such as heart rate, alertness, physical coordination, clearness of thought, and problem-solving abilities. Compare the results for the same drug in different people.

4. Write down what you do (such as jogging or waking up early) that makes you feel energetic or positive (a natural upper). In particular, note how long the feeling lasts. Compare these natural stimulatory activities with those of your friends.

5. Write down what you do to calm yourself down, particularly if you are upset and hurting emotionally (natural downers such as eating or sleeping). Compare it with those of your friends.

6. Write down what you do that gives you a feeling of being in a different environment or world such as lying in the sun, day dreaming, going to church, or fasting (a natural all arounder). Compare it with what you did when you were very young to achieve the same effect (i.e., spinning in a circle, closing your eyes real tight, etc.).

7. Discuss the different ways the body tries to keep itself in balance internally (i.e., you're out of breath--you breath deeper; it's too bright outside--your pupils become smaller; you're tired--you sleep; you have an acid stomach--you eat different foods to counteract the acidity).

8. Name and discuss the different degrees of anger that you have felt in your life, from annoyance to hatred, and how you dealt with each of those emotions. In particular, discuss the different degrees of emotion and the fact that they can be handled in a variety of ways (i.e. relaxation, exercise, talking).

9. Do some role playing: One scenario is that a mother and father have found that their son or daughter got bad grades on the last report card. In one case, anger flows on both sides. In another scenario, the three people try to negotiate an agreement as to what to do to improve grades. (In one case, the anger prevents a solution. In the other, an attempt is made to find a solution).

10. Have people in the audience give their impression, through role playing, of someone who is using crack, heroin, LSD, or marijuana.

11. Do a survey of your group asking, "Do you know anyone that is using drugs, and what kinds are they using?" This might give you a sense of the extent of drug use in your community.

12. Discuss how each person in your group would handle the stress of
• a date
• a driver's exam
• a fight with a parent or relative
• some physical abnormality.

13. Discuss the appropriate times that each member of the group has taken legal psychoactive drugs, either in a medical situation or a social situation.

14. Do some role playing: You're at a party and a friend offers you some crack cocaine. You want to say no, but your friend keeps pushing you, trying to embarrass you. Act out what you would say or do.

15. Have members of the audience rent and view a film in which drug use is a central theme. Have them talk about how the character in the film changed because of the use of a drug. Some suggested titles are
• Days of Wine and Roses (alcohol)
• I'm Dancing As Fast As I Can (Valium)
• Long Day's Journey Into Night
•   (morphine)
• Fat City (alcohol)
• Less Than Zero (cocaine)
• French Connection II (heroin)
• A Star Is Born (alcohol)
• Taxi Driver (amphetamines)
• Lady Sings the Blues (heroin)
• Hoosiers (alcohol)
• Sid and Nancy (heroin)
• Clean and Sober (cocaine and alcohol)

16. Have your friends list things that they feel are important to their character or personality, i.e. friends, parents, education, sport's activity, church, TV, etc. Then have them estimate how important each one is by representing it as a slice of a circle. Compare circle diagrams and note how similar or different you are. (This is a way to show the importance of real activities that give the pleasure some seek through drugs.)

17. Divide a group into two sides, one to support legalization of all drugs and the other to argue against them. Let the groups research their position for one week, then debate the issue.

THE HAIGHT-ASHBURY CLINICS

The Haight-Ashbury Free Medical Clinic began admitting patients on June 7, 1967 under the auspices of David Smith, M.D., in a second floor flat at the corner of Haight and Clayton Streets in San Francisco. This was at the beginning of the "Summer of Love," when thousands of young people followed the philosophy of "Turn on, tune in and drop out." Many of them were involved in a variety of experimental lifestyles which included the use of drugs such as LSD and marijuana.

In rapid succession, starting in 1968, the clinic staff dealt with successive waves of high dose intravenous methamphetamine abuse, high dose intravenous and oral barbiturate abuse, intravenous heroin abuse, and now high dose snorting and smoking cocaine abuse. Treatment modalities that were developed for each of these drug epidemics are still used at the clinic and in drug treatment programs throughout the country.

Since 1967, the clinic has started and nurtured a number of community health projects. The various sections of the clinic, housed in 8 buildings throughout the Haight Ashbury district of San Francisco include:

- The Medical Section
- Drug Detoxification, Rehabilitation and Aftercare Section
- Women's Needs Section
- Training and Education Section
- Jail Psychiatric Services Section
- Rock Medicine/Emergency Medical Services Section
- Urban Health Study - AIDS Research and Prevention
- Haight-Ashbury Alcohol Treatment Services Section
- HIV Risk Reduction Program
- Bill Pone Memorial Unit for Asian-Pacific-American Substance Abusers
- Primary Prevention Project for Inner City Youth
- Stimulant Abuse Unit
- Glide/Haight-Ashbury Institute on Black Chemical Abuse
- Smith House, a Social Model Residential Detox for Women Alcohol Abusers.

THE DRUG DETOXIFICATION, REHABILITATION, AND AFTERCARE SECTION

Since its inception as part of the original Free Clinic in 1967, the Detox Project has operated in the belief that chemical dependence, no matter what the substance, is a treatable and preventable family disease from which individuals affected can and do progress into productive, contented, meaningful, and healthy lives. To facilitate this, the project relies on a treatment philosophy which is non-judgmental, non-punitive, confidential, sympathetic, and supportive. Over 90% of the Project's client population enters into the recovery services on their own in a desire to address their drug problems.

As of June 1988, the Detox Project had treated some 30,000 substance abusers. It interacts with 90 to 130 individuals each day. Over 26,000 client contacts are made each year.

Currently, 35% to 40% of the clientele are in treatment for opiate/opioid problems (heroin, methadone, codeine, etc.); 25% to 30% for stimulant problems (cocaine, crank, speed, diet pills, etc.); 17% to 20% for alcohol problems; 6% to 10% for sedative problems (Valium, Quaalude, Doriden, barbiturates, etc); and 1% to 3% for psychedelic drug problems (marijuana, PCP, LSD, MDA, MDMA, etc). The Project also treats a significant number of clients with problems stemming from their use of caffeine, nicotine, chocolate, and sugar. These numbers are not included in the above statistics.

In recognition of unmet community needs involving chemical dependencies, the Detox Project's ancillary services, listed on the previous page, provide a multi-faceted approach. These consist of

- **The Bill Pone Memorial Unit** serving Asian Pacific American substance abusers (100 to 120 clients a month).

- **Prevention Project** providing educational services, K through college (100 presentations each year and five award winning films). Presently, this is run in coordination with the local community "Boys and Girls Club."

- **The Stimulant Abuse Unit** addressing the growing epidemic of stimulant abuse (100 to 125 clients a month).

- **HIV Risk Reduction Program** providing community information about AIDS.

- **Haight-Ashbury Alcohol Treatment Services** providing a full range of treatment targeted to alcohol abuse in the community. Additionally, Smith House provides residential alcohol treatment services to female alcoholics. The alcohol programs treat some 120 to 130 clients at any one time.

• **The Training and Education Project** provides educational resources in chemical dependency issues. It covers diagnostic and treatment issues through consultation, direct training, technical assistance, presentations, and its international and domestic visitor's program. The project sponsors several national conferences including ones on "MDMA (Ecstasy)," "Adolescent Alcoholism and Drug Abuse," and "Drug Testing in the Work-place." The largest conference is the annual Plaza House conference in July. The project provides expert consultation on all aspects of chemical dependency. The project also produces a number of clinical articles and books throughout the year and supports the Journal of Psychoactive Drugs, which is published by Haight-Ashbury Publications.

• **Glide/Haight-Ashbury Institute on Black Chemical Abuse,** housed at Glide Memorial Church, focuses treatment, prevention, and community intervention efforts on the special needs of the black crack, alcohol, and drug-abusing populations of the San Francisco Bay Area. Raising the Black community's awareness and understanding of chemical dependencies is another major goal of the project.

• **Smith House,** opened in August 1988, is a short term, inpatient, social model alcohol detoxification program, targeted for women alcoholics in need of acute treatment services. The major goal of this program is to stabilize women alcoholics through detoxification and to then shepherd them into long term aftercare and recovery services.

HAIGHT-ASHBURY FREE MEDICAL CLINIC

STILL FREE AFTER ALL THESE YEARS

ABOUT THE AUTHORS

DARRYL S. INABA, Pharm. D., is the director of the Haight-Ashbury Drug Detox Clinic and has been with the clinic since 1967. He's a graduate of the University of California, San Francisco, School of Pharmacy, where he is retained as an associate clinical professor. In addition, he maintains a monthly caseload of 20 to 25 clients at the clinic, as well as delivering more than 150 lectures a year to treatment, law enforcement, educational, prevention, and youth groups.

During Dr. Inaba's career in the field of substance abuse treatment, education, research, and prevention, he has authored more than 50 papers and has been a consultant and writer on at least two dozen film and video projects. He has also been instrumental in the development of innovative treatment approaches to service special segments of society. Dr. Inaba is nationally recognized and has received a number of awards for his work including the Long Foundation's Clinical Teaching Award, The Japanese Community Youth Consul Leadership Award, The California Drug and Alcohol Abuse Administrator's Treatment Award, and some two dozen other formal acknowledgments.

As Director of Training and Education for the Clinic, Dr. Inaba is deeply involved in expanding the educational resources and mission of the Clinic.

WILLIAM E. COHEN, formerly a partner in Biomed Arts Associates Inc., a medical/scientific, audio-visual company based in San Francisco, has written and directed more than 70 documentaries and educational films, filmed and edited hundreds more, and worked in television news as a cameraman, editor, writer, and producer for 15 years. His documentaries have appeared on ABC and PBS (NOVA).

His awards include two National Emmy Awards, the Peabody, Grand Prize at the San Francisco International Film Festival as well as dozens of first place awards at major film festivals throughout the world.

His interest in the field of substance abuse began with "Psychoactive," a general purpose drug education film. His other films on drugs include "Uppers, Downers, All Arounders," "The Haight-Ashbury Cocaine Film," "Smokable Cocaine," " A Matter of Balance," and "From Opium to Heroin." All of these films were made with Dr. Inaba.

Currently he is making a series of videotapes with Dr. Inaba and Cinemed called the Haight-Ashbury Lecture Series to provide the latest information on drugs of abuse and related issues, and to make this information available nationwide.

BIBLIOGRAPHY

There are hundreds of articles, books, and pamphlets that we have used. Included are those we found most valuable. They are arranged in order of their importance to our research.

Silver, Gary & Aldrich, Michael *The Dope Chronicles: 1850-1950.* San Francisco, CA: Harper and Row Publishers, 1979.

Weil, Andrew & Rosen, Winifred. *Chocolate to Morphine: Understanding Mind-Active Drugs.* Boston, MA: Houghton Mifflin Co., 1983.

The Diagram Group. *The Brain: A User's Manual.* Rockville Centre, NY: Berkeley, 1979.

Cohen, Sydney. *The Chemical Mind: The Neurochemistry of Addictive Disorders.* Minneapolis, MN: CompCare Publishers, 1988.

Brecher, Edward M. & the Editors of Consumer Reports. *Licit & Illicit Drugs.* Boston, MA, Toronto, Canada: Little, Brown and Co., 1972.

Zerkin, Leif & Novey, Jeffrey H., Editors. *Journal of Psychoactive Drugs, 1967 to the present.* Available through Haight-Ashbury Publications, 409 Clayton Street, San Francisco, CA, 94117.

Johnston, Lloyd D., et. al. *Monitoring the Future: Use of Licit and Illicit Drugs by America's High School Students 1975-1984.* Washington DC: DHHS publication No. (ADM) 85-1394, 1985.

Chilnick, Lawrence D., et. al. *The Coke Book.* New York, New York: Berkeley Books, 1984.

Smith, David E. & Wesson, Donald R. Editors. *Treating the Cocaine Abuser.* Center City, MN: Hazeldon Foundation, 1985. Available from Haight-Ashbury Publications, 409 Clayton Street, San Francisco, CA 94117.

Seymour, Richard B. & Smith, David E. *Drugfree: A Unique, Positive Approach to Staying Off Alcohol and Other Drugs.* New York, NY: Facts On File, 1987. Available from Haight-Ashbury Publications, 409 Clayton Street, San Francisco, CA 94117.

Seymour, Richard B. & Smith, David E. *The Guide to Psychoactive Drugs.* New York, NY: Harrington, 1987-Available from Haight-Ashbury Publications, 409 Clayton Street, San Francisco, CA 94117.

Smith, David E., et. al. *A Multicultural View of Drug Abuse.* Cambridge, MA: Schenkman Publishing, Inc., 1978.

Smith, David E. and Wesson, Donald R. *The Benzodiazepines.* Hingham, MA: MTP Press, Limited, 1985.

Blum, Richard H. *Society and Drugs.* San Francisco, CA: Jossey-Bass, 1969.

Briggs, et .al. *Drugs in Pregnancy and Lactation.* Baltimore, MD: Williams and Wilkins, 1986.

Milkman, Harvey & Sunderwirth, Stanley. *Craving for Ecstasy: The Consciousness and Chemistry of Escape.* Lexington, MA: Lexington Books, 1987.

Goodman, Louis S. & Gilman, Alfred, Editors. *The Pharmacological Basis of Therapeutics,* 6th Edition. New York, NY: MacMillan Publishing Co., 1980.

Schultes, Richard Evans & Hoffman, Albert. *Plants of the Gods: Origins of Hallucinogenic Use.* New York, NY: McGraw Hill Book Co., 1979.

Irwin, Samuel. *Drugs of Abuse: An Introduction to Their Actions and Potential Hazards* (26 page pamphlet). Phoenix, AZ: Do It Now Publications, 1984.

Marlatt, G. Alan & Gordon, Judith R. *Relapse Prevention: Maintenance Strategies in the Treatment of Addictive Behaviors.* New York, NY: Guilford Press, 1985.

Stafford, Peter. *Psychedelics Encyclopedia.* Los Angeles, CA: J.P. Tarcher, 1982.

Ray, Oakley S. *Drugs, Society and Human Behavior.* St. Louis, MO: C.V. Mosby, 1972.

American Medical Association. *Drug Abuse: A Guide for the Primary Care Physician.* Monroe, WI: American Medical Association, 1981.

Liepman, Michael R., et. al. *Family Medicine Curriculum Guide to Substance Abuse.* Kansas City, MO: The Society of Teachers of Family Medicine, 1986.

Julien, Robert M. *A Primer of Drug Action, Fifth Edition.* New York, NY: WH Freeman and Company, 1988.

Beschner, George & Friedman, Alfred. *Youth Drug Abuse.* Lexington, MA: Lexington Books, 1979.

Lettieri, D.J., et. al. *Theories on Drug Abuse.* Washington, DC: DHHS Publication No. (ADM) 84-967, 1984.

Bell, C.S. & Battjes, R. *Prevention Research: Deterring Drug Abuse Among Children and Adolescents.* Washington, DC: DHHS Publications No. (ADM) 85-1334, 1985.

Chiang, C.N. & Lee, C.C. *Prenatal Drug Exposure: Kinetics and Dynamics.* Washington, DC: DHHS Publication No. (ADM) 85-1413, 1985.

Sorensen, James L. & Bernal, Guillermo. *A Family Like Yours: Breaking Patterns of Drug Abuse.* San Francisco, CA: Harper & Row, 1987.

Weil, Andrew. *The Natural Mind.* Boston, MA: Houghton-Mifflin, 1972.

Musto, David F. *The American Disease-Origins of Narcotic Control:* New Haven, CT: Yale University Press, 1985.

INDEX

Note: All page numbers and headings in boldface type indicate the primary source for information

Note: All page numbers and headings in boldface type indicate the primary source for information

"Crystal," 52, 70, (also see amphetamines)
Cylert, 52, 75
Cytocells, 43

D

D-Phenylalanine, 74
Dalmane, 73, 113, 119, 130
Dark Ages, 15
Darvon, 24, 41, 43, 86, 92, 100, 101, 102, 108, 109, 130, 178, 190, 199, 206
Datura, 137, 143
DEA, 22, 85, 95, 104
Deadly nightshade, 137
Decadron, 191
Decongestant, 70, 76
Deficiency (of neurotransmitters), 126, 221-224
Deja vu, 151
Delirium, 115, 143, 160
delusions, 140, (also see hallucinations)
Demerol, 24, 44, 86, 89, **100,** 103, 130, **162,** 178
Dendrite, 35
Dependence
    emotional (see the individual drugs)
    physical, 26-27
    psychic, 217
    tissue, **43-44,** 101, 217
Depletion of neurotransmitters, 74, 126, 221
DEPRESSANTS, 79-127, (also see **DOWNERS** or the specific drug)

Depression, 61, 66, 69, 72, 74, 77, 87, 127, 129, 154, 227, (also see cocaine)
    respiratory d., 61, 71, 129, 144
Desensitization (see tolerance)
Designer drugs, **162-163**
    d. heroin, 100
    d. psychedelics, 143
Desoxyn, 52
Desryl, 73
Detection period, 206
Detoxification, 74, 109, 224-226, 241
Detroit, 186
"Devil," 147
Dexadiet, 53
Dexamyl, 70
Dexatrim, 53
Dexadrine (dexies), 52, 70, 71
Dextroamphetamine, 52, 71
Dextromethamphetamine, 52
Dextromethorphan, 207
diabetes, 77, 103, 199
Diacetyl morphine (see heroin)
Diagnosis, 224-225
Dianabol, 190
Diarrhea, 27, 92, 127, 178
Diazepam, 113, 119, (also see Valium)
DIET PILLS, 24, 52, 70, 75, 186, 187
Diethylpropion, 52
Digestion, 127
Dilantin, 182
Dilaudid, 24, 89, **99,** 101, 130, 206
"Dillies," 89

Dilution of drugs, 61, 102, (also see adulteration)
Dimethyl sulfoxide, 193
Dimethyl tryptamine, 136
"Dipping" "dip," 53, 80, 187
"Dirty basing," 65
Disinhibition, 123, 125
Dispositional tolerance, 41
Distill, 123, 124
Diuretic, 193
DMSO, 193
DMT, 136, 137, **142**
Dolophine (see methadone)
DOM, 136
Doonsbury, 233
Dopamine (DA), 36, 37, 38, 59, 73, 120, (also see neurotransmitters)
Dope Chronicles, 10
Doriden, 22, 24, 98, 114, 115, 121, 206, (also see loads, sets, set-ups)
Dose, 140, 188
"Double trouble," 113
DOWNERS (DEPRESSANTS), 24, 85-133
    see **ALCOHOL**
    see **OPIATES & OPIOIDS**
    see **SEDATIVE-HYPNOTICS**
    (also see the specific drugs)
Drambui, 123
Driving, 84, 125, 188
Drug circulation
Drug Detoxification, Rehabilitation, and Aftercare Project of the Haight-Ashbury Clinics, 241
Drug Enforcement Administration (see DEA)
"Drug Free Workplace," 204

Note: All page numbers and headings in boldface type indicate the primary source for information

Note: All page numbers and headings in boldface type indicate the primary source for information

Iran, 96, 104
Isobutyl nitrite, 22, 25, 160-161
Italy, 96, 104
Itching, 93

J

Jamaica, 68
Janus Institute, 205
Java, Island of, 56
"Java," 53
"Jelly beans," 114
Jessor, Richard, Ph.D., 189
"Jesus' opium," 96
Jimsonweed, 137
"Joe," 53
Johnston, Lloyd, Ph.D, 186
"Joint," 137, 152
"Joy plant," 90
"Jungle vine," 134
"Junk," 89
Juvenile hall, 186

K

Kahlua, 123
Karposi's sarcoma, 201
Kava root, kava-kava, 137
Kerosine, 65, 160
Ketamine (Ketalar, Ketaject, Super-K), 138, 145
Kidney, 46, 127, 160
Kindergarten, 188
"Kindling," 62
King George, 16
"KJ," 144
"Knockout drops," 114
Krakatoa, 187
"Krystal," 70, 137

"Krystal joint," 137

L

L-acetyl alpha-methadol (LAAM, LAM), 89
Lacquer thinner, 160
"Lady," 52
Laos, 19
Lasix, 193
Latency, 206, 208
Laudanum, 89
Laughing gas (see nitrous oxide)
Learning, 188
Leary, Dr. Timothy, 19, 26, 139
Legal costs (work), 194
Legal intoxication, 124
Legal speed, 53
Legal stimulants, 73
Lethargy, 72, (also see depression)
Librium (Libs, Libritabs), 24, 73, 113, 117-121, 130
Lidocaine, 193
Lighter fluid, 160
Limbic system, 123, 138, (also see reward/pleasure center)
Light beer, 24, 123
Liquid paper, 160
Liver, 25, **46-47,** 77, 116, 121, 124, 125, 126, 127, 128, **129, 130,** 141, 148, 160, 187, 191, **199**
"Loads," 89, 98, 114
"Locker Room," 25, 160
Longitudinal prevention, 237

Long term memory (see memory)
"LOOKALIKES," 24, 53
l. sedative hypnotics, 86, **87**
l. stimulants, **76**
Lorazepam, 113, 119
Los Angeles, 186, 187
Low risk, 186
LSD, 23, 25, 26, 37, 38, 40, 136, 137, 138, **139-140**
history, 19
"Ludes," 114
Lungs, 28, 66, 78, 79, 80, 151, 161, (also see inhalation, crack, nicotine, smoking)
Lysergic acid diethylamide (see LSD)

M

"M," 89
Mace, 137, 143
Mafia, 91, 97, 105
Magic mushrooms)see psilocybin)
Magnesium citrate, 192
"Mainlining," 200, (see I.V. drug use)
Manco Capac, 15
"Mandrake," 165
Manic depressive illness (see dual diagnosis)
MARIJUANA, 22, 25, 38, 45, 134, 135, 136, **137,** 138, **146-154,** 162, 179, 180, 181, 186, 188, 190, 199, 205, 206, 207, 219, 233, 234, 237, 240
amotivational syndrome (see apathy)

effects, 151
glaucoma, 150, 152
hashish, 150
history, 14
memory, 152
plants, 149
potency, 146, 148, 159
tracking ability, 151
urine test, 207
withdrawal, 154, 224
Matrix Laboratories, 39
McKinley, President William, 17
MDA, 14, 25, 38, 136, 137, **143,** 162
MDE, 143
MDMA, 11, 25, 38, 136, **143,** 162
Media (crack), 64, 68, 219
Melfiat, 52
Melting point, 66
Memory, 138, **152**
Menstrual cycle, 94
Mental illness (see dual diagnosis)
Mental retardation, 171, 174
Meperidine (see Demerol)
Meprobamate, 114, 121
Meprotabs, 114
Mescaline (peyote), 16, 25, 134, 136, 138, 142, 145, 179
Met-enkephalin, 38, 126, 218, 221
METABOLISM, 42, 46-47, **54, 199**
fetal m., 172, 173, 177, 181, 182
Metabolites, 148
Metallic paint, 25, 160

"Meth" (see methamphetamines or amphetamines)
Meth labs, 69
Methadone, 24, 89, **99,** 101, 130, 165, 185, 206, 207, 225
Methadrine, 69-74
Methamphetamines, 69-74, 240
Methaprylon, 114
Methaqualone (see Quaalude)
Methyl alcohol, 63
Methylenediozyamphetamine, 23
Methylphenidate (Ritalin), 52
"Mexican brown," 89, 95, 97
"Mexican reds," 113
Mexican "tar," 67, 73, 89, 95, 96, 97, 103
Mexico, 70, 96, 97, 142
Micrograms (mics), 139
Midol, 207
Miltown, 18, 24, 114, 115, 121
Miscarriage, 67, 94, 172, 175, 176, 178, 183
Misrepresentation, 76, 89, 97
"Miss Emma," 89
Mitchum, Robert, 146
Mitochondria, 43
MMDA, 136, 143
Model cement, 160
Moloch the god, 147
Money (see costs)
Monamine autoreceptor, 39
Mood, 75, 138
Morning glory seeds, 136, 138, **142**
"Morph," 89

Morphine, 16, 28, 86, 91, 92, 98, **99,** 101, 109
"Mota," 147
Motrin, 193, 205, 207
MPPP, 11, 100, **162**
MPTP, 100, 103, 162
Mrs. Winslows Soothing Syrup, 98
"Mud," 53
Multi-cultural prevention, 237
Multiple diagnises, 229
Multi-leveled prevention, 236
"Murphy," 89
Muscles, 62, 87, 93, 113, 161, 178, 182, 201, 217
"Muscling," 28, 91
Muscular coordination, 115
Muscular system, 127
Mushrooms (see psilocybin)
Myristican, 137

N

N.A. (Narcotics Anonymous), 110, 111, 189, 226, 229
Nail polish remover, 156
Naloxone (Narcan), 100, 102
Naltrexone (Trexan), 100, 109, 225
Narcan (see Naloxone)
Narcotics, 85, 88
Nasal passages, 58
Natural high, 62
Nature of drugs, 40
"Nebbies," 113
NEEDLE USE, 94, **103,** 171, 178, **200-203,** (also see I.V. use)

Note: All page numbers and headings in boldface type indicate the primary source for information

Note: All page numbers and headings in boldface type indicate the primary source for information

"Whack," 67, 165
Whiskey, 123, 124, 175
"Whites," 52, 190
Whiteout, 160
"Window pane" (LSD), 23,
  28, 136, 139
Wine, 24, 124, 175
Wine cooler, 24
WITHDRAWAL, 43-44, 73,
  77, 79, 94, 101, 102, 107,
  113, 115, 117-120, 154, 173,
  175, 177, 178, 181, 182,
  217, 224
Wolfbane, 137
Work, 69, 110, 170, **194-197,**
  204
Work shrinkage, 194
"Works," 200, (also see
  needle use)
World War II, 18, 69

X

Xanax, 24, 113, **117-119,** 181-
  206
"XTC" (see ecstasy)

Y

Yage, 136, **143**
"Yellows, yellow jackets,
  yellow bullets," 113
Yopo, 142
YOUTH, 170, **186-189**

Z

"Zoom," 160

*Note: All page numbers and headings in boldface
type indicate the primary source for information*

FILMS/VIDEOTAPES MADE WITH THE HAIGHT-ASHBURY DETOX CLINIC

Uppers, Downers, All Arounders
Part One-The Effects (30 minutes)
Part Two-The Drugs (30 minutes)

Part One examines how the physical and emotional centers of the central nervous system are affected by psychoactive drugs. It describes and visualizes tolerance, withdrawal, tissue dependence, and other consequences of drug use and abuse. It also classifies psychoactive drugs, i.e. uppers (stimulants), downers (depressants), all arounders (psychedelics) and inhalants; and it examines the various levels of drug seeking behavior.

Part Two identifies the most commonly used psychoactive drugs such as marijuana, cocaine, heroin, Valium, crank, etc., classifies them by effect, and shows how they are metabolized. It also gives a short history of drug use.

The Haight-ashbury Cocaine Film: Physiology, Compulsion, and Recovery (35 minutes)

This non-judgmental, teaching film/tape details what cocaine is and how it manipulates brain chemicals. By using computer graphics, animation, and personal interviews, "The Haight-Ashbury Cocaine Film" demonstrates how cocaine inhibits the natural balance of the brain's chemistry, and can replace basic survival mechanisms such as sleeping, eating, and the sex drive, with the compulsive use of cocaine.

Smokable Cocaine: The Haight-Ashbury Crack Film (28 minutes)

This film/tape details how freebase and crack manipulate brain chemistry, how freebase and crack are made, why they are used so compulsively, and how smokable cocaine abuse can be treated.

A Matter Of Balance
(23 minutes)

This film/tape teaches the physiology and brain chemistry of psychoactive drugs in a manner that is easy to understand. It starts with the thesis that the body tries to keep itself in balance no matter what and psychoactive drugs only act to disturb that balance.

From Opium To Heroin (32 minutes)

The film/tape is the most complete show available on the subject of opiates. By using animation, live action, and client interviews, it explains the topic in a comprehensive fashion. Besides describing the effects, the film examines tolerance, tissue dependence, withdrawal, overdose, needle use and AIDS, addiction, and recovery.

The Haight-Ashbury Lecture Series-
60 to 90 minutes each. **Available 1990**

For information on these and other productions, please contact
CINEMED INC.
P.O. BOX 96
ASHLAND, OR 97520
1-800 888-0617 or (503) 488-2805